Cost–Benefit Analysis

Cost–benefit analysis (CBA) is the systematic and analytical process of comparing benefits and costs in evaluating the desirability of a project or programme, often of a social nature and for society as a whole. CBA is fundamental to government decision-making and can be an effective tool for making informed decisions on the use of society's scarce resources. This book highlights the main concepts and principles of cost–benefit analysis used in real life cases and actual applications. It contains rich case study material and examples of real life CBA applications with the emphasis on both physical and non-physical projects and infrastructure developments in Asia and beyond. The book also discusses techniques frequently used in applied CBA.

Part I of the book introduces the historical background and theory of CBA. Part II presents frequently discussed theories and topics in CBA, including commonly used techniques in applied CBA. Part III introduces new applications in CBA, such as the recent trend of using behavioural economics. Finally, in Part IV, case studies illustrate how CBA is applied in real life. Questions for readers and students to ponder are raised at the end of each chapter in this final section.

The scope of the case studies is more than just physical infrastructure and includes public sector social policies and programmes in health, education and social welfare, as well as the environment. The case studies, many of which have taken or are to take place in developing countries, provide a rich background to the principles of the method and are accompanied by a wealth of explanatory material. In each case, there are illustrations of how the key concepts and principles of CBA are used. The case studies analysed include:

- the Three Gorges Dam in China;
- the 2008 Beijing Olympic Games;
- the costs of global warming; and
- the Jamuna Bridge in Bangladesh.

As well as being suitable for courses in cost–benefit analysis, public finance, the environment and health economics, this book should be of interest to all public policy decision-makers and planners.

Euston Quah is Head of Economics at the Nanyang Technological University (NTU), Singapore. He is co-author, with E. J. Mishan, of the fifth edition of *Cost–Benefit Analysis*, also published by Routledge.

Raymond Toh is an Economist at the Singapore Land Transport Authority.

Cost–Benefit Analysis

Cases and materials

Euston Quah and Raymond Toh

Routledge
Taylor & Francis Group

LONDON AND NEW YORK

First published 2012
by Routledge
2 Park Square, Milton Park, Abingdon, Oxon OX14 4RN

Simultaneously published in the USA and Canada
by Routledge
711 Third Avenue, New York, NY 10017

Routledge is an imprint of the Taylor & Francis Group, an informa business

British Library Cataloguing in Publication Data
A catalogue record for this book is available from the British Library

Library of Congress Cataloging-in-Publication Data
Quah, Euston.
   Cost–benefit analysis : cases and materials / by Euston Quah and
   Raymond Toh.
     p. cm.
   Includes bibliographical references and index.
   ISBN 978-0-415-55880-8 (hb) – ISBN 978-0-415-56226-3 (pb) –
   ISBN 978-0-203-69754-2 (eb) 1. Externalities (Economics) 2. Public
   goods–Cost effectiveness–Case studies. I. Toh, Raymond. II. Title.

HB846.3.Q34 2011

338.5'1–dc22

2011015853

ISBN: 978-0-415-55880-8 (hbk)
ISBN: 978-0-415-56226-3 (pbk)
ISBN: 978-0-203-69754 -2 (ebk)

Typeset in Times New Roman
by Sunrise Setting Ltd

Printed and bound in Great Britain by the MPG Books Group

Contents

Figures

Tables

Foreword

In the first edition of my Cost–Benefit Analysis (CBA) book, I introduced the method of compounding forward to a terminal value in order to expose the implicit assumption that benefits and cost are continually re-invested at the discount rate in the more commonly-used discounted present value (DPV) method of discounting future benefits and costs to the present. My recommended compounded terminal value (CTV) approach would reconcile the rankings of projects derived from the (corrected) Internal Rate of Return (IRR) criterion with those from the (corrected) DPV criterion. Needless to remark, recognition of this fact did not often percolate into the all-too-many teaching manuals on the subject.

On the other hand, I have to recognize that in all earlier editions of my CBA book, including the fifth edition with Euston Quah, our guiding concern was just how any particular change should be measured, if we were to abide by the theoretical economist's method of basing it on the subjective valuation of the persons concerned – a counsel of perfection! Bearing in mind, however, that in any actual calculation, it is virtually impossible to realize, one has recourse to proxies. For instance, an approximate measure of consumer surplus by the area under the demand curve serves as an excellent proxy for the more fastidious Hicksian measures[1].

Again, in the choice of investment criteria, we need not be overly concerned. Provided only that the ranking of alternative projects is the desideratum, simple recourse to DPV may suffice. This may be confirmed by discounting the stream of cost and benefits first by r (the average rate of time preference) alone and then by p (the actuarial rate of return on new investment) alone. Assuming r and p remain relatively unchanged over the relevant period of time, the rankings of alternative projects should be similar.

Insufficient attention is paid in CBA manuals to what may transpire to be a crucial difference between CV^{12} and CV^{21} (CV being shorthand for Compensation Variation as defined by Hicks), where CV^{12} is the most a person or group is willing to pay for a good (or for the removal of a 'bad') and CV^{21} is the minimum sum acceptable to forgo it. The two are not necessarily equal.

Needless to emphasize, adopting people's subjective valuations has to be accepted as the only valid measurement in any CBA (or in any valuation exercise). Consequently, any 'utility' or 'politico' weighting has to be dismissed.

The worst offence in this regard would be to derive the weights via reference to the predilections of the policy-makers of a given country – thereby effectively subverting not only the economic checks on policies favoured, but (inadvertently) rationalizing the resulting pseudo economics to justify the country's existing policies.

It has to be noted that, notwithstanding the general acceptance of adopting people's subjective valuations as the basic data in a CBA, there can no economic rationale in determining the degree of uncertainty that has perforce been wholly arbitrary. This arbitrariness is by far the weakest aspect of a CBA since it may result in different conclusions being reached by different economists.

Finally it has to be accepted that the outcome of a CBA, even when uncertainty is ignored, is far from being (morally) compelling. Assuming a resulting figure from CBA is positive (say it were $10 billion and ignoring, for argument's sake, the wide band of uncertainty), it can only be understood as a potential Pareto improvement of $10 billion. What is more, this preceding adjective 'potential' does not refer to any anticipated development but simply to its being conditional on some possible future occurrence. One, moreover, that is unlikely to occur.

Thus, when the economist offers a figure, or range of figures, purporting to be derived from a CBA calculation, he has to make this clear to the political role-makers.

I have highlighted some issues in the practice of CBA. There are other equally important matters, of course, and they will be discussed in greater scope and depth in the subsequent chapters. On that note, I wish all readers a fruitful and enjoyable journey through the pages that follow.

E. J. Mishan
Professor of Economics, London School of Economics

Preface

Cost–Benefit Analysis is an exciting subject. It is a valuable tool available in economics to analyse proposed projects as well as post-project developments. Projects is a broad term for referring to physical projects, such as infrastructures, and also in the context of programmes and policies, such as proposed educational programmes or a health policy to reduce incidences of certain diseases.

There are already many good cost–benefit textbooks covering the principles, as well as more advanced ones covering certain aspects of cost–benefit analysis. There are also theoretical cost–benefit texts; but few provide simple illustrations of actual case studies on projects that have utilized cost–benefit analysis. Understanding the theoretical background and the welfare economics behind cost–benefit analysis is already daunting, let alone applying the principles to a real cost–benefit exercise of a proposed project.

This book aims to show real life applications behind project evaluations using cost–benefit analysis, and to highlight special topics in cost–benefit analysis which are often used in such studies. These topics may involve valuation of non-market goods, including a novel approach utilizing pair-wise comparisons to supplement valuations; value of statistical life; benefit transfer methods; discounting principles and decision criteria; and methods dealing with cost of diseases and air-pollution studies. In addition, there is a special contribution by the eminent economist, Jack Knetsch, on how recent behavioural economics can affect cost–benefit studies.

This book will appeal to students and educators of cost–benefit analysis courses at university level and all institutions of higher learning that offer the subject. It will also be very useful to research practitioners who want a quick reference to applications of cost–benefit analysis as well as to be updated with relevant techniques in cost–benefit analysis. Policy- and decision-makers will find the materials in this book very handy and relevant to their needs in understanding resource allocation decisions. The book also provides a comprehensive bibliography which should be useful for all engaged in the further study, research and applications of cost–benefit analysis.

We are very grateful to the special contributions by Professor Jack Knetsch, Dr Chia Wai Mun and Ms Christabelle Soh. We thank our research assistants, Jen Wei, Warrick Wee and J. H. A. Kamika, for their invaluable and efficient assistance in preparing this book. We thank Professor E. J. Mishan for contributing his foreword to the book as well as his generous comments along the way. We would love to hear from our readers. Please send your comments and other suggestions to ecsquahe@ntu.edu.sg, for the attention of Professor Euston Quah.

Euston Quah and Raymond Toh
Authors

Part I

Background and theory of cost–benefit analysis

1 Introduction

The idea behind cost–benefit analysis (CBA) is not a novel one. In fact, on a day-to-day basis, most people would employ, knowingly or unknowingly, decision methods similar to that of CBA – if the benefits outweigh the costs, then an action is taken, otherwise it is not. For want of a convenient term, we shall name the usual decision-making process, profit-and-loss accounting.

The question then arises – if the basic idea behind the two is similar, why then, is there a need for CBA? Why not simply allow individual decisions based on profit-and-loss accounting to organize the economy?

First, it is a matter of reference. For the most part, the area that CBA addresses is the economy of a whole country, while everyday profit-and-loss analysis only concerns individual person(s). The effects (both benefits and costs) of a person's action are not limited to the person. Yet, individual person(s) make choices based only on the benefits and costs accruing to him/her. Naturally, one can expect the social optimum to deviate from that reached by private profit-and-loss accounting. Of course, if we were to assume that markets for every good exist and that all markets are perfectly competitive, then both CBA and the sum of individual profit-and-loss calculations would yield the same outcome.

Second, as a natural extension of the differing frames of reference, what enters the computation as a benefit and what enters the computation as a cost will naturally differ between CBA and profit-and-loss accounting. Externalities, for example, will escape the individuals' profit-and-loss accounting but will be included in CBA. Transfer payments, on the other hand, provide a counter-example as they may enter profit-and-loss accounts but find no place in CBA.

Third, not only do the items to be included in each type of analysis differ, how they are to be valued also differs. In profit-and-loss accounting, items may be valued at their market prices whereas in CBA items are always valued at their opportunity cost. In the case of providing employment for an otherwise unemployed person, for example: to a firm, the wages paid to that unit of labour constitute a type of cost in the profit-and-loss accounts; in a CBA, however, the cost of employing that unit of labour is zero[1] since he/she would have produced nothing otherwise.

There are many textbooks providing more detailed treatment of the topic but this is not one of them; this is a case study book. Nonetheless, a brief review of the principles and the steps involved in conducting a CBA are presented to provide a quick refresher for seasoned practitioners and some basic grounding for readers new to the subject.

Some of the principles of CBA were highlighted in previous paragraphs. A more formal framework would be to think of the principles in terms of relevance, shadow prices, spillover effects and constraints. These correspond to the three steps in conducting a CBA, which are: deciding which items to include (relevance); computing the value of the items (shadow prices and spillover effects); and arriving at a conclusion that provides informed advice to the decision-maker (constraints).

Relevance concerns itself with the inclusion and exclusion of items. This is wholly dependent on the accounting stance, which, for CBA, is typically the whole country. Common sense would dictate that passing an item from one's left hand to one's right hand does not constitute a benefit or cost to oneself. Neither would one consider the sum of the cost of an item and the alternative use of the money as the total cost of the item. The parallels with CBA are obvious. First, a CBA must not include transfer payments as an item. Second, double-counting should be avoided. Both constitute the basic principles of CBA regarding relevance.

Shadow prices (sometimes referred to as accounting prices) constitute the true valuation of items. The true value may be thought of as the opportunity cost. Market prices are subject to much distortion either via taxation/subsidies in competitive markets or through rent-seeking behaviour in non-competitive markets and hence do not accurately reflect the opportunity costs. The principle here is to always adjust market prices to correct for distortions, if any, to obtain shadow prices that are reflective of opportunity costs.

Spillover effects may be thought of as an extension of shadow prices. Shadow prices reflect the true private value of an item. However, certain items have spillover effects (also known as externalities) that cause the social value of the item to differ from its private value. For example, in the production of certain goods, noise and smoke may be by-products that negatively affect the general population residing nearby, whose discomfort (cost) is not registered by the market. Two principles regarding spillover effects are: if present, the value of spillover effects should always be included in the CBA and such values are to be derived from the minimum compensation the parties directly affected are willing to accept.

Finally, every CBA faces a number of constraints. These constraints may or may not be political in nature but regardless of the constraint type, the CBA practitioner must work within them. As such, if the decision-maker only commissions a practitioner to find out whether a particular project yields net benefits and is thus worth funding, the practitioner can only provide information as to whether the specific project yields benefits, even if there are other more worthy projects with greater net benefits. This principle of only working within constraints necessarily means that decision-makers must take care in selecting the initial constraints to prevent situations in which a better solution is not considered due to the constraints.

Having summarized the principles of CBA, we conclude with a preview of the chapters to come.

Part I presents the background and theory of CBA and consists of this introductory chapter and the next one on the history and recent developments in CBA.

Part II deals with the theories and topics frequently discussed in CBA. Here, the reader will find discussions of the practical aspects of CBA including: valuation matters, benefit transfers, discounting issues, the value of a statistical life, the economic cost of air pollution on health and the economic cost of diseases. The relevant chapters follow the above order.

Part III introduces new applications in CBA. In this section, readers will become acquainted with the pair-wise comparison, a novel approach in valuation, as well as the lessons CBA can draw from recent developments in behavioural economics.

Part IV is a compilation of cases and materials for CBA. It provides multiple examples of CBA that cover a broad spectrum of project types from projects to improve health to those that further science. The cases reflect a geographical balance with a slight emphasis on Asia: cases are included from all five populated continents but with a higher proportion from Asia.

2 History and scope of cost–benefit analysis

If understood in the loose sense of weighing costs against benefits in decision-making, cost–benefit analysis (CBA) has probably existed for as long as there have been (rational) humans. In the more narrow definition as the technical subject this book is concerned with, CBA may reasonably find its formal[1] beginnings in the United States Flood Control Act of 1936. In this chapter, we explore the history and major developments (both in theory and application) of CBA and briefly review the more recent developments that have influenced its future direction.

History of cost–benefit analysis

While CBA only became a formal subject of study in 1936, many of the theoretical underpinnings were developed a long time before that. Chief among them are the concepts of consumer surplus and externalities, which are the main aspects that distinguish CBA from traditional profit-and-loss accounting.

The concept of consumer surplus may be attributed to Jules Dupuit, a French civil engineer and economist who noted in 1844 (Dupuit, 1844) that users of a toll bridge enjoyed its services more than the toll they paid to use it. Dupuit named this additional enjoyment 'relative utility', which later became known as Alfred Marshall's 'consumer surplus'[2].

The idea of externalities, on the other hand, was a concept developed by the English welfare economist, Arthur Cecil Pigou, in the 1920s. Pigou argued that the private and public economic product were not necessarily the same and in his *Economics of Welfare* (Pigou, 1952) published much later, he cited child labour and factory pollution, among other externalities, to illustrate his point.

The key relation of the above two concepts to CBA was that they identified how social welfare could be measured (consumer surplus) and how previously ignored factors could contribute to or subtract from it (externalities). These came into prominence when the US Flood Control Act, which mandated that proposed projects were to be evaluated to ascertain that the benefits (whomsoever they accrued to) outweighed the associated cost, was enacted in 1936. The significance of the Act lay in the fact that an exercise in measuring the net benefits to society invariably required the consideration of external effects and social welfare. This signalled a shift in policy evaluation towards the consideration of net social benefits as opposed to a simple financial appraisal from the perspective of the producer – the norm of the time (Mishan and Quah, 2007).

However, while it became clear what aspects ought to be included, there was still a lack of consensus on how they could be valued, as the Act did not include guidelines as to how CBA and valuation studies were to be conducted.

This lack of standardized procedures and techniques was to persist for the decade following the Flood Control Act. It was not until 1946 when the US Federal Inter-Agency River Basin Committee's Subcommittee on Benefits and Costs, an inter-agency group, produced the *Proposed Practices for Economic Analysis of River Basin Projects* (1950; revised 1958) that a standardized procedure was put forth. The need for a common standard across agencies was necessary as, in the years following the enactment of the Flood Control Act, multiple agencies developed individual guidelines and procedures that appeared to do little more than justify projects that had already been decided upon. The eventual recommendations put forth by the group became more commonly known later on as the shortened *Green Book*.

While significant, the *Green Book* was still considerably incomplete in its guidelines and was later complemented by the *Budget Circular A-47* that the Bureau of Budget put forth six years later in 1952. As with the *Green Book*, the *Budget Circular A-47* was an attempt to standardize CBA across all US agencies. Of importance is the fact that the combined effect of the two publications not only served the initial inter-agency CBA standardization purposes, but it also represented a first attempt at aligning CBA practices with economic theory.

It was the latter result that caught the interest of academic circles. The late 1950s to 1970s saw the rapid development and refinement of CBA theories and techniques as economists tried to reconcile CBA practices in relation to economics. Foremost amongst the economists of this era were Eckstein, Krutilla and McKean, who, in seminal papers published in the latter part of the 1950s (Eckstein, 1958; Krutilla and Eckstein, 1958; McKean, 1958), laid the firm theoretical framework for CBA based on neoclassical welfare economics on which current CBA practices still stand. It is interesting to note that although in the 1960s and 1970s there was an especial increase in numerous publications on subjects pertaining to how non-market goods ought to be valued, most of the ideas and techniques put forth were, to a greater or lesser extent, variants of the contingent valuation method (CVM), hedonic pricing and the travel cost method. It was also during this period that these methods were first applied to the valuation of non-market goods (Davis, 1963; Ridker and Henning, 1967; Clawson and Knetsch, 1966).

While the valuation theories and techniques were still undergoing refinement in the 1970s, the criterion by which proposed projects might pass muster was well established by the 1930s. Nowadays known as the Kaldor–Hicks criterion[3], it required the net money measure of gains, from a proposed project, to be positive, regardless of the effects of distribution. Otherwise known as a potential Pareto improvement, the criterion was developed after a prolonged debate amongst welfare economists about the viability of inter-personal comparisons of utility triggered by the repealing of the Corn Laws and in recognition of the impossibility (or at least, great unlikelihood) of achieving Pareto improvements (Mishan, 1981a,b).

At the same time that the theories and techniques of CBA were being developed, the use of it was increasingly being institutionalized. Apart from the growth in economics literature concerning CBA, the 1960s also witnessed the implementation of CBA at the national level in the US, Canada and the UK. President Lyndon Johnson of the US put into effect the planning–programme–budget system (PPBS) at the federal government level in 1965 (Hirsch, 1966). This was later reinforced by President Ronald Reagan's Executive Order 12291 in 1980, which mandated that projects affecting the economy by more than a hundred million dollars annually had to undergo Regulatory Impact Analysis to ensure that they met the efficiency (Kaldor–Hicks) criterion (The US National Archives and Records Administration, n.d.). Thirteen years later, President Clinton issued Executive Order 12866 in 1993, which was largely similar in nature (The US National Archives and Records Administration, 1993). In Canada, aided by Sewell *et al.*'s *Guide to Benefit–Cost Analysis* (1965), the government adopted a similar PPBS in 1967. In the same year, the release of the *Government White Paper* in the UK institutionalized the CBA practice (Mishan and Quah, 2007). The institutionalization of CBA by these three countries resulted in an unprecedented increase in its application, especially with regard to proposed public projects. One of the more notable examples was the evaluation of the Third London Airport in the UK (Roskill, 1970, 1971).

On the academic front, the exploration of CBA and normative economics (Mishan, 1971, 1981b) also added a new dimension to the growing literature.

It was only a matter of time before the practice was similarly institutionalized at the international level. The OECD adopted CBA in its project evaluations in 1969; the UN did so in 1972; and the World Bank followed in 1975 (Squire and Van der Tak, 1975). The international application of CBA was first made explicit at the Earth Summit in 1992 where a consensus was reached that required public sector projects, for which countries requested funding support, to pass the CBA test. Subsequent international agreements have often included items to a similar effect.

Recent developments

In more recent history, two developments that could have potentially far-reaching effects on CBA have emerged. The first is the growing number of valuation databases; the second is the development of a new branch of economics – behavioural economics.

The establishment of valuation databases, where the results of valuation studies are meticulously recorded, has thus far been limited to valuation studies of environmental goods. At present, there appear to be at least four databases of this sort, the most comprehensive being the Environmental Valuation Reference Inventory (EVRI) which was established in the late 1990s. Other databases also seem to have been established around this period or later.

The databases were set up to facilitate a valuation method known as benefit transfer that rose to prominence, not coincidentally, in the early 1990s. Benefit transfer is, in essence, the practice of assigning a value to an item based on the established value of another similar item. The exact methodology and associated issues are covered in the later chapter on benefit transfers.

Nonetheless, from the brief description, it should be clear that the method required an origin from which values could be 'transferred'. That is where the databases entered the picture. The databases provided a ready source from which CBA practitioners could derive values for items in their studies without employing any of the conventional methods.

Most experts still agree that the conventional methods yield more accurate value estimates. However, with the increased ease of obtaining transferred values, one can reasonably expect that future CBAs will utilize fewer conventional methods and more benefit transfers. As such, it is not improbable that future CBA developments will occur along the lines of developing more accurate transfer techniques as opposed to further refinement of the conventional methods.

The other recent development that has had an impact on CBA is the growth in the relatively young branch of behavioural economics. Studies in behavioural economics have sparked off new controversy regarding the validity of certain CBA techniques, with valuation methods being the most readily debated topics. The more technical nature of the issue will be further explored in Chapter 10, which discusses behavioural economics and CBA. Suffice to say, such challenges will provide an impetus for the further development and refinement of methods and techniques that account for behavioural biases and more importantly, answer the central and seemingly innocuous question at the heart of all CBA – do the benefits of a proposed project outweigh its cost and if so, by how much would society benefit?

Part II

Topics and issues frequently discussed in cost–benefit analysis

3   Valuation issues and methods

All decisions involve certain trade-offs. Policies are no exception. Where the trade-offs can be easily and accurately measured, it is easy to decide on courses of action that maximize welfare. However, there are instances where the trade-off involves items for which there are no existing values to refer to. Consider the following cases:

1   The Singapore government launched a bid to hold the inaugural Youth Olympic Games (YOG) in 2010. One of the cases made in favour of submitting the bid in 2008, despite the costs involved, was that it would increase national pride.
2   The Copenhagen summit was widely perceived to be unconstructive as not many countries readily embraced the emissions targets. Among others, a common argument against steep emissions reduction was that it would hamper growth and the alleviation of poverty.
3   Residents of Penang, Malaysia commonly lament the loss of heritage sites as the state develops and urban infrastructure replaces old buildings.

The three cases highlighted are similar, in that the trade-offs involve non-market goods (pride, environmental conservation and heritage). This poses a problem, because the lack of defined markets means that we cannot use the pricing mechanism to ascertain the value of these goods in conducting cost–benefit analysis (CBA).

While the idea of monetizing the environment and feelings such as national pride may be offensive to some, one should consider the relative merits of such a practice against the alternatives.

First, not specifically taking the loss of these goods into account is equivalent to assigning a value of zero to them. This is very likely to cause an over-consumption of such goods that diminish their value – a phenomenon observed countless times throughout humanity's history.

Second, practices that take into account the impact on such non-market goods without placing a specific value on them may be socially inefficient. To illustrate, one may employ the political system of one-person-one-vote referendums to collectively decide whether to undertake projects that damage the environment. However, a major drawback of this method is that it does not take into account the intensity of preferences. Under such a system, it is possible that certain projects that the majority have a marginal preference for and the minority have strong preferences against would be carried out, although they have deleterious effects on social welfare.

Having delineated the rationale for putting money values on non-market goods, the three most common economic valuation techniques are discussed.

Economic valuation techniques

In the CBA literature, valuation techniques typically revolve around deriving a demand curve for the good in question in order to compute its value. The three most commonly used techniques are the contingent valuation method (CVM), hedonic pricing and the travel cost method.

Contingent valuation method

The CVM is, by far, the most direct and intuitive method to derive values for non-market goods. Essentially, it involves eliciting the maximum amount that people are willing to pay for welfare improvements and the minimum that they are willing to accept as compensation for welfare loss, to derive a demand curve for the good in question.

To do so, one designs a survey that measures people's responses to a hypothetical change in an attribute or amenity in terms of the maximum they would be willing to pay to enjoy a benefit, or the minimum they would be willing to accept to forgo it. The amount that they are willing to pay or accept would logically be the monetary sum that leaves them at the same level of welfare as before. The process may involve simply asking respondents to state a single value or more sophisticated methods like bidding, where respondents are asked whether they would be willing to pay (or accept) successively lower (or higher) amounts to derive the maximum (or minimum) willingness-to-pay (or acceptance). We shall abbreviate the willingness-to-pay and accept as WTP and WTA respectively, for the rest of the chapter. The WTP or WTA of the survey sample (whichever the case may be) is then extrapolated for the whole population and adjusted where necessary. The values are totalled to provide an estimate of the area under the demand curve for the hypothetical change in that variable, which may be interpreted as the value of the good.

We illustrate one CVM approach with a hypothetical example. Suppose we wanted to measure the value of an increase in green cover for a particular city in conducting a CBA for a citywide greening project. For simplicity's sake, let us assume that pre-tests have revealed that survey participants can effectively separate the benefits of increased green cover from other environmental goods. Instead of eliciting WTP values, we may ask participants whether they would approve the project if it cost $5, $10, $20, $50 or $100 respectively. Each value is presented to only 20 per cent of the participants. Let us imagine the survey reveals the approval rates in Table 3.1.

Table 3.1 Approval rates for hypothetical greening project

Project cost $	Approval rate %
5	95
10	85
20	65
50	30
100	5

If the population of the city is one million, the estimated aggregate number of approvals for each cost will be as shown in Table 3.2 and can be plotted as a demand curve as illustrated in Figure 3.1.

The area under the demand curve is the total WTP for the project, which may be interpreted as the value for increased green cover. In this case, it can be approximated by taking the sum of the area of the four trapezoids, which would yield the value of $34,750,000.

Table 3.2 Aggregate approvals for hypothetical greening project

Cost $	Aggregate approvals Approval % × 1,000,000
5	950,000
10	850,000
20	650,000
50	300,000
100	50,000

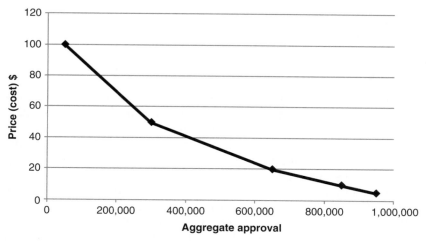

Figure 3.1 Demand curve for hypothetical greening project.

An important caveat has to be made here. That is, for most non-market goods, especially environmental goods, apart from the usual use demand, option demand, as first put forward by Weisbrod (1964), and existence demand are likely to be significant and ought to be accounted for in the CVM. The two concepts are similar but not equal. Option demand is the willingness of consumers to pay to keep a good available for future use while existence demand is the willingness-to-pay to keep a good in existence even if one never has any intention to use it. The applicability to environmental goods is obvious; most people would be willing to pay to preserve a natural area so that they can visit it in the future and a great number would do so simply for the sake of knowing that they have done some good. Hence, in conducting CVM, option and existence values should be measured.

While the CVM is highly intuitive and straightforward, it has two key weaknesses. The first is the susceptibility to survey bias; the other is the susceptibility to behavioural bias.

Most survey bias may be corrected by proper survey design. However, strategic bias is one major source of bias that may not be easily dealt with. This is the case when survey respondents over- or understate their WTP or WTA for strategic reasons. This is illustrated clearly by the following scenario. Imagine a surveyor asks a participant to state his/her WTP for a natural park's usage to ascertain the park's value. If the participant thinks that his/her WTP amount will be used to formulate charges for using the park, he/she will have an incentive to understate his/her true WTP. Similarly, if a participant thinks that his/her WTA amount will be used to formulate compensation, he/she will have an incentive to overstate the amount. To minimize strategic bias, great care has to be taken in the survey design to avoid giving participants the impression that charging and compensation are in any way related to the survey.

Apart from survey bias, CVM, being reliant on surveys, are also susceptible to behavioural biases. The exact behavioural effects on valuation will be expanded further in Chapter 10, on behavioural economics and CBA. Suffice to say, a common criticism of the CVM is that the values derived may not be accurate due to the possibility of behavioural bias.

Hedonic pricing

Hedonic pricing is an alternative valuation technique. The key underlying principle is to use price differentials in existing markets as proxies of prices with certain attributes. Property markets provide a good example here. Let us assume we want to compute the value of a reduction in ambient noise levels. To do so with hedonic pricing, we may compare the prices of two properties, which are similar in every way except for the ambient noise level. Suppose property A is worth $2 million and has an average ambient noise level of 20 decibels (dB) while property B is worth $1 million and has an average ambient noise level of 35 dB. What we can infer then, is that the 'price' of a reduction of noise by 15 dB is $1 million.

The previous example is overly simplified to illustrate the principle behind hedonic pricing. Typically, hedonic pricing models are more complex than that even though the reasoning that underpins the method is the same. In actual hedonic pricing models, it is common to apply multiple regression techniques to find out the marginal effect of a particular attribute on price. This can then be used to find out the value of that attribute. We illustrate this with a simple example. Suppose data on property prices reveals that prices were well-estimated by the following function:

$$p = \sum_{i=1}^{n} b_i x_i$$

where p represents the price of the property, x_i represents the attributes (e.g. x_1 is the distance from a train station, x_2 is the noise level, etc), b_i measures the effect of the attribute on house prices and n is the total number of attributes.

Let us imagine that in the above specification x_2 is the ambient noise level as measured in decibels and its corresponding coefficient b_2 is equal to -10. In such a scenario, the value of a reduction in ambient noise level by 10 dB would be $100.

The key criticism of hedonic pricing is that it requires the strict assumption of perfect markets to yield accurate estimates. If people wish to move but cannot due to some reason or another, the market for property will be imperfect and property price differentials will not reflect the true 'price' of various attributes. In addition, other factors may distort market prices such as imperfectly competitive market structures and government intervention in the form of taxes and subsidies.

To overcome these problems, an alternative method of examining the prices of goods that yield the desired outcomes known as the Defensive Expenditure approach has been proposed (European Commission, 2000). For example, to find out the value of noise reduction, one can simply look at the cost of soundproofing one's home. If the cost of soundproofing one's home is $1,000 then we may infer that the value of noise reduction is $1,000. However, this method is not without its flaws either. The main problem with this method is the difficulty in separating the multiple uses of certain goods. For example, thicker windowpanes contribute to lowering a home's noise penetration as well as providing increased thermal insulation. The price of thicker windowpanes thus reflects the value of noise reduction as well as increased warmth. Hence, using the price of thicker windowpanes, as an estimate of the value of noise reduction, results in an overestimation of its value. Such limitations should be kept in mind when hedonic price models are employed.

Travel cost method

The travel cost method is a more recent development in valuation techniques. It is also known as the Hotelling–Clawson–Knetsch technique and is most often applied to estimate the value of recreational sites such as marine parks, mountain resorts and wilderness areas in North America. The main idea is to derive a demand curve by using the cost of travel as a proxy for price. First, a sample of the user-population is stratified according to the distance from the target site. The stratification involves separating the surrounding areas into concentric zones with the target site in the centre. For each zone, an average zonal participation rate is then computed.

The average zonal participation rate is then plotted against the travel cost. This graph will allow us to estimate the change in total visitation for any change in the travel cost by estimating the change in the average zonal participation and multiplying it by the zonal population before totalling. The demand curve is then derived by postulating that people will respond to a dollar increase in the price in the same way that they would respond to a dollar increase in travel costs.

As this method is more complex, we will illustrate its workings via the use of a numerical example. Imagine we wanted to estimate the annual value of a hypothetical park. The user populations come from cities A, B and C with certain characteristics where all flow variables are measured on a per annum basis (see Table 3.3).

Using the data on the number of trips per million and the travel cost for the three cities, we may then use linear extrapolation (or any other form) to estimate the relation between trips and cost. The relation is plotted in Figure 3.2.

We hypothesize that if entrance fees were introduced, each dollar increase in entrance fees would have the same effect as a dollar increase in travel costs. Hence, from Figure 3.2, we can estimate the number of trips made per thousand of population for each city if there were an entrance fee of $0, $5, $10, $15 and $20. Figure 3.3 shows the process for a $5 entrance fee. A, B and C mark out the

Table 3.3 Hypothetical data on park use, population and travel costs of three cities

City	Trips (annual)	Population	Trips per 1,000 population	Miles (round trip)	Travel cost (total $)
A	1,600	2,000	800	50	5.00
B	6,000	10,000	600	100	10.00
C	2,400	6,000	400	150	15.00

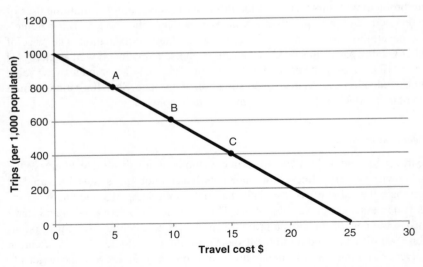

Figure 3.2 Relationship between trips per thousand of population and travel cost.

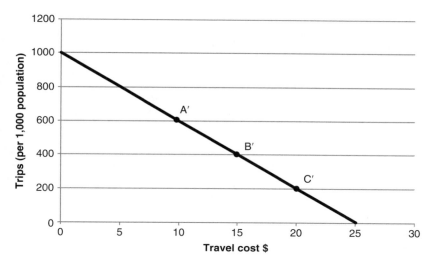

Figure 3.3 Estimated trips per thousand of population with a $5 entrance fee.

estimated trips per thousand population for each town when a $5 entrance fee is imposed. Table 3.4 shows the estimated trips per thousand of population for all three cities when differing entrance fees are imposed.

The trips per thousand of population can then be multiplied by the respective populations of each city and summed up to get the total visits (trips) for each entrance fee (price). The process is illustrated by Table 3.5.

Finally, a demand curve can be estimated by plotting the price against the total number of trips, as exhibited in Figure 3.4.

As with CVM, the value of the park may be estimated as the area under the demand curve. For this particular example, the value of the park is approximately $73,000 per annum.

As with other valuation methods, the travel cost method is not ideal. First, the method implicitly ignores option demand (people's WTP to maintain the site even though they currently do not use it) as the final demand is derived from an

Table 3.4 Estimated trips per thousand of population for various entrance fees

Price (entrance fee) $	Trips per thousand of population		
	A	B	C
0	800	600	400
5	600	400	200
10	400	200	0
15	200	0	0
20	0	0	

Table 3.5 Total visits made for various entrance fees

Price (entrance fee) $	Total visits Trips per 1,000 of population × 1,000 of population			
	A	B	C	Total
0	1,600	6,000	2,400	10,000
5	1,200	4,000	1,200	6,400
10	800	2,000	0	2,800
15	400	0	0	400
20	0	0	0	0

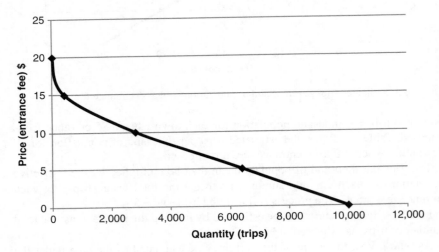

Figure 3.4 Demand curve for hypothetical park.

interpolation of actual trips made which only reflects use demand. Second, as people spend both time and money in visiting recreational sites, the travel cost method, which only takes into account monetary expenditure, tends to understate the true value. Third, the value derived is only accurate to the degree by which visitors' travels are directed to the particular site only. However, when people go sightseeing, they tend to visit a few places in one trip and it is difficult to separate the value of each site from the rest. Fourth, visitors need to be spread out geographically at sufficient distance in order to have travel costs that vary adequately. This restricts the application of the method. Finally, the travel cost method makes the implausible assumption that whole populations, from which the visitors are drawn, have similar preferences.

Having explained how each technique is conducted and the weaknesses of each method, we now present examples of actual valuation studies that have made use of the methods mentioned. The valuation method, author/s, year, valuation item and the estimated value of the item in the studies are all presented in Table 3.6.

Table 3.6 Examples of valuation studies using differing valuation techniques

Valuation method	Author (year)	Valuation item	Estimated item value
Contingent valuation method (CVM)	Quah and Tan (1999)	Scenic view of East Coast Park (Singapore)	Present value of Singapore dollars S$2.1–7.2 billion
	Amirnejah et al. (2006)	Existence value of North Forests (Iran)	US$30.12 per household per annum
	Aabø (2005)	Public libraries (Norway)	400–2,000 Kr per household per annum
	Hammitt and Zhou (2006)	Air-pollution-related health risk (China)	Prevention of a cold episode: US$3–6 per episode Prevention of chronic bronchitis: US$500–1,000 per case
Hedonic pricing	Dewenter et al. (2007)	Mobile phone brand name Premiums (Germany)	Brand premium in the range $57–172
	Day et al. (2007)	Noise avoidance in Birmingham (UK)	Road noise reduction (1dB)[1]: £31.49–201.16 per annum (1997 value) Rail noise reduction (1dB)[1]: £83.61–1,488.88 per annum (1997 value)
	Kong et al. (2007)	Percentage of urban green landscape within 0.3 km radius in Jinan City (China)	63.55 yuan per percentage point increase
Travel cost method	Shrestha et al. (2007)	Nature-based recreation in public natural areas of Apalachicola River, Florida (US)	US$74.18 per visit day US$484.56 million per annum
	Fleming and Cook (2008)	Lake McKenzie (Australia)	AU$13.7–31.8 million per annum AU$104.30–242.84 per person per visit
	Gürlük and Rehber (2008)	Recreational value for bird-watching at Lake Manyas (Turkey)	US$103.23 million per annum
	Jeuland et al. (2010)	Private benefits of 'free' cholera vaccine in Beira (Mozambique)	US$0.85 per complete treatment (of two doses)

[1] Value depends on original noise level.

Non-economic valuation techniques

The valuation techniques and examples discussed thus far (CVM, hedonic pricing and the travel cost method) are all economic valuation techniques because they involve estimations of demand curves. However, there are times when policy-makers rely on non-economic methods for efficiency reasons. These techniques include the dose–response function, where a relationship between a stressor and a receptor is identified to determine both safe and hazardous levels for the stressor, the defensive expenditure approach, which takes the value of an item as the amount people are observed to spend in order to protect themselves from a decline in the availability of the good, and the replacement cost method where the value of an item is estimated as the cost of replacing it. As these are closer to heuristic rules-of-thumb that have little economic basis than proper estimation procedures, we shall not elaborate further on each method. In general, the CBA practitioner is advised to use economic methods to yield more accurate and reliable estimates to aid optimal decision-making.

Conclusion

In conclusion, we summarize the various valuation techniques with Figure 3.5.

The continual development and refinement of valuation techniques provide little excuse for the practitioner not to explicitly take into account monetary values of externalities and non-market goods. The development of the paired-comparison approach (to be discussed in Chapter 9) is a good example. However, in utilizing any valuation technique, the practitioner should bear in mind the

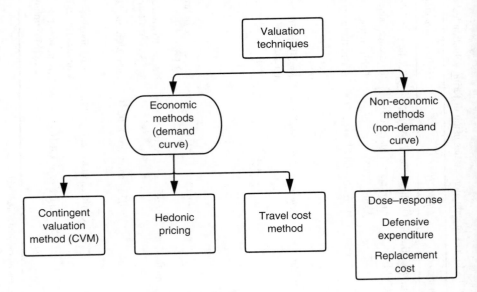

Figure 3.5 Overview of valuation techniques.

possible limitations and constraints. The choice of valuation method ought not to be arbitrary. For any item, the optimal valuation tool depends on the context of the CBA. Should the markets within the CBA frame prove to be close to perfect, hedonic pricing may produce the most accurate estimations. Otherwise, CVM or the travel cost method may be preferable.

Further, where time and cost impose impossible constraints, the practitioner may turn to the use of non-economic valuation techniques. That said, it is recommended that a superior alternative known as the benefit transfer method is applied instead. As benefit transfer is the subject of the next chapter, we shall not elaborate here.

Lastly, in the unlikely scenario where all valuation techniques fail to work, the practitioner always has the option of falling back on the familiar recourse of presenting the item separately from the rest of the CBA and letting the policy-maker decide whether the trade-off is worth it. This approach is, however, greatly discouraged and should be avoided as far as possible.

4   Benefit transfers

Contributed by Christabelle N. E. Soh[1]

In Chapter 3, valuation techniques such as the contingent valuation method (CVM), hedonic pricing and the travel cost method were introduced. We may think of these as methods that elicit indigenous valuations since they are based on primary localized data. They represent the ideal in computing item values.

In practice, however, one may not have the luxury of time and/or funds to carry out the above methods. It is not uncommon for a practitioner to have to produce a cost–benefit analysis (CBA) within a short span of time, especially if a proposed project is time-sensitive. Neither do government bodies always have the available funds to conduct proper valuation studies. Under such circumstances, the practitioner may have to use plug-in values derived from other studies. This transfer of values from a secondary source is termed benefit transfer. Boyle and Bergstrom (1992, p. 657) provide a more formal definition where benefit transfer is defined as 'the transfer of existing estimates of non-market values to a new study which is different from the study for which the values were originally estimated'. In keeping with the general literature, we refer to the new study site (to which values are transferred) as the policy site and the original site (where values are transferred from) as the study site. Depending on the similitude of the policy site and the study site, adjustments may have to be made to the value before transference.

Types of benefit transfers and the steps involved

Benefit transfers may be broadly classified into two types – value transfers and function transfers. As the name suggests, value transfers involve plugging in values, either adjusted or unadjusted, from other study sites into the policy context. These values may be transferred from a single point (point-estimate value transfer) or from an average of several studies (measure of central-tendency value transfer). Function transfers, on the other hand, involve the transference of statistical models that define relationships between the collected data of a study site (Rosenberger and Loomis, 2003).

In certain cases, government agencies may have existing databases of values of certain items[2] that practitioners are encouraged to adopt. Some practitioners prefer a separate classification for such methods. Here, for simplicity, we will refer to these transfers as point-estimate value transfers.

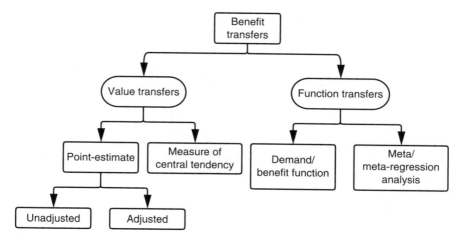

Figure 4.1 A classification of benefit transfer methods.

A classification of benefit transfer methods is presented in Figure 4.1.

Value transfers

The first broad classification, value transfers, may be subdivided into point-estimate value transfers and measure of central-tendency value transfers.

Point-estimate value transfer

A point-estimate value transfer is the transfer of an item's value from a single study site to the policy site. In conducting a point-estimate value transfer, practitioners may choose whether to adjust the value to be transferred. An unadjusted value is the easiest to transfer and may be justified if the original study site is not significantly different from the policy site. To assess the degree of similarity of the study and policy sites, practitioners have to take into account the socioeconomic characteristics of the populations at the two sites (e.g. income levels); the physical nature of both sites; the similarity of the proposed projects for each site (e.g. incremental improvements versus overhaul); the time frame of the projects (i.e. inter-temporal differences[3]); and the market characteristics of both sites (Bateman *et al.*, 2000; Boardman *et al.*, 2006). Should the above characteristics be largely similar between the study and policy sites, unadjusted transfers may be reasonably accurate and hence, justifiable.

In such transfers, the practitioner searches through the existing valuation studies, identifies a completed study of a study site suitably similar to the policy site, selects the value of the item required and then uses it as the value of the item for the policy site.

Realistically speaking, it is rare for the study and the policy sites to be similar enough for an unadjusted value transfer to be accurate. In such instances, the value to be transferred will have to be adjusted. Among other factors, such adjustments can take the form of adjusting the value for income, the stock of the good available in the region, differences in project impacts and differences in time. Apart from scaling to adjust for the factors mentioned, expert judgment may also be employed for the adjustment, as was the fashion in the 1970s and 1980s. Alternatively, the practitioner may choose to only transfer values of subsamples of the original study that have similar characteristics to the policy site. Such transference, however, is subject to the availability of data from the original study. The current preferred method is to systemically adjust the values for differences in site characteristics or survey method differences by looking at how both factors affect the estimated values (i.e. the role of the factors in the value's function). This transfer method, however, falls under the classification of function transfers, which will be explained in later paragraphs.

For adjusted point-estimate value transfers, the steps involved are to search through the existing valuation studies, identify a completed valuation study for the item in question (preferably for a site similar to the policy site to reduce the amount of adjustment required), decide in what way the selected value needs adjusting, make the necessary adjustments and then use the result as the value of the item for the policy site.

Measure of central-tendency value transfer

Measure of central-tendency value transfer is the transference of an average value of an item across a number of relevant study sites to the policy site. To carry out a measure of central-tendency value transfer, the practitioner searches for all relevant valuation studies for the item in question, computes a measure of central-tendency of the values (i.e. mean, median, etc.) and uses the result as the value of the item for the policy site.

Unlike point-estimate value transfers, transfers of measures of central-tendency do not lend themselves well to adjustments. The reason is relatively straightforward. Values of measures of central-tendency do not accrue to any particular study site and hence do not have comparable site characteristics to adjust for.

Function transfers

The other class of benefit transfers is function transfers. The two main types of function transfers are demand transfers and meta transfers, also known as the more technical-sounding benefit function transfers and meta-regression analysis function transfers, respectively. We will use the latter names for the rest of this chapter.

Benefit function transfer

Benefit function transfers involve transferring a known relationship (the demand function) between the willingness-to-pay (WTP) and the study site factors related to the respondents, from a single original study to a new policy site. For example, if regression analysis of an original study shows that the WTP is a linear function of income and male–female ratio with coefficients of 0.5 and 0.4 respectively (i.e. WTP = 0.5 (Income) + 0.4 (Male:Female)), then the WTP of the policy site can be estimated by plugging the income level and male–female ratio into the expression. The drawback of this method is that the practitioner still has to collect data on the policy site, albeit a different type compared to indigenous value elicitations. Where such data is readily available, benefit function transfers are efficient both in terms of cost and time. Where they are not, it might be better to employ some other transfer method or conduct an original study. Another failing of this method is its inability to account for differences in physical site characteristics and valuation methods. For example, open-ended value elicitation typically leads to lower valuations than dichotomous choices. However, such discrepancies cannot be adjusted for if benefit function transfer is used.

To conduct a benefit function transfer, the practitioner must first search through the existing valuation studies to select a completed valuation study for the desired item (a study on a site similar to the policy site is preferred for higher accuracy). Here, we assume data on the affected populations at both sites is available. If not, in the selection of the original study, the practitioner must limit the choices to studies in which the affected population's profile is documented and also collect data on the profile of the policy site's affected population. The next step is to decide what the selected value needs to be adjusted for and regress the study site value on the study site parameters to obtain the value function. The final step is to plug in the policy site parameters into the value function to compute the value of the item for the policy site.

Meta-regression analysis function transfer

Meta-regression analysis function transfers are similar to benefit function transfers in that a function is transferred. However, in demand function transfers, the function is transferred from only one original study, which necessarily restricts the independent variables to only site characteristics related to the respondents. In meta-regression analysis function transfers, the function is derived from more than one study, which allows for variations in the study site's physical characteristics, the value-elicitation approach and the survey methodology. This allows these cross-study differences to be included as independent variables. To illustrate, dummy variables may be used to code for the type of item being valued (e.g. 'old forest'=1 versus 'young forest'=0), the value-elicitation method (e.g. 'stated preference'=1 versus 'revealed preference'=0), the survey method (e.g. 'by phone'=1 versus 'by mail'=0) and others. As in benefit function transfers, once the relationship between the value and the independent variables is established, the practitioner only has to plug in the values of the independent variable of the policy site to compute the desired valuation of the item.

The steps in a meta-regression analysis function transfer are largely similar to those of a benefit function transfer. First, the practitioner must search through the existing valuation studies and make a database of all relevant studies. Here, each study should be meticulously coded for differences in the valuation item, aspects of the methodology and other facets of the affected population's profile. Second, the practitioner establishes the relation between the value of the item and all of the previously mentioned parameters (or a selection based on the practitioner's judgment) by running a regression of the value on the independent variables. A value function is thus obtained. Finally, the practitioner plugs in the policy site parameters into the value function to compute the value of the item for the policy site.

Table 4.1 identifies examples of valuation studies in which the various benefit transfer methods have been applied. For each case, the study details, transfer source, transfer method, as well as the original and estimated values of the item are presented.

Having explained the rationale behind benefit transfers and the different benefit transfer techniques, we will now answer the two questions that are most relevant to practitioners – what are the limitations of benefit transfer and, in general, which transfer technique performs best?

Limitations of benefit transfers

The literature on the criticisms and limitations of benefit transfer is rich. We can, however, summarize them along the lines of five fundamental limitations.

First, benefit transfer relies on extracting values from existing studies. Any inaccuracy in the original valuation is carried over during the transfer. Hence, the accuracy of the transferred value is necessarily constrained by the accuracy of the original study. Where the quality of the original study is poor, the results of the benefit transfer will be poor.

Related to the above, the second limitation of the benefit transfer method, stemming from its dependence on primary studies, is that the (lack of) availability of relevant studies constrains the potential use of this method. If no relevant primary study can be sourced, there can be no value to be transferred. This limitation is especially relevant for value transfers. For function transfers, however, in particular meta-regression analysis function transfers, even physical site characteristics and original valuation methodology may be adjusted for. Hence, in theory, we could pool *all* valuation studies into a database and the values of *any* item may be obtained via meta-regression analysis function transfer that adjusts for the type of site. Doing so would significantly increase the potential pool of studies a practitioner may draw from. While that is so, it must also be noted that this argument is purely theoretical and is based solely on the perspective of wanting to have the largest number of studies from which values can be transferred. In practice, such actions would result in a huge loss of accuracy.

Apart from the issue of whether the above limitation more strongly applies to value or function transfers, we note that this limitation is likely to be less relevant over time as the stock of valuation studies increases. The continued development of valuation study databases (e.g. EVRI[4], Envalue, ValueBaseSWE[5]) will further add to the ease of finding relevant studies to transfer required values from.

Table 4.1 Cases of benefit transfers

Study		Source		Benefit transfer methodology		Values		
Year	Title of study (author/s)	Year	Title of study (author/s)	Transfer type	Adjusted for	Item	Original	Transferred
2007	The Economic Value of Iowa's Natural Resources (Otto et al., 2007)	2005	Updated Outdoor Recreation Use Values on National Forests and Other Public Lands (Loomis et al., 1991)	Unadjusted point-estimate value transfer	Nil	Value per activity day for recreational activities in Iowan parks	(2007 US$): Camping: 33.11 Fishing: 32.91 Hunting: 47.45 Trail use (general recreation): 16.88 Wild-life viewing: 31.29 General use: 16.88	Exactly the same
2003	The Economic Cost of Particulate Air Pollution on Health in Singapore (Quah and Tan, 1999)	1995	Assessing the Health Costs of Particulate Air Pollution in the UK (Pearce and Crowards, 1995)	Adjusted point-estimate value transfer	Income	Value of statistical life in Singapore	(1999 US$) 2.98 million	(1999 US$) 3 million
2007	Introducing Willingness-to-pay for Noise Changes into a Transport Appraisal: An Application of Benefit Transfer (Nellthorp et al., 2007)	2004	The Valuation of Transport-Related Noise in Birmingham (Bateman et al., 2004)	Adjusted point-estimate value transfer	Income Time Household tenure	Mean value of noise reduction by 1dB in the interval of 45–50dB per household per annum in the United Kingdom	(1997 £) 10.2	(2002 £) 13.7

Continued

Table 4.1 Cases of benefit transfers (continued)

Study		Source		Benefit transfer methodology		Values		
Year	Title of study (author/s)	Year	Title of study (author/s)	Transfer type	Adjusted for	Item	Original	Transferred
2004	The Economic Value of Marine Recreational Fishing: Applying Benefit Transfer to Marine Recreational Fisheries Statistics Survey (MRFSS) (Jeong and Haab, 2004)	1994–1997	The Economic Value of New England and Mid-Atlantic Sportfishing in 1994 (Hicks et al., 1999) The Economic Value of Marine Recreational Fishing in the Southeast United States: 1997 Southeast Economic Data Analysis (Haab et al., 2000)	Benefit function transfer	Travel cost Travel time (where wage rate is not available) No. of intercept sites Historic harvest rate Species distribution	Mean access value per fishing trip for states along the northeast and southeast of the United States	(Only selected states shown) (1994 US$) Connecticut: 5.31 Delaware: 2.42 (1997 US$) Georgia: 3.41 North Carolina: 37.19	(Only selected states shown) (1994 US$) Connecticut: 5.90 Delaware: 3.40 (1997 US$) Georgia: 2.19 North Carolina: 25.44
2007	Meta-functional Benefit Transfer for Wetland Valuation: Making the Most of Small Samples (Moeltner and Woodward, 2009)	1991–2004	Nine primary studies on the economic valuation of wetlands in the United States[1]	Meta-analysis function transfer	Wetland type Wetland acreage Household income Percentage of active users Policy scenario	Mean and total value of wetlands in eastern Nevada to Nevadan residents only	Varies between the nine studies	(US$, base year unavailable) 4.749 per household 3,567,616 in total

[1] Loomis et al., 1991; Roberts and Leitch, 1997; Tkac, 2002; Hanemann et al., 1991; Whitehead and Blomquist, 1991; Mullarkey, 1997; Blomquist and Whitehead, 1998; Poor, 1999; and Klocek, 2004.

The third limitation lies in the degree of similitude between the policy and study sites. Although there are mechanisms to adjust for most differences, each adjustment invariably causes some loss of accuracy. As such, the greater the difference between the policy and study site, the less accurate the transferred values and hence, the less efficient the benefit transfer.

The subjectivity involved in benefit transfers constitutes the fourth limitation. In the process of transferring benefits, the practitioner must make any number of value judgments. For instance, in function transfers, the choice of independent variables that enter the demand function depend on the assumptions of the model, which in turn, are based on the value judgment of the practitioner. Similarly, in value transfers, what the original value ought to be adjusted for is also at the practitioner's discretion. However, logically, as in ideal CBA practices, items that enter a CBA ought to be valued from the viewpoint of the affected parties. Following through this line of reasoning, the fact that benefit transfers increase the role of the practitioner while diminishing the influence of the affected parties would very likely result in a greater loss of accuracy.

The final limitation concerns the methodological bias in primary studies. Apart from the issue of the quality of the original study constraining the quality of the transferred value, methodological bias also creates other problems in benefit transfers. For value transfers and benefit function transfers, it presents a problem as such bias cannot be accounted for and corrected in the transfer process. These transfers that do not explicitly account for the methodological bias in the original studies implicitly accept them in their valuations. For meta-regression analysis function transfers, there is the issue of what a practitioner is supposed to do if or when it is discovered that different methods consistently produced different value estimates (e.g. CVM consistently yielding higher/lower estimates than hedonic pricing, CVM by phone producing higher/lower estimates than by face-to-face surveys, etc.). There are no absolute guidelines with regard to what should be done about the above. Clearly, if a particular method can be shown to consistently produce more accurate value estimates than others, then adjustments should always be made to correct the methodological bias caused by other methods. However, the evidence on the superiority of indigenous valuation techniques is mixed at best. Besides, if one method can be shown to consistently produce better estimates than the rest, there would not be such an array of varying methods used in primary studies in the first place. The lack of best practice in indigenous valuation techniques demands that practitioners exercise their value judgments, adding to the subjectivity of the transferred value.

Having discussed the general limitations of benefit transfers, let us move on to the last section of the chapter – the specifics as to whether certain methods of transfer outperform the rest.

Comparison of benefit transfer methods

In terms of broad comparisons, there seems to be some consensus that on average, function transfers provide more accurate estimates than value transfers.

Rosenberger and Loomis (2003) reached this conclusion by observing the percentage difference between the transferred and actual values across 13 sites in which both benefit transfer and indigenous value elicitation were employed. They go on to state that meta-regression function transfers provided better estimates than benefit function transfers. Groothuis (2005) reached a similar conclusion and further showed that the degree of error caused by benefit function transfers were significantly less than value transfers when the original study employed CVM. However, Rosenberger and Loomis (2003) also acknowledged that misapplications of function transfers could result in very significant errors.

The evidence largely supports the idea that function transfers, especially meta-regression analysis transfers, outperform value transfers. However, accuracy of transfer is only one facet of efficiency; application limitations are another. With regard to application limitations, there is, first, the issue of degree of applicability. Function transfers require a minimum amount of information for the regression analysis to be robust. Value transfers, on the other hand, may be carried out as long as one original study may be found. The continued increase in the stock of valuation studies will work in favour of function transfers. However, the stricter requirement of a minimum number of studies will always render function transfers less applicable, even if only slightly.

Second, there is the issue of time. Both methods require exhaustive searches of the literature. However, in function transfers, additional time has to be spent on coding the various aspects of the original studies while this step is not necessary for value transfer. In this light, value transfer may be more time-efficient than function transfers.

In summary, while function transfers provide more accurate value estimates, value transfers are more time- (and hence cost-) effective. As such, there is not a constant optimal method and the practitioner has to exercise judgment as to which method best suits the CBA purposes, taking into account accuracy issues, as well as time and cost constraints.

Conclusion

To conclude the chapter, we take note of a few caveats in conducting benefit transfers. First, while benefit transfers may be relatively more efficient in both costs and time, it should never be the first option. Benefit transfers only provide recourse when indigenous valuation methods are not possible; it is not an alternative. Where possible, practitioners should always opt for indigenous valuation methods. Second, practitioners should always be aware of the limitations of benefit transfers and the ensuing accuracy issues. Third, related to the issues of accuracy, benefit transfers typically provide a range of transferable values. Hence, it is only when the CBA criteria are met for the whole range of values (i.e. when sensitivity analysis yields consistent results) that the practitioner may comfortably provide a recommendation.

5 Simple mathematics of discounting and decision criteria

A typical problem in the cost and benefit analysis process is valuing the cost of the investment against a stream of net benefits that will accrue sometime in the distant future, over the life cycle of the project. This problem is relevant to both public and private sector investments; however, it is more pertinent to the former because of the longer project life spans of public investments.

A simple and naive way to value the investment is to simply add up all the costs and benefits then, if the total sum of the social benefits is more than the total sum of the social costs, the project is deemed beneficial and can be embarked on. An alternative approach is to find out the average return of the investment by dividing the excess returns over the initial outlay over the number of years the project is expected to last.

However, these approaches, though simple to apply, are naive and inadequate when applied to practical problems. The opportunity cost of the investment is incurred at the point the project is embarked on and the net benefits will only occur sometime in the future. People are not indifferent to $100 now or $100 in ten years' time and when given a choice they prefer consumption today rather in the future. Following this, it is easy to see that people will prefer a stream of benefits that accrue earlier in the project's lifecycle rather than a large sum that only appears at the end of the project. These problems demonstrate that a simple summation of the costs and benefits will be inadequate and therefore it is necessary to take account of the time horizon of the investment.

Decision criteria approaches

There are several approaches to account for the time horizon of an investment – the first (and most commonly used) method is to use some discount rate to reduce the investment stream to the present value. This is the net present value (NPV) method. The second method is the benefit–cost (B–C) ratio, which compares the size of the total discounted benefit relative to the total discounted cost of the project. The third method is to find out the average rate of return on the initial outlay, also called the internal rate of return (IRR) method. Finally, a complex technique called the terminal value (TV) method can also be adopted if we want to avoid the "reinvestment" problem inherent in the NPV and IRR methods. We shall discuss each of these methods in detail in the following sections.

Net present value

The NPV discounts a stream of benefits and costs to the present value. The simplified formula is given as follows:

$$NPV = -K_0 + \sum_{t=1}^{N} \frac{B_t}{(1+r)^t} - \sum_{t=1}^{N} \frac{C_t}{(1+r)^t}$$

where K_0 is the initial capital investment, B_t is the benefit in the time period t, C_t is the cost in the time period t, r is the discount rate and N is the time horizon of the project or investment K_0.

The first term in the formula is the value of the capital outlay. As it is invested in the present time period, we need not discount it further. The second and third terms are called the present value of the benefits and costs respectively. They are the discounted value of future benefits and costs at the present time period.

We can simplify the formula further if we take the difference of the benefits and costs for each time period to obtain the net benefits. The net benefit can be negative or positive and the outcome is not affected by the simplification of the formula. We restate the simplified NPV formula as follows:

$$NPV = -K_0 + \sum_{t=1}^{N} \frac{NB_t}{(1+r)^t}$$

where NB_t is the net benefit in the time period t, which is given as $B_t - C_t$.

From the formula, it is clear that the necessary instrument in this method is an appropriate discount rate (r) by which the net benefits are to be discounted. We will discuss further the discount rate later, but for now, it is sufficient to say that when the future net benefits are brought back into the present value and compared against the original cost of investment, the NPV of the project can be positive, negative or zero. The outcome depends on the initial capital cost, the size of the net benefits over the investment horizon and the discount rate chosen.

When the NPV is positive, a project is beneficial to society as the investment brings more future net benefits than the cost of the project. When the NPV is negative, then the project does not bring about sufficient benefits to society for the sacrifice of the consumption that could be made in lieu of the investment, and hence the project should not be embarked upon.

Benefit–Cost ratio

This is similar to the NPV method, where the stream of benefits and costs are discounted to the present value. The B–C ratio is obtained by dividing the present value of benefits over the present value of the costs and including the investment outlay. The formula is given as follows:

$$BC = \frac{\sum_{t=1}^{N}\frac{B_t}{(1+r)^t}}{K_0 + \sum_{t=1}^{N}\frac{C_t}{(1+r)^t}}$$

We can clearly see a relationship between the B–C ratio and NPV methods. When the NPV of the project is zero, than the B–C ratio will be equal to one. When the B–C ration is more than one, it implies that the NPV is more than zero and the project is beneficial to society. Conversely, when the B–C ratio is less than one, then the project is not beneficial to society and NPV will be negative.

Internal rate of return

The formula for determining the IRR is no different from the above methods. However, the difference lies in the instrument of concern. Instead of finding the net benefits of the project over and above the cost of the project, we are trying to discover the discount rate that will reduce the stream of net benefits and the initial investment outlay to zero. In other words, the IRR seeks to find out the level of return or yield that is necessary to make a stream of net benefits equal to the initial outlay, K_0. The formula is given as

$$-K_0 + \sum_{t=1}^{N}\frac{B_t}{(1+r)^t} - \sum_{t=1}^{N}\frac{C_t}{(1+r)^t} = -K_0 + \sum_{t=1}^{N}\frac{NB_t}{(1+r)^t} = 0$$

Although it may look difficult to obtain a solution, and trial and error is required to obtain an approximation of the discount rate, with present computing power, this problem can be solved easily by using a solver tool in a spreadsheet.

Apart from the computation issue, another issue with the IRR method is that it is possible to obtain more than one IRR *if the direction of the net benefits changes from positive to negative* for particular years, in other words, the solution is not unique and this makes decision making inappropriate. However, this should not worry practitioners because the problem does not generally occur unless the changes in net benefit are very significant in absolute terms. An analysis of the stream of costs and benefits will be necessary to determine whether the profile is acceptable before making any decisions.

For decision-making, we can compare the obtained IRR with the prevailing social discount rate and if the IRR is higher than the social discount rate, then the project is worth investing in. However, it is difficult to decide what discount rate is suitable (we will discuss this in the later section – What discount rate to use?). To avoid this problem, the decision-maker can decide whether the calculated IRR is sufficiently high for society based on his/her judgment. If a higher rate of return is required, then the project is not worth investing in and the converse is true as well. This neat solution avoids the need to refer to a social discount rate, but it is highly subjective and may render the decision unsound.

Terminal value

All the above methods assume that it is possible to reinvest all the project proceeds during the life of the project at the same discount rate or IRR. This implicit assumption is important and has bearing on the theoretical fundamentals of the methods. Clearly, it may not be realistic to make such an assumption especially if some of the benefits, if not all, are consumed and not reinvested. Furthermore, when the benefit has non-monetary value, then reinvestment of the proceeds is not appropriate. Even if we can assume that these benefits can be reinvested, it may not be reasonable to hold that the rate of return will be the same throughout the whole project. Hence, academics have developed a new method, called the terminal value (TV) method, to circumvent the 'reinvestment' problem.

To calculate the terminal value, we need to have information about the proportion of annual benefits that are reinvested and the appropriate rate of returns for such reinvestments. With this information, we can compound forward the benefits to the end of the project life. Similarly, the costs and initial capital investment are compounded forward. This way, we obtain the net benefits calculated at the terminal value (or end of the project life) rather than at the present value. The formula can be expressed as follows:

$$TV = -K_0(1+r)^N + \sum_{t=1}^{N} B_{1,t} + \sum_{t=1}^{N} B_{2,t}(1+r_t)^{N-t} - \sum_{t=1}^{N} C_t(1+r_t)^{N-t}$$

where $B_{1,t}$ is the benefit in the time period t which is consumed or not reinvested, $B_{2,t}$ is the benefit in the time period t which is reinvested and r_t is the rate of compounding relevant for each time period t.

The advent of computers has made it easier to carry out the complex calculations with different rate of returns for each time period. However, readers should be aware that the TV method is not commonly used because sometimes the information on the reinvestment proportion and separate reinvestment interest rates is severely lacking. If we simplify the assumptions and use the same rate of returns and full reinvestment of the benefits, then discounting or compounding the stream of net benefits will yield the same results. Therefore, conventional methods of NPV, B–C ratio and IRR are preferred by practitioners as it is simpler to understand and we shall focus our discussion on these methods. For readers who are interested in the theoretical development of the TV method, it is recommended to refer to Mishan and Quah (2007, chapters 30–31) for details.

Decision criteria illustrated

The usefulness of the NPV, B–C ratio or IRR approaches is that the time dimension of the investment problem is taken into consideration. We will illustrate this point more clearly with the following example, as shown in Table 5.1.

(Note: whenever we calculate NPV, B–C ratio and IRR, we have to be careful to use the appropriate sign.)

Table 5.1 Illustrating and comparing different calculation methods

	Initial investment (t = 0)	Benefits and costs ($)					Decision criteria				
			t = 1	t = 2	t = 3	t = 4	Total return	Average return	Net present value at 10%	B–C ratio	Internal rate of return
Project 1	100	B	40	60	80	100	40	10%	7.18	1.03	13%
		C	20	30	40	50					
Project 2	100	B	70	70	70	70	40	10%	14.71	1.07	18%
		C	20	30	40	50					

Note: This table compares the calculations of different decision criteria. Project 2 is the preferred base for the different criteria such as NPV, B–C ratio and IRR.

We see that there are two projects that have a similar investment outlay of $100 and identical total return and average returns. The difference arises when the net benefits are accrued. If naive approaches were used to evaluate the two projects, it would be impossible to decide between the two projects because the absolute return is the same.

However, it is clear that the net benefits of Project 2 are accrued earlier over the investment horizon. As future benefits that are discounted heavily, the NPV of Project 2 is greater than Project 1. It has a higher B–C ratio at 1.07 and has a higher IRR at 18 per cent. Therefore, based on the above calculations and criteria, it is easy to conclude that Project 2 will be preferred.

The decision to invest in Project 2 and not Project 1 only is based on the assumption that there is a limited budget and that the projects are mutually exclusive. If sufficient resources are available, we can invest in both projects. If we have several projects to decide on and a budget constraint, then it is more appropriate to rank the projects before making decisions.

Assuming that the investment horizons are the same for each of the projects, Table 5.2 suggests that if we have a budget constraint of $120, then using the NPV criterion, we will prefer Project 3. On the other hand, if we rank the B–C ratio and work down the list of the projects until the capital budget is exhausted, we can find that a combination of Projects 1 and 2 will yield a higher NPV than Project 3 alone and a net gain of $50 is possible. Hence, when we have several projects to compare, it is appropriate to find out all feasible combinations of projects that can be financed within the budget constraints and to work out the NPV of each combination for comparison. It should be noted that the investment must keep within budget as the B–C ratio will not be appropriate when the budget is violated.

Table 5.2 Comparing decision criteria

	Project 1	*Project 2*	*Project 3*	*Project 4 (Projects 1 and 2 combined)*
Investment cost ($)	40	80	120	120
PV of benefits ($)	70	150	200	220
PV of costs ($)	10	40	60	50
Decision criteria:				
NPV ($)	20	30	40	50
B–C ratio	1.4	1.25	1.25	1.29
IRR (assuming 2 periods only)	50%	37%	17%	42%

Note: This table shows that if the budget constraint is $120, then Project 4 (a combination of Projects 1 and 2) is better than Project 3.

What discount rate to use?

We have until now deferred the question of what discount rate to use when calculating NPV and B–C ratio. This will be dealt with in this section.

The main criticism of the approach of NPV is the choice of an appropriate discount rate. It is commonly assumed that the discount rate to be used is one that reflects society's rate of time preference. In other words, if society is indifferent between having $100 million today and $110 million next year, the time preference is 10 per cent per annum. However, this is only correct under certain circumstances.

One circumstance is that the rate of preference does not change with the amount of investment. Will society's rate of time preference be the same if the amount of investment forgone is not $100 million but $200 million? It is possible that as a result of higher investment, society may require higher discount. Furthermore, if the time horizon is longer, it is possible for the rate of discount to vary.

Even if it is possible to simplify the assumption by assuming one single social rate of discount, there are other problems with choosing a discount rate for long-term investments with uncertain benefits.

As a guideline, it is common to use discount rates that equate to the cost of borrowing close to the timeframe of the investment horizon (Lyon, 1990). For example, for an investment with a ten-year horizon, the analyst can use the Government's ten-year bond, adjusted for the necessary risk premium, as the discount rate. The assumption of this approach to the discount rates is that the rates used should be consistent with current market real interest rates and savings rate reflecting the true market's view of the capital investment today.

Nonetheless, it is still debatable what correct discount rate should be used when doing cost and benefit analysis.

When Lord Stern (Stern, 2006) published his review on climate change, he used a near-zero discount to calculate the net benefits of taking action against climate change. A discount rate that is close to zero means that the cost of borrowing from the future is low, and future benefits and costs are worth about the same as today. A higher discount rate implies that today's value is worth more than the future.

Illustrating this principle with some numerical examples, we see that $100 today would be worth very little in 10 or 20 years time if the discount rate is high (see Table 5.3).

Therefore, we can see that a long-term project is less attractive if a very high discount rate is used. The implication is that society will not be investing too far into the future today and will prefer shorter-term projects. And the converse is true for low discount rates.

Lord Stern used a near-zero rate in his report and concluded that it is necessary to take action against climate change. In doing so, he had implicitly regarded the value of the benefits accrued to society many generations in the future to be as important as for today's generation. Therefore, it is obvious that he would conclude that it is necessary for today's society to make some sacrifice for the sake

Table 5.3 Impact of discount rate on project evaluation

Discount rate %	1 year $	5 years $	10 years $	20 years $
0	100	100	100	100
1	99.0	95.1	90.5	82.0
5	95.2	78.4	61.4	37.7
10	90.9	62.1	38.6	14.9
20	83.3	40.2	16.2	2.6

Note: The impact of discounting on $100 at different discount rates and time frames.

of the future. However, when there are so many uncertainties over the benefits of climate change investments, and the fact that they are accrued so far into the future, it remains to be seen whether such investment is more worthwhile and attractive compared with other investments, such as education, that deliver clear benefits in the near future.

In practice, it takes some value judgment to decide what discount rate is appropriate for the project. As discussed earlier, one way to avoid the problem is to use the IRR method. The average return rate calculated from the IRR can be viewed as the maximum threshold discount rate for the project to remain positive. When the IRR is larger than the borrowing rates by a large margin, the project will give net positive benefit regardless of the discount rate used. In other words, the project is worth investing in. The decision-maker should be only more careful when the IRR is close to the borrowing rate.

When adopting the NPV method or the B–C ratio, it is necessary to test out the impact of the decision with different assumptions of the discount rate. This is known as sensitivity testing. By testing the sensitivity of the project appraisal towards the discount rates, the decision-maker can decide whether it is important to be particular about the discount rate used in the appraisal process. If it is not particularly sensitive, the guideline of using the prevailing cost of borrowing close to the project investment horizon to value the investment should be sufficient. The IRR will also be able to provide the upper boundary of the sensitivity test that will turn the NPV of the project from positive to negative.

6 Value of a statistical life in Singapore

With additional contributions by Chia Wai Mun[1]

Introduction

Most often, cost–benefit analysis involves the evaluation of a wide range of health, transportation and environmental public projects that impose costs on society in exchange for the reduction in fatality risk. Therefore, a comparison between the costs of reducing risk and the benefits of such reduction is necessary. However, such a comparison between costs and benefits is challenging because it often requires an estimate of the economic value of a statistical life (VOSL).

Although the VOSL literature began to be established in economics in the late 1970s and early 1980s, policy-makers viewed the idea of placing a value on human life as being immoral. As a result, in early government studies particularly in the United States, the human capital measure given by the average present value of the lost earnings of those affected by a policy was presented as the measure of the economic benefits of reducing fatality risks. This measure, which is often used in court cases to compensate for wrongful death, is easy to calculate. However, for many reasons, this human capital measure is no longer well accepted. One main reason is that people with low income would be attributed very low values of human capital, making this measure ethically debatable. Besides, such a measure only takes into account material losses such as an individual's productive capacity without appraising the intangible aspects such as joy of life, health and the prevention of sorrow, pain and distress.

The economic approach of valuing life or, more specifically, valuing the risks of death, is quite different and more appealing than an accounting procedure based on one's income where the value of an individual's life is calculated as the present value of future earnings. The economic approach of valuing the risks of death requires estimating the rate at which an individual would trade monetary wealth for a small change to the chance of dying within a specified time-period. VOSL, in economics, is a technical term used to evaluate the trade-off between risks of death and monetary wealth. It is neither commonly attached to individual's lives nor used to compare the value of one person's life relative to another's. The word 'statistical' implies that the valuation of a statistical life is concerned with the valuation of changes in the level of risk exposure rather than valuation of the life of a specific individual. When one expends wealth to avoid potentially fatal risks (i.e. willingness-to-pay) or accepts wealth to take such risks (i.e. willingness-to-accept), the trade-off between wealth and the probability of death is implicitly defined.

In VOSL literature, the concept can be measured by a person's willingness-to-pay (WTP) or willingness-to-accept (WTA). WTP is the maximum monetary amount an individual is willing to sacrifice for a reduction in the risks of death, while WTA stands, in contrast, for the minimum amount an individual is willing to accept for an increase in the risks of death. WTP and WTA values are individual trade-offs in terms of the expenditure needed for improving safety and reducing risks versus alternative types of consumption. These values are explicitly intended to reflect preferences, perceptions and attitudes toward risk of those affected. Totalling such a measure across individuals can provide an estimated VOSL.

In practice, estimating VOSL can be time consuming and costly. While the bulk of studies have been conducted in many developed countries, particularly the United States and Western Europe, no such study has been conducted in Singapore. Therefore, it has been common practice to use a benefit transfer approach to transfer such values, with adjustments, for income differentials across countries. That is, from countries where these values have been made available (usually based on US or European studies) to countries where these values have not been estimated. Generally, the transferred value is scaled by the ratio of per capita income of the country in which the value does not exist, to the per capita income of the country of which the value is adapted, to correct for the income differential between the two countries. The adapted value is then adjusted using the elasticity of WTP with respect to income, which measures the responsiveness of WTP for a small percentage change in income.

The benefit transfer approach, even though widely used, seems to introduce some unique issues and challenges making this practice subject to controversy and scrutiny. These issues include how to convert values from one currency to another, how to account for differences in quantifiable characteristics between countries such as income and how to account for differences in non-quantifiable characteristics such as cultural differences.

Estimates of WTP to reduce the risk of mortality, and hence VOSL, unfortunately do not exist for Singapore. Therefore, without any primary data, performing a benefit transfer becomes the only feasible alternative by transferring information from existing studies that have applied different methods. Motivated by the lack of indigenous estimates of VOSL which in turn provides a reference point for assessing public policies, this study aims to be the first to elicit Singaporeans' WTP for the risk of mortality reduction using a contingent valuation survey. The results obtained from the survey are used to derive estimates of VOSL for Singapore. The effects of age, health status and other endogenous variables on the VOSL and WTP are also evaluated.

In the next section we discuss the survey methodology used to elicit Singaporean WTP to reduce the baseline risk of death. The survey and regression results are presented in the third section. The final section presents the conclusions of the study.

Contingent valuation survey in the estimation of indigenous VOSL in Singapore

The objectives of the survey were first, to estimate, on average, the amount a Singaporean is willing to pay for reducing mortality risk, and second, to examine the effects of population characteristics, such as age, health status, personal income, household income, gender, occupation and educational attainment, on WTP. Following the work of Krupnick *et al.* (2002) and Alberini *et al.* (2004), the present study reports the Singaporean results. A target population aged 40 and above was chosen because the present demographic structure suggests that more than 55 per cent of the population are aged 40–75, and this more elderly population tends to benefit disproportionately from health and environmental programmes. We asked people how much they were willing to pay for an abstract private good that will reduce their risk of dying, over a 10-year interval, by 5 in 10,000 and 1 in 10,000. The chances of dying over a 10-year period with risk in the order of 10^{-3} are equivalent to annual risk changes in the order of 10^{-4}.

Design of questionnaire

Personal interviews were conducted and respondents presented with background information on the top five causes of death in Singapore to help them to understand the current level of risk. There were three pre-survey screening criteria:

1   only respondents aged 40 to 75 are invited to participate in the survey;
2   only Singaporeans and Singapore's permanent residents were invited to participate in the survey;
3   following the use of grids to represent probabilities in mortality risk reductions, as shown in Krupnick *et al.* (2002), only respondents who understood the concept of risk reduction were invited to participate in the survey.

The questionnaire was divided into five sections. Section I began with some demographic questions which include respondents' personal and family health information. Section II introduced the simple concept of probability by using two graphs: one that shows the chance of death of five in 1,000 (five coloured grid squares out of 1,000) and another shows the chance of death of 10 in 1,000 (10 coloured grid squares out of 1,000) over the next ten years. The respondent is asked which of the two shows the higher risk of death. Section III presented the leading causes of death in Singapore. Section IV elicited WTP for risk reductions of a given magnitude, occurring at a specified time, using dichotomous choice methods. Respondents were randomly assigned to one of the two subsamples. As shown in Table 6.1, respondents in one subsample (wave 1 or subsample 1) were first asked if they were willing to pay for a product that, when used and paid for over the next ten years, would reduce baseline risk by 5 in 1,000 over the 10-year period, that is, by 5 in 10,000 annually. In the second WTP question, risks are reduced by 1 in 1,000, that is, by 1 in 10,000 annually. Respondents in the second

Table 6.1 Order of questions

Group of respondents	Current risk reduction		Future risk reduction valued
	Initial risk reduction valued	Second risk reduction valued	
Subsample 1 ($n = 557$)	5 in 1,000	1 in 1,000	5 in 1,000
Subsample 2 ($n = 243$)	1 in 1,000	5 in 1,000	5 in 1,000

subsample (wave 2 or subsample 2) were given the 1 in 1,000 risk change question first. Section V documented the respondents' characteristics such as gender, race, level of education, occupation, personal income and household income.

Early studies typically used open-ended WTP questions, that is, they asked respondents for their maximal WTP for a particular risk reduction. In recent years, however, closed-ended formats have become increasingly popular. In this study, the bid figures and bid structure used in the questionnaire were adapted from a contingent valuation study of Canada by Krupnick *et al.* (2002) where the figures are adjusted by the exchange rate of the two countries and inflated by an average inflation rate, to be expressed in 2007 Singapore dollars. All respondents were asked a set of follow-up dichotomous choice questions to obtain more information about WTP. All WTP dichotomous choice questions answered by 'No–No' responses were followed by a question asking if the respondent was willing to pay anything at all and if so, how much. Respondents were then asked, on a 1–5 scale, their degree of certainty about their responses.

Administration of the survey

A total of 800 people were invited to take part in the survey in December 2007 through a door-to-door personal interview. Survey areas were selected to cover various housing areas in Singapore. These include Yishun (North), Redhill (South), Tampines (East), Boon Lay (West), Bukit Timah (Central), Choa Chu Kang and Sengkang. The 800 respondents were distributed among these seven survey areas and the block numbers in each area were picked randomly. Since housing blocks in Singapore have block numbers of one to three digits, a card was randomly chosen from a pack of cards bearing numbers zero to nine for the first digit and recorded. The card was then returned to the pack for reshuffling and another card was chosen in the same way for the second and third digits. The survey was conducted randomly at every fifth housing unit.

Descriptive statistics of the sample

The target population was people between 40 and 75 years of age, and the sub-sample size of respondents in different age groups is consistent with Singapore's population demographic structure, as shown in Table 6.2.

Table 6.3 shows the descriptive statistics and the population characteristics of the entire sample and each subsample. The average age was 52 years. Both genders had equal representation in the sample with 76 per cent of the sample aged between 40 and 59, and 24 per cent of the sample aged above 60. The average

Table 6.2 Sample demographic structure and Singapore's population demographic structure

Age range	Sample (%)		Singapore's population (%)	
	Males	*Females*	*Males*	*Females*
40–44	11	11	10	10
45–49	10	13	10	10
50–54	8	10	9	9
55–59	9	6	7	7
60–64	5	4	4	4
65–69	3	3	3	4
70 and over	4	4	5	7

Note: Data on Singapore's population demographic structure is obtained from the Department of Statistics, Singapore.

Table 6.3 Characteristics of respondents

Variable name	Mean (std. dev)		
	Subsample 1 (n = 557)	*Subsample 2 (n = 243)*	*Total sample (n = 800)*
Age	52.63 (8.95)	52.94 (8.92)	52.72 (8.94)
Male	49%	47%	49%
Race			
Chinese	72%	69%	71%
Malay	13%	18%	15%
India	13%	11%	12%
Years of education	9.8 (4.17)	10.21 (3.93)	10 (4.06)
Annual household income, S$	49,447 (28,570)	54,810 (31,344)	51,074 (29,553)
Annual personal income, S$	25,137 (18,873)	25,405 (18,670)	25,218 (18,800)
Health status			
General health status score (1–100)	63.4 (8.1)	63.9 (13.0)	63.5 (13.4)
Physical functioning score (1–100)	64.0 (13.0)	63.0 (13.0)	63.8 (13.0)
Social functioning score (1–100)	63.0 (14.1)	64.0 (14.3)	63.3 (14.2)
Vitality score (1–100)	63.9 (13.6)	64.4 (14.7)	63.1 (13.9)
Mental health score (1–100)	59.1 (8.1)	59.5 (7.5)	58.4 (7.9)
Average current baseline risk	6.3 (9.1)	6 (7.3)	6.2 (8.5)

educational attainment was 10 years of schooling with more than 70 per cent having completed secondary school. However, only 12 per cent of the sample had completed university.

The average household income and personal income were around S$51,074 and S$25,218, respectively. The average individual in the sample had a higher level of educational attainment, with 10 years of schooling, compared with the average Singaporean having an average of 9.3 years of schooling.

Table 6.3 also reports the average index scores of general health status, physical functioning, social functioning, vitality and mental health. The reported average current baseline risk shows that the mortality risk for the survey respondents is 6.2 per 1,000 people.

Survey and regression results

Risk comprehension

Using a grid graph, similar to that of Krupnick *et al.* (2002) as shown in Figure 6.1, the probability choice test question was designed to ask respondents which of the two persons has the higher risk of death, when risks were represented using coloured squares on the grid. The probability question also asked respondents which one of these people they would rather be. Only respondents who chose the correct answer, that is, they preferred to be the person with the lower risk, were invited to participate in the survey. By this process, we cleaned the sample by

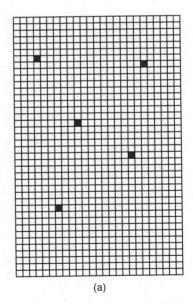
(a)

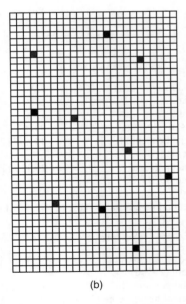
(b)

Figure 6.1 Grid graph used to introduce probability concept: (a) risk of 5 in 1,000 and (b) risk of 1 in 1,000.

dropping respondents who chose the incorrect answer in both the first and second probability tests.

WTP responses: current risk reductions

Similar to the work of Krupnick *et al.* (2002), when respondents were asked to value more than one commodity within an interview, WTP tends to be affected by the order in which the commodities are presented. As a result, we only selected to analyse WTP for the first risk reductions presented in the questionnaire. For respondents in subsample 1 and subsample 2, we examined WTP for risk reductions equal to 5 in 1,000 and 1 in 1,000, respectively.

In a VOSL study using contingent valuation survey, an external scope test is passed when the mean WTP of respondents faced with the larger risk change is significantly larger than the mean WTP of respondents faced with the smaller risk change, for example, if the percentage of people willing to pay for the 5 in 1,000 mortality risk reduction is higher than the 1 in 1,000 mortality risk reduction for every initial bid value. An internal scope test is passed when a respondent's WTP increases with the size of the risk reduction.

Figure 6.2 shows the percentage of respondents giving a 'yes' response to the initial payment questions. Generally, our survey results passed the external scope test where the mean WTP of respondents faced with 5 in 1,000 mortality risk reduction was larger than the mean WTP of respondents faced with 1 in 1,000 mortality risk reduction. Additionally, economic theory suggests that the proportion of people willing to pay should be inversely related to the bid amount. While this is generally true for the results of 5 in 1,000 mortality risk reduction, the same does not apply to 1 in 1,000 mortality risk reduction as the second lowest bid value of S$400 has the highest 'yes' response. The small sample size might be the contributing factor leading to the above observation.

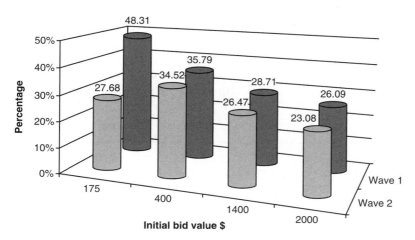

Figure 6.2 Percentage of 'yes' responses by bid value.

Respondents who replied 'no' to both initial and follow-up bids were asked whether they were willing to pay anything at all for the abstract product that delivers risk reduction. In this survey, as shown in Table 6.4, 24 per cent and 33 per cent of respondents refused to pay any amount for the 5 in 1,000 (subsample 1) and the 1 in 1,000 (subsample 2) mortality risk reduction, respectively. Consistent with other contingent valuation studies, the number of zero responses is large but the percentage is smaller for the larger risk reduction.

Following convention, an interval data/continuous data variant of the tobit model, also commonly known as the spike model, is used as a statistical framework to model WTP. Table 6.5 reports the mean WTP and VOSL figures for the 5 in 1,000 (Subsample 1) and 1 in 1,000 (Subsample 2) mortality risk reductions. As shown in Table 6.5, the mean WTP for the 5 in 1,000 mortality risk reduction that takes place over the next ten years is S$422.73 (2007 S$) per year with a standard deviation of S$37.18, while the corresponding mean WTP for the 1 in 1,000 mortality risk reduction is S$205.44 with standard deviation of (S$53.60). A Wald test was also conducted to test for whether there was a significant difference between mean WTP for the 5 in 1,000 and the 1 in 1,000 mortality risk reductions. The test showed a Wald statistic of 147.55 with a p-value of 0, which implies that the mean WTP for the 5 in 1,000 mortality risk reduction is statistically greater than the mean WTP for the 1 in 1,000 mortality risk reduction. In other words, we can confirm that our survey passes the external scope test mentioned earlier and the mean WTP is proven sensitive to the size of mortality risk reductions. As in Krupnick *et al.* (2002), WTP is not directly proportional to the size of mortality risk reductions as mean WTP for the 5 in 1,000 mortality risk reduction is less than 5 times of the mean for the 1 in 1,000 mortality risk reduction, where we see a Wald statistic of 19.47 with p-value of 0.

The VOSL figures were computed by dividing the corresponding annual mean WTP figure by the size of the annual mortality risk reductions, that is, 5 in 10,000 or 1 in 10,000. As shown in Table 6.5, the VOSL was S$845,460 (US$615,950) for the 5 in 1,000 mortality risk reduction and S$2.05 million (US$1.49 million) for the 1 in 1,000 mortality risk reduction. The VOSLs are calculated assuming

Table 6.4 Percentage of zero responses

Subsample (sample size)	No. of zero responses	% of subsample
Subsample 1 ($n = 557$)	135	24
Subsample 2 ($n = 243$)	80	33

Table 6.5 WTP and VOSL figures in 2007 S$

Subsample (sample size)	WTP (std. dev) S$	VOSL S$
Subsample 1 ($n = 557$)	422.73 (37.18)	845,460
Subsample 2 ($n = 243$)	205.44 (53.60)	2,054,400

risk change is evenly distributed over the 10-year period. Because the payment and the risk change are discounted over the same time period using the same discount rate, the choice of discount rate in this scenario is irrelevant.

Sensitivity of WTP to age: 5 in 1,000 mortality risk reduction

An important issue for decision-makers is whether the VOSL increases or decreases with age. From the theoretical perspective, the age-pattern of the VOSL is ambiguous (Johansson, 2002). From the empirical perspective, there seems to be some support of an inverted-U shape for the age-pattern of the VOSL, i.e. the VOSL increases with age to peak at some age and then starts to decline. Shepard and Zeckhauser (1982 and 1984) were among the first to report this result. In a Swedish contingent valuation study of the WTP for a new medical treatment, Johannesson *et al.* (1997) also report an inverted-U shape for the age-pattern of the VOSL. Drawing on labour market data for the US, Kneisner *et al.* (2006) found a similar result.

Will an older and/or less healthy individual be willing to pay less for mortality risk reductions compared to a younger and/or healthy individual? An answer to this question can be found by regressing WTP on age and health status variables by controlling other factors such as personal and household income, and level of educational attainment. Table 6.6 presents the regression results based on interval regression using observations collected in subsample 1, that is, the 5 in 1,000 mortality risk reduction. Three model specifications were estimated.

Table 6.6 Internal validity of WTP for 5 in 1,000 risk change

Variable	Coefficient (z-statistic)		
	Specification 1	Specification 2	Specification 3
Intercept	510.92 (1.34)	565.16 (1.48)	−89.05 (−0.32)
Age	−9.30** (−2.13)	−11.66** (−2.46)	
Age²		0.61 (1.27)	
Age 40–49			108.73 (1.16)
Age 50–59			−26.31 (−0.23)
Age 60–70			28.99 (0.24)
Male	3.69 (0.05)	0.25 (0.01)	−4.85 (−0.07)
Bottom 28% of distribution of income in the sample (dummy)	−583.35*** (−3.69)	−577.83*** (−6.68)	−581.94*** (−6.72)
Education (years of schooling)	−6.82 (−0.66)	−4.24 (10.45)	−1.26 (−0.13)
Mental health score	10.63** (2.46)	10.58** (2.45)	10.86** (2.50)
Scale parameter	779.16 (1.04)	781.33 (1.04)	781.33 (1.04)
Log likelihood	−1339.55	−1338.74	−1340.58

Note: The symbols *, ** and *** indicate statistical significance at the 10%, 5% and 1% levels, respectively.

Table 6.7 Mean WTP by age in 2007 S$

Age range	Predicted mean WTP	Standard deviation
Ages 40–49 (n = 248)	$505.63	59.15
Ages 50–59 (n = 184)	$397.70	49.02
Ages 60–69 (n = 79)	$322.36	122.54
Ages 70 and over (n = 47)	$141.41	193.53

In specification 1, we estimated only a linear relationship between age and WTP. In specification 2, we estimated a nonlinear relationship by allowing the squared value of age to enter into the specification. In specification 3, we allowed more flexibility in the relationship by including different age-group dummy variables.[2] Our results from specifications 1 and 2, showed a statistically significant relationship between the mean WTP and age. The negative coefficients suggest that the mean WTP is declining with age, i.e. the elderly are less willing to pay for mortality risk reductions.

To determine the effect of age on WTP, we further divided the sample into four different age groups: 40–49, 50–59, 60–69 and 70 or above. Interval regression was estimated using a tobit/spike model, which includes only the intercept. Table 6.7 shows the estimates of WTP for each age group.

Table 6.7 shows that the mean WTP is declining with age. Generally, the mean WTP for younger people aged 40–49 and 50–59 is about S$506 and S$398, respectively. This figure drops further to S$322 for people age 60–69, and continues to decline to only S$141 for elderly aged 70 and above. The relationship between VOSL and age is less clear. Abelson (2003) points out that based on models of lifetime consumption, theoretical studies tend to find that the VOSL rises until about the age of 40 years and then falls. However, based on other empirical studies (for example, Krupnick *et al.*, 2002), the mean WTP falls with age, but only after age 70 years.

Other determinants of WTP for 5 in 1,000 mortality risk reduction

To examine the effect of health, income, occupation and other covariates on the mean WTP we ran interval regression for the 5 in 1,000 mortality risk reduction. Table 6.8 presents the estimation results where ages, household income, level of educational attainment and occupational dummy variables,[2] such as white-collar workers and the self-employed, are found significant. Age is negatively related to WTP and household income is positively related to WTP. Additionally, white-collar workers and those who are self-employed tend to be more willing to pay for mortality risk reductions. Surprisingly, more educated people are found less willing to pay for mortality risk reductions.

Table 6.8 Variables contributing to WTP

Variable	Estimate	z-statistic
Intercept	−1187.10***	−2.72
Baseline risk:		
Male	−75.78	−0.99
Age^2	−0.092**	−2.53
Chinese	170.37	0.73
Malay	192.58	0.78
Indian	367.91	1.49
Individual characteristics:		
Personal income (S$)	0.054	1.43
Household income (S$)	0.051***	2.61
Education (years)	−33.91***	−3.08
Physical health status	4.27	1.08
General health status	−1.41	−0.34
Social functioning	6.59	0.06

Note: The symbols *, ** and *** indicate statistical significance at the 10%, 5% and 1% levels, respectively.

Conclusions

This is the first study deriving indigenous values of a statistical life for Singapore. It is a contingent valuation survey conducted to elicit Singaporeans' willingness-to-pay (WTP) to reduce the baseline risk of death by 5 in 10,000 and 1 in 10,000. From a sample size of 800, aged 40 to 75 years, the mean of WTP translates into values of a statistical life of S$850,000 (US$615,950) and S$2.05 million (US$1.49 million), respectively. These values can be used as a critical input in cost–benefit analysis of proposed project, regulations and policies in Singapore. From the study, we also found that there is a significant inverse relationship between the mean WTP and age. Other important variables affecting the mean WTP are mental health, household income, age, occupation and level of educational attainment.

Through this study, however, we found that refining VOSLs for the specific characteristics of the affected population at risk remains an important priority for government agencies in the conduct of economic analyses. Improving the applications of VOSLs in this way can result in more informed government interventions to address market failures related to environmental, health and safety mortality risks.

7 Estimating the economic cost of air pollution on health

Contributed by Chia Wai Mun[1]

A number of developing countries around the world face the dual challenge of sustaining their rapid pace of development while simultaneously ensuring that this development occurs in a sustainable manner. Industrialization coupled with surging populations has resulted in severe environmental degradation, a key aspect being air pollution. Pollutants such as sulphur dioxide, nitrogen oxide, lead, ozone and particulate matter have primarily caused the most significant and obvious damage to air quality in cities worldwide. In such a scenario, it becomes imperative for governments and industries to have a useful and accurate method to estimate the economic cost of air pollution, for policy-making, regulation, surveillance and innovation. This chapter closely examines one such method of estimating the economic cost of air pollution with case studies to examine its use.

Particulate matter in the atmosphere refers to any dust, dirt, smoke and liquid droplets emitted into the atmosphere through industrial activity, vehicles, construction, fires and windblown dust. Particulate matter may also originate through the condensation of emitted gases into tiny droplets. Particulate matter is not only found to be widespread, but is also considered to be the most damaging, and measures relating to particulate matter in the air are used to create a useful measure of the economic cost of air pollution.

Concentration of particulate matter in the air is expressed in micrograms of particles per cubic metre of air sampled ($\mu g/m^3$). The particulate size measure is known as PM_{10} and includes all particles with an aerodynamic diameter of 10 μm or less. These particles are a health concern as they can penetrate deep into the sensitive lower regions of the respiratory tract and are known as inhalable particles.

Studies examining the effects of exposure to air pollution identify PM_{10} as the pollutant most responsible for the life-shortening effect of dirty air. The biggest concerns with respect to human health include adverse effects on breathing, aggravation of existing respiratory and cardiovascular disease, change to the body's immunity against foreign materials, lung tissue damage, carcinogenesis and premature death. The reduction in immunity and an increased susceptibility to respiratory infections also leads to an increase in the incidence of pneumonia in more vulnerable sections of the general population.

Establishing the link between increased emissions and human health is more straightforward. The next step entails establishing a link between the predicted health effects and the corresponding economic cost. For the health effects, the monetarization approach determines such values according to individuals' stated preferences or willingness-to-pay (WTP). The argument for this approach is that the basis for most judgments regarding changes in human well-being are people's preferences. Similarly, changes in human mortality and morbidity, which are vital aspects of human well-being, should also be valued, based on what individuals are willing to pay for better health or the compensations they are willing to accept to forgo an improvement in health. A vital moral and ethical issue arises when this economic analysis is undertaken. Conflicts arise between the ethical validity of assigning a value to a human life and the need for economic analysis. To clarify, the value of a statistical life (VOSL) is unrelated to the value of a human life.

The VOSL can be defined as the value of a small change in the risks associated with an unnamed member of a large group dying (Dixon *et al.*, 1994). It represents an individual's WTP for a marginal reduction in the risk of being dead. The calculation of VOSL can be achieved by several approaches – hedonic value methods: property-value approach, compensating wage differential approach, preventive expenditures approach and contingent valuation method (CVM).

The valuation of reduced morbidity can also be calculated through measures of an individual's WTP or by using cost of illness (COI) approaches. COI measures the total COI that is imposed on society including the value of lost productivity (loss in earnings) due to illness, medical costs like hospital care, medicine, the services of doctors and nurses and other out-of-pocket expenditure.

Several studies have been conducted to determine the economic costs of air pollution damage to human health from PM_{10}. The economic cost of health damage per capita in developing countries appears to be fairly consistent in the range of US\$15 to US\$247. Most of these studies conducted use consensus dose–response functions (DRFs) in the estimation of the economic cost of air pollution. This implies that the costs of particulate air pollution in terms of its impact on human health is largely determined by the size of the population at risk and the unit economic values used to value the increase in mortality and morbidity.

The methodology

Estimating the economic cost of particulate air pollution on health in a particular city or region involves using the damage function/dose–response approach. This approach measures the effects of premature death (mortality effects) and the effects of health deterioration (morbidity effects) of particulate air pollution. Subsequently, the economic values of these health impacts are calculated in terms of the statistical lives that could be saved and the COI incurred.

The procedure can be adopted through three steps:

1   Determine the ambient concentration of the pollutant, PM_{10}, in the city or region being analysed for pollution costs.
2   Apply the damage function approach using dose–response relationships to estimate the health impact of this PM_{10} pollution (where the health impacts

considered are the increase in mortality and morbidity). This is one of the most accepted methodologies of doing so.

3   Assign an economic/monetary value to the increase in mortality and morbidity.

Examining the second step in detail, the damage–response functions are adopted from Ostro (1994) and Rowe *et al.* (1995) and are used to estimate the health effects of air pollution, specifically of PM_{10}. The strength of this approach is its simplicity and its easy interpretation. For this stage, we need to determine a few factors.

First, we need to develop estimates of the effects of air pollution on various health outcomes, as DRFs link variations in ambient levels of pollutants to certain health effects. For this we calculate the partial derivate of slope of the DRF to provide an estimate of the change in a given health effect associated with a change in air quality.

Second, we multiply this partial derivative (slope of the DRF) by the population at risk of the air pollutant under consideration. For some pollution related health effects, this might include the entire population exposed to air pollution, whereas for other effects, there may be particularly sensitive subgroups such as the children, the elderly or asthmatics to account for.

Third, we look at the change in air quality under consideration. This is calculated as the deviation between the actual ambient levels of air pollutant and the acceptable average concentration of air pollutant. As a result, the change in air pollution is dependent on both the policy under consideration (to determine the acceptable concentration) and the available data (to determine the actual ambient level of air pollutants). Usually, the relevant change in air pollution can be calculated by using either the change from current air pollution levels to some ambient air quality standard or a given percentage of reduction, such as 5 or 10 per cent.

The estimated health impact can be calculated by the relationship

$$\Delta H_{ij} = a_{ij} \times \text{POP}_i \times \Delta A_j \tag{7.1}$$

where ΔH_{ij} is the change in the population's risk of health impact i due to pollutant j, a_{ij} is the slope from the dose–response curve for health impact i due to pollutant j, POP_i is the population at risk of health effect i and ΔA_j is the change in ambient concentration of air pollutant j.

Methodology for evaluating the mortality cost

DRFs relate information on changes in the ambient air quality of different pollutants for different health outcomes. The changes in ambient air pollution levels of different types of pollutants can then be statistically related to any observed changes in morbidity and mortality in a population. However, different studies estimate different coefficients for such an effect. So, we can use three alternative assumptions about health estimates, giving the central estimate the most weight. The high and low end estimates are calculated by increasing and decreasing the coefficient by one estimated standard deviation respectively. According to a paper by Ostro (1994), the suggestion is to use 0.062, 0.096 and 0.13 as the lower, central and upper coefficient, respectively, for the estimator of percentage change in mortality.

Using the DRF in Equation (7.1), the number of cases of premature mortality due to PM_{10} can be expressed as

$$\Delta \text{Mortality} = b \times \Delta PM_{10} \times \text{crude mortality rate} \times POP \tag{7.2}$$

where b is the mortality coefficient determined above (0.062, 0.096 and 0.13 for lower, central and higher estimate, respectively) and POP is the population exposed to risk.

To complete the estimation of health effects, it is possible to calculate the economic valuation of this effect. This can be developed from estimates of the WTP for reducing risk, to attach values to the expected changes in premature mortality or a modified COI approach to value changes in morbidity. Thus, the change in value (ΔT_i) of the health effects due to change in air pollution under consideration is the summation of all effects and can be presented by

$$\Delta T = \sum V_i \Delta H_i \tag{7.3}$$

where T is the economic value of the health effects, V_i is the willingness-to-pay to reduce a particular type of health risk and H_i is the reduction in a particular health risk.

Due to the substantial uncertainty about much of the research on which these estimates are based, upper and lower boundary estimates are provided to indicate the ranges within which the actual health effects are likely to fall.

Although the valuation of mortality and morbidity is important to cost–benefit analysis of air pollution programmes, relevant studies are fairly limited in scope. Using the benefit transfer approach (BTA, as described earlier, in Chapter 4), it is assumed that the stated preferences of people in the developed countries will be similar to those of people in any developed region being analysed, for the economic cost of air pollution. Transfer of these values may neglect factors that would cause people to value health differently, yet despite these drawbacks, these are cost advantages in terms of time and resources.

In the third step, for the estimation of the monetary valuation of premature mortality due to $PM_{10,}$ the VOSL in the United States is adjusted to derive the VOSL for the region or city in question. This adjustment to the $VOSL_{US}$ is done using purchasing power parity (PPP) estimates of GDP per capita of the United States and the region being analysed. Thus, $VOSL_{Region}$ can be computed based on the following expression:

$$VOSL_{Region} = VOSL_{US} \times \left(\frac{GDP_{Region}}{GDP_{US}} \right)^e \tag{7.4}$$

where $VOSL_{Region}$ is the value of a statistical life for the region in question in a particular year, $VOSL_{US}$ is the value of a statistical life for the United States in the same year's prices, GDP_{Region} is the GDP of the region in question, GDP_{US} is the GDP of the United States and e is the elasticity of WTP with respect to income.

Methodology for evaluating the morbidity cost

A similar approach can also been used to estimate the effects of changes in air quality on air pollution-related illnesses (morbidity). Again, to determine morbidity coefficients of the morbidity effect of PM_{10} concentration we turn to Rowe *et al.* (1995). The coefficients relate to the effect of the increase in the number of morbidity cases due to:

1   respiratory health admissions (RHA);
2   emergency room visits (ERV);
3   restricted activity days (RAD);
4   lower respiratory illness in children (LRI);
5   asthma attacks;
6   respiratory symptoms; or
7   chronic bronchitis.

The increase in the number of morbidity cases can be estimated using the equation

$$\Delta\text{Morbidity} = c_i \times \text{POP} \times \Delta PM_{10} \tag{7.5}$$

where c_i is the morbidity coefficient for each measure of morbidity effect (extrapolated from Rowe *et al.* (1995)) and POP is the population exposed to risk.

For the estimation of the monetary valuation of PM_{10}-related morbidity we use pre-determined unit values for each morbidity effect estimated in the United States (adapted from Rowe *et al.* (1995) see Table 7.1) with various adjustments. The morbidity unit value for the region in question is expressed using the equation

$$MUV_{Region} = MUV_{US} \times \left(\frac{GDP_{Region}}{GDP_{US}}\right)^e \tag{7.6}$$

where MUV_{Region} is the morbidity unit value for the region in question in a particular year, MUV_{US} is the morbidity unit value for the United States in the same year's prices, GDP_{Region} is the GDP of the region in question, GDP_{US} is the GDP of the United States and e is the elasticity of WTP with respect to income.

Note that under the BTA we not only transfer the DRFs from established work, but also transfer the economic unit values of the effects of mortality and morbidity.

Table 7.1 Mortality and morbidity effects of a 1 µg/m³ change in PM₁₀ using benefit transfer

Mortality and morbidity	Lower estimate	Central estimate	Upper estimate
Mortality	0.062	0.096	0.13
RHA/100,000	0.657	1.2	1.73
ERV/100,000	11.6	23.7	35.4
RAD	0.029	0.058	0.078
LRI	0.001	0.0017	0.0024
Asthma attacks	0.033	0.058	0.196
Respiratory symptoms	0.08	0.168	0.256
Chronic bronchitis/100,000	3	6.12	9.3

Source: Rowe *et al.* (1995).

The appropriateness and rationale for benefit transfer

When estimating the cost of air pollution, we require a number of pieces of information: population at risk of air pollution; the level of ambient concentration of the air pollutant in question; the crude mortality rate (to estimate mortality effects of the pollutant); coefficients (relating to mortality and morbidity) of the DRFs; and the unit economic values of the effects of mortality and morbidity.

Unfortunately, we do not have the indigenous DRFs and unit values for most regions that we would like to examine for the costs of air pollution. As a result, it remains necessary to use DRFs and unit economic values for mortality and morbidity effects estimated in the developed countries to derive the cost of particulate air pollution in other developed regions being analysed.

There are a variety of approaches to making a benefit transfer. However, the existing approach to benefit transfer outperforms the others and was developed by Alberini *et al.* (1997). The BTA involves the use of the estimates from a particular environmental impact valuation study in one area to estimate the economic value of environmental impact of a similar study in another area. The underlying assumption is that the latter project will have a similar impact (Pearce *et al.*, 1994). The process of data collection to establish indigenous DRFs and values can be extremely costly and time consuming, making the above-mentioned approach all the more desirable (Krupnick *et al.*, 1993).

It remains necessary, however, to make sure that the implicit assumption behind such a transfer of DRFs from developed countries should be fulfilled. This implicit assumption is that the relationship between the levels of air pollution and the consequent health effects in the developed countries can be extrapolated to estimate the health impact of particulate air pollution in the region being analysed. This restricts any possible estimation of the economic costs of air pollution using this approach just to developed cities. Similarly, for the transfer of unit economic values of the mortality and morbidity, it is implicitly assumed that the stated preferences of people in the developed countries are similar to those of the people residing in the region being analysed.

Besides restricting the number of countries or regions that can be analysed using such an approach, extrapolation DRFs and unit economic values from developed countries do have their drawbacks:

1   Transfer of DRFs may not be valid if the local context contains factors that would affect their function. For example, differences in baseline health or nutrition, access to healthcare, demographics and occupational exposure may cause a level of pollution to cause more damage.
2   Transfer of values may also neglect factors that would cause people to value health differently. For example, the concept of what constitutes full health may differ with culture and not only with income.
3   There are other environmental factors specific to location and culture, and the inter-play of these factors limits the reliability of the BTA in assessing environmental impacts.

In spite of these limitations, the cost advantages in terms of time and resources of benefit transfer continue to encourage its use for the economic cost analysis of developed regions. Furthermore, for the case of particulate matter, there appears to be a consensus in the DRFs and many related studies converge (as observed by Pearce, 1996). Finally, a brief review by Khatun (1997) has shown that the available studies for developing countries suggest a dose–response coefficient similar to those estimated for developed economies.

Case studies

The economic cost of air pollution in Singapore

By using the method described above, we can estimate the economic cost of air pollution in Singapore. The mortality and morbidity effects of the ambient concentration of PM_{10} in Singapore are estimated by using Singapore-specific data on the ambient concentration of PM_{10}, the crude mortality rate and the population at risk of air pollution, combined with the coefficients of the DRFs obtained from Ostro (1994) and Rowe *et al.* (1995).

Following the DRF in Equation (7.2), the level of premature mortality due to PM_{10} can be expressed as

$$\Delta\text{Mortality} = b \times \Delta PM_{10} \times 1,100 \times \text{crude mortality rate} \times \text{POP} \qquad (7.7)$$

where b is the mortality coefficient determined above (0.062, 0.096 and 0.13 for lower, central and higher estimate, respectively) and POP is the population exposed to risk.

First, for Singapore, since the annual level of PM_{10} in 2009 was higher than the WHO air quality guidelines (WHO–AQG) of 20 $\mu g/m^3$ by 15 $\mu g/m^3$, we determined a change of 15 $\mu g/m^3$ and took ΔPM_{10} to be 15. The population exposed to particulate air pollution is equal to the total population in Singapore.

This assumption can be justified by its small geographical area. According to the Singstat Time Series Online, the crude mortality rate in Singapore is 4.3 per 1,000 and the size of its population (POP) was 4,987,000 in 2009.

Based on this information, the mortality effect of PM_{10} in Singapore can be estimated, by the relationship above, to be

$$\Delta\text{Mortality} = 0.096 \times 15 \times 1,100 \times 0.0043 \times 4,987,600 = 309 \qquad (7.8)$$

This figure is obtained using the central estimate of 0.096. Similarly, the upper and lower estimates of the total number of mortalities are 418 and 199, respectively.

Table 7.2 presents the results of the estimation of the morbidity effects of particulate air pollution for Singapore using Equation (7.5) and the morbidity coefficients. Note that for the estimation of the number of RADs due to PM_{10}, only the adult population is considered since they are the main participants in the work force, and for the estimation of the number of LRI in children, only the population under the age of 15 is considered. All other estimates are computed using the entire population figure of 4,987,000.

Second, to estimate the mortality costs, we transferred the estimates from countries where WTP studies have been conducted to Singapore's case using Equation (7.4).

1   The $VOSL_{US}$ in 2009 prices is calculated as US$7.0725 million.
2   Per capita GDP at PPP for Singapore was $50,523(in international dollars) and for the United States was $46,381(in international dollars) for the year 2009. Hence, the ratio of Singapore's GDP per capital to the United States GDP per capital is 1.0893.
3   For the elasticity of WTP with respect to income, e, we assume a value of 0.32. It is argued that environmental amenities such as clean air are not luxury goods and hence the income elasticity of WTP to avoid illness is less than 1. Empirical evidence from some studies also supports this argument.

Table 7.2 Mortality and morbidity effects (number of cases) of a 15 µg/m³ change in PM_{10} using benefit transfer

	Lower estimate	*Central estimate*	*Upper estimate*
Mortality	199	309	418
Morbidity			
RHA	492	898	1,294
ERV	8,678	17,731	26,484
RAD (1,000)	1,190	2,380	3,201
LRI	10,019	17,031	24,044
Asthma attacks (1,000)	2,469	4,339	14,664
Respiratory symptoms (1,000)	5,985	12,569	19,152
Chronic bronchitis	2,244	4,579	6,958

Source: Author's calculation.

For example, the Alberini *et al.* (1997) study in Taiwan estimated an income elasticity of WTP of about 0.32, while the Loehman *et al.* (1979) study estimated that the income elasticity is between 0.26 and 0.6. These empirical studies all suggest that WTP is lower in a low income country than in a higher income country, but less than proportionally to the income differential. Thus, for the estimation of the $VOSL_{Singapore}$, the income elasticity is assumed to be equal to that in Taiwan, which is 0.32.

4   This gives us a $VOSL_{Singapore}$ of US$7.27 million.

Similarly, in estimating the morbidity cost, we transfer estimates from countries where morbidity unit values have been computed to the Singapore case using Equation (7.6). Note that in estimating the cost of RAD, 20 per cent of RAD results in lost workdays and the remaining 80 per cent of the RAD values at one-third of the daily average wages. Taking an exchange rate of US$1=S$1.4034, the monthly average wages in Singapore for 2009 is approximately US$2,964. Making an additional assumption that people work for 20 days every month, the daily wage rate in 2009 is US$148. As a central estimate we obtain the cost of RAD in Singapore as US$164.61 million. All the findings of the unit values of morbidity are summarized in the Table 7.3.

Finally, based on Equation (7.3), we compute the economic costs due to changes in levels of PM_{10}. For the central estimate of the mortality cost, we multiply the number of cases of mortality by the estimate for $VOSL_{Singapore}$ in 2009 using the BTA. This is calculated as $309 \times US\$7,072,500 = US\$2,244.72$ million. The estimated morbidity costs are summarized in Table 7.4, along with the total health damage cost due to particulate air pollution in Singapore.

The total estimated economic cost of health damage attributable to PM_{10} in Singapore is US$3,745.26 million (central estimate), which is about 2.04 per cent of the total GDP of Singapore in 2009. Based on these estimates, premature mortality accounts for about 60 per cent of health costs and other illnesses account for 40 per cent as shown in Table 7.4.

Table 7.3 Unit values for morbidity effects in 2009 (US$) using benefit transfer

	Lower estimate	*Central estimate*	*Upper estimate*
Morbidity			
RHA	9,820.9	19,641.6	29,462.5
ERV	370.8	741.5	1,112.3
RAD (1,000)	NA	69.2	NA
LRI	NA	NA	NA
Asthma attacks (1,000)	18.0	50.2	80.2
Respiratory symptoms (1,000)	8.0	14.0	20.1
Chronic bronchitis	NA	193,739.1	NA

Source: Author's calculation.

Table 7.4 Costs of mortality and morbidity due to a 15 µg/m³ change in PM₁₀ in 2009 (US$ million)

	Lower estimate	*Central estimate*	*Upper estimate*
Mortality	1,449.71	2,244.72	3,039.72
Morbidity			
RHA	4.8	13.1	29.5
ERV	3.2	13.1	29.5
RAD	82.3	164.6	221.4
LRI	NA	NA	NA
Asthma attacks	44.5	217.7	1,176.4
Respiratory symptoms	48.1	175.9	384.8
Chronic bronchitis	NA	911.6	NA

Source: Author's calculation.

An application to Jakarta

Dose–response relationships are mostly based on data from the United States, Canada and the United Kingdom, relating to information on changes in the air quality and pollution levels for different pollutants and health outcomes. Through an approach similar to the one described above, Ostro (1994) applies previous work from Europe and the United States to Jakarta.

When coefficients listed in Table 7.5 are applied to Jakarta, Ostro estimates the health impacts associated with decreasing particulate levels to Indonesian standards (from current levels to 90 µg/m³) and WHO standards (from current pollution levels to 75 µg/m³). Many parts of Jakarta city had PM₁₀ levels ranging between 100 and 200, with certain 'hot spots' having readings of 300 or 350. Table 7.6 shows the derived health benefits of reducing particulate matter to the Indonesian standard of 90 µg/m³.

Under the central estimate of the dose–response relationships, Ostro estimated that each year the benefits of reducing the PM₁₀ levels to Indonesian standards for a population of 8.2 million people in the Indonesian capital include a reduction of

Table 7.5 Morbidity effects of 10 µg/m³ change in PM₁₀

Morbidity	*Central estimate*	*High estimate*
RHA/100,000	12.0	15.6
ERV/100,000	235.4	342.5
RAD/person	0.575	0.903
LRI/child/per asthmatic	0.0169	0.0238
Asthma attacks/per asthmatic[1]	0.326	2.73
Respiratory symptoms/person	1.83	2.74
Chronic bronchitis/100,000	61.2	91.8

Source: Ostro (1994).

[1] Applies to the 8.25% of the Indonesian population that is assumed to be asthmatic.

Table 7.6 Health effects of reducing PM_{10} levels to Indonesian standards of 90 $\mu g/m^3$ for Jakarta

Health effect	Central estimate
Premature mortality	1,200
Hospital admissions	2,000
ERV	40,600
RAD	6,330,000
LRI	104,000
Asthma attacks	464,000
Respiratory symptoms	31,000,000
Chronic bronchitis	9,600

Source: Ostro (1994).

1,200 premature deaths, 2,000 fewer hospital admissions, 40,600 fewer emergency room visits and more than 6 million fewer restricted activity days, among many other benefits.

However, to estimate the right investments and control options to be undertaken, any policy-maker would like to compare the benefits to the costs. The economic benefits, as noted below are largely due to the health costs avoided and reduced premature deaths. In this case, monetary values were not placed on the health outcomes. Yet, presenting the impact of particulate air pollution as in Tables 7.5 and 7.6 can be a powerful message for policy-makers.

Limitations of the methodology

This methodology is limited in two respects. First, this methodology uses DRFs and unit economic values for mortality and morbidity effects estimated in developed countries for the estimation of the cost of particulate air pollution. In a strict sense, these adopted values do not apply to the region being analysed (in this case, Singapore). Second, as Pearce (1996) noted, a major weakness of air pollution-damage literature has been the focus on outdoor pollution. In terms of human person hours, 89 per cent of all developed-country person hours are spent indoors, leaving only 11 per cent of time spent outdoors. In developing countries, the percentage of time spent indoors and outdoors are 70 per cent and 30 per cent, respectively. In other words, in developed countries the major part of an individual's time is spent indoors, away from the direct effect of particulate air pollution, not outdoors. However, given the paucity of data on indoor air quality, only outdoor air quality is considered in this analysis. In view of these limitations, the findings of this methodology are to be treated as indicative rather than conclusive.

This discussion also highlights the uncertainties involved in economic valuations of environmental amenities like clean air. These uncertainties include doubts about the authenticity of the impacts on health, possible statistical invalidities and a lack of consensus regarding the monetary valuation of various types of benefits. To reduce such uncertainties, the best approach is to establish dose–response relationships of local and regional PM_{10} and conduct studies investigating the value that residents actually place on clean air. Such data collection to establish DRFs and values will not be easy or cheap, but these efforts could then provide the impetus for more in-depth analysis of environmental impacts.

8 Economic cost of diseases

Cost–benefit analysis (CBA) is most commonly applied by government or regulatory bodies, both national and international, to evaluate if certain policies are worth undertaking. Further, of the policies brought under the domain of CBA a significant proportion are related to reducing the incidence of particular diseases. As such, this chapter discusses how the economic cost of disease, and hence the benefits from reducing the incidence of the disease, is typically measured. The steps involved in the measurement are then illustrated through a study of the economic cost of dengue, an infectious tropical disease, in Singapore.

Types of economic cost pertaining to diseases

If an individual were to compile a list of all the costs involved in falling ill, he/she would most likely state items like 'medical costs', 'loss of wages' and the 'general misery of being sick'. Similarly, the costs of any disease may be broadly classified into:

1 the expenditure on medical care;
2 the loss of current production; and
3 the pain and discomfort associated with the disease.

The expenditure on medical care would include the costs of the services provided by all medical personnel, the cost of drugs prescribed and the equipment and facilities required.

The loss of current production has two components. First, there is the loss of earnings from having to take time off due to treatment and convalescence. Second, the loss of earnings from reduced productivity due to having been weakened by the disease.

The third category, the pain and associated discomfort, is the hardest to measure. While it is undoubtedly a cost, a standardized and reliable measure has yet to be developed. Most current procedures are arbitrary in nature.

Although the above classification provides a useful framework for calculating the economic costs of diseases, a common criticism levelled at it is the absence of explicit links to economic principles (Mishan and Quah, 2007). However, the criticisms are of a more theoretical nature and we will not discuss it in detail here.

Instead, we present an actual study of the cost of dengue in Singapore, to illustrate the method discussed above.

Economic cost of dengue in Singapore

Introduction

Recent reports on dengue, a mosquito-borne disease, have documented a sobering increase in the number of incidences and deaths. The disease without doubt is currently one of the most common arthropod-borne diseases worldwide, representing a major health and economic burden to many tropical and subtropical countries. Cases of dengue fever (DF) were described more than 200 years ago and histories of dengue and dengue epidemics were documented (Ehrenkranz *et al.*, 1971; Halstead, 1980; Pinheiro, 1989; Gubler, 1991; Halstead, 1992; and Gubler and Trent, 1994). After the Second World War, populations of most of the most important mosquito vector, *Aedes aegypti,* were suppressed. The control campaigns, however, were abandoned in the early 1970s and the vector re-established itself in virtually all of the countries that had vector control campaigns and further expanded into a few new areas. This re-establishment of the vector has resulted in the dengue viruses spreading rapidly around the globe. During the last two decades, all countries in the tropical regions (Singapore included) have experienced a marked increase in the incidence of both DF and dengue haemorrhagic fever (DHF). Globally, an average of 25,000 cases of DHF per year were reported from 1956–80. From 1981–85, the number increased to 137,504. From 1986–90, the average number of reported DHF cases per year increased to 267,692. The World Health Organization (in 2006) estimated that approximately two billion people are living in tropical and subtropical countries and an additional 120 million each year are travelling to these countries. Therefore a large share of the world population is at risk of contracting dengue.

The widespread distribution and rising incidence of dengue virus infection worldwide and the large numbers of people afflicted have resulted in dengue being classified by national and international public health authorities as an emerging or re-emerging infectious disease (Gubler and Clark, 1995; LeDuc, 1996). Although Torres (1997) argued that the estimated loss associated with the disease is in the same order of magnitude as tuberculosis, sexually transmitted diseases (excluding HIV/AIDS), Chagas disease, Leishmaniasis or intestinal Helminths, only rarely are studies found focusing on the disease burden of dengue. Estimates of the total direct and indirect costs from the 1977 epidemic in Puerto Rico are found ranging from US$6.1 million to US$15.6 million (Von Allmen *et al.*, 1979). The 1980 epidemic in Cuba, with 344,203 reported cases, cost US$103 million. Another outbreak in 1980 in Thailand was estimated to cost approximately US$6.8 million. Recently, a study (Torres, 1997) on the impact of an outbreak in rural Puerto Rico has shown a loss of income attributable to the disease of US$305 per household or US$125 per person. The direct costs of DHF in Thailand in 1994 were estimated to be US$13.36 million for 51,688 cases (Sornmani *et al.*, 1995). When indirect costs were included, the cost of DHF was estimated to be between US$19.3 million and US$51.9 million.

Like many other countries, the incidence of the disease in Singapore has shown cyclical peaks and troughs since 1980. More importantly, every three to four years a reduction in dengue incidence is followed immediately by a two to three years increase in reported incidence. The new peaks in the incidence have been consistently higher than those observed in the previous cycles. For instance, when the first peak was observed in 1982, only 216 cases were reported. Subsequently, 436 cases were reported in 1987, followed by 2,878 cases in 1992, 5,258 cases in 1998 and more recently 14,209 cases in 2005. Despite the large number of victims, no comprehensive study has been found to estimate not only the disease burden of dengue but also the economic cost of dengue.

It is imperative to know the magnitude of the health consequences that are attributed to dengue as such knowledge is necessary for performing a cost–benefit analysis for devising cost-effective abatement strategies and guiding policy decisions. The objective of this study is to assess and evaluate the economic cost of dengue in Singapore using primary data from 1980 to 2007. Special attention focuses on the most recent cycle of 1999–2005. The estimated economic cost of dengue is provided for first, for a low incidence year in 2000, second, for a high incidence year in 2005, and third, the more recent medium incidence years of 2006 and 2007. The assessment and evaluation is the first step in developing a more consistent national approach to dengue management. In this study, a two-step procedure is adopted. First, the incidence of dengue is determined. Second, economic (monetary) values of mortality and morbidity are calculated to estimate the health impact in terms of an increase in mortality and morbidity due to dengue. Other costs, such as the cost of dengue prevention and control incurred by various government agencies, are also included. The cost from lost tourism is identified as an important economic cost of dengue to Singapore. However, as no formal study has been found showing the impact of dengue on the number of tourist arrivals, it is therefore viewed as an important cost but not included in our study. Figure 8.1 summarizes the estimation methodology.

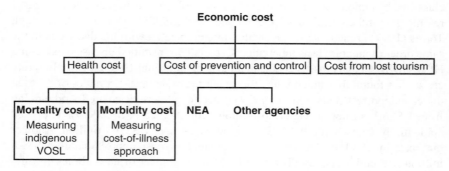

Figure 8.1 Estimation methodology.

The study is structured as follows. Section two provides an overview of the incidence of dengue in Singapore. Section three describes the proposed methodology for estimating the economic cost associated with dengue. This section also details the baseline assumptions that are required for such estimations. Section four provides the results and discussions of the economic cost associated with dengue in the four cycles. The section also specifically compares the morbidity and mortality costs of dengue in low and high incidence years. Section five concludes the discussion.

Overview of incidence of dengue in Singapore

This section provides a brief overview of the incidence of dengue in Singapore from 1980 to 2008. Figure 8.2 splits the data into cycles. From the four cycles, three interesting observations are documented. First, the incidence of the disease has shown cyclical peaks and troughs since 1980. Second, the incidence of dengue transmission has increased significantly in Singapore. Since 1987, the number of reported cases of DF has been significant. Importantly, every three to four years a reduction in dengue incidence is followed immediately by a two to three year increase in reported cases. Further, the new peaks have been higher than those observed in the previous cycle. For instance, from the peak of 436 in 1987, the incidence of dengue increased to 2,878 in 1992, to 5,258 in 1998 and up to 14,209 in 2005. Overall, the average annual DF incidence increased by 562.2 per cent (first to second cycle), by 76.3 per cent (second to third cycle) and 86.9 per cent (third to fourth cycle). Third, the length of each cycle has lengthened from five years to six years and then to seven years.

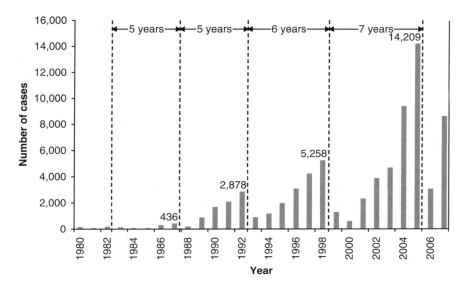

Figure 8.2 Dengue cycles, 1980–2007.

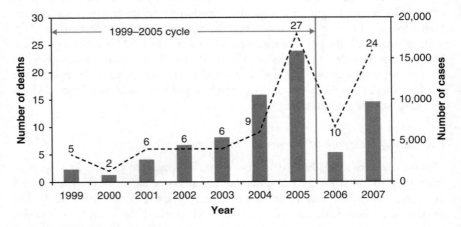

Figure 8.3 Dengue cycle 1999–2005.

Figure 8.3 shows the number of deaths from 1999 to 2007. The highest number of deaths is observed in 2005. This is probably because of the significant outbreak of 14,209 cases reported in 2005. Anecdotal evidence from Singapore seems to suggest that the number of deaths was higher for adults aged 15 years and above. For instance, patients over 15 years old represented all the nine deaths reported in 2004, the 25 out of 27 deaths reported in 2005 and nine out of ten deaths reported in 2006.

Methodology

The estimation in this study measures the health cost associated with dengue in terms of morbidity and mortality costs. The morbidity cost is estimated using a commonly known approach, the cost-of-illness approach, which concentrates on the aspects of the value of health that are well defined with observable quantities, as well as directly measurable. Medical expenditures and forgone earnings due to illness are considered. The cost-of-illness approach regards people as productive agents who yield a continuing return in the future. The expenditure and value of any resources used in promoting health are referred to as the direct cost-of-illness. The loss of labour earnings due to sickness and the lost product of labour are considered as the indirect cost-of-illness. The mortality cost is measured using the values of a statistical life (VOSL) in Singapore. Other costs, such as the cost of dengue prevention and control incurred by various government agencies, are also included.

Estimation of direct morbidity cost

In estimating the direct morbidity costs covering costs of treatment, the average number of days of illness and the cost of healthcare are estimated. Based on the

Table 8.1 Number of patients hospitalized on various types of wards (2006–2007)

Ward	Number hospitalized	%	Bill size per day 50ᵗʰ percentile S$	Total bill size 90ᵗʰ percentile S$
Ward A	164	17.41	438.95	1,624.11
Ward B1	108	11.46	321.17	1,188.34
Ward B2	263	27.92	126.55	468.25
Ward C	407	43.21	78.80	291.57
Total	942	100.00		

Source: Data obtained from website of the Ministry of Health, Singapore, http://www.moh.gov.sg/mohcorp/statistics.aspx?id=242, between 1 May 2006 and 30 April 2007.

data provided by the Ministry of Health, the average number of days of hospitalization is 3.7 days per person admitted with dengue.

The level of expenditure on hospitalization bills is obtained from the website of the Ministry of Health. The data obtained is for the period of 1 May 2006 to 30 April 2007. The average bill sizes per day for various wards are calculated by dividing the total bill sizes by the average number of days spent at different hospitals. After calculating the average bill sizes per day for each hospital, the average bill sizes for different wards are computed and summarized in Table 8.1. The 50th percentile indicates that 50 per cent of patients pay this amount or less and 50 per cent pay more. This figure provides an estimate of the typical bill size for patients. For instance, a typical patient pays S$438.95 per day for Ward A, S$321.17 per day for Ward B1, S$126.55 per day for Ward B2 and S$78.80 per day for Ward C. The total bill sizes are obtained by multiplying the bill sizes per day by the average number of days of hospitalization i.e. 3.7 days. Table 8.1 also shows that 17.41 per cent of patients stayed in Ward A, 11.46 per cent in Ward B1, 27.92 per cent in Ward B2 and 43.21per cent in Ward C. The weighted average of the total bill size is obtained. It is found that the weighted average bill size is S$675.70 for each incidence of dengue.

Estimation of indirect morbidity cost

In estimating the indirect morbidity costs for the cost of lost productivity, Singapore Statistics Online reveals that the monthly average wage in Singapore for 2007 is S$3,773. By assuming that people work for 22 days in a month, the daily average rate is computed as S$171.50. The total cost of lost productivity for each dengue incidence is computed by multiplying the daily average rate by the number of days of lost productivity. Another study by NEA also indicates that 60 per cent of symptomatic dengue goes unreported. Therefore, it is assumed that the number of days of lost productivity varies with the degree of severity. The unreported cases are assumed to be least severe and the number of days of lost productivity is three days, followed by five days for reported but not hospitalized cases and ten days for reported and hospitalized cases.

Table 8.2 Total cost of prevention and control

Year	Government agencies S$ million	NEA S$ million	Total S$ million
1999	1.47	14.70	16.17
2000	1.46	14.60	16.06
2001	1.62	16.20	17.82
2002	1.62	16.20	17.82
2003	2.50	25.00	27.50
2004	2.50	25.00	27.50
2005	5.15	51.50	56.65
2006	10.00	52.30	62.30
2007	88.40	63.50	151.89

Source: Based on data from the National Environment Agency (NEA), Singapore and other sources.

Estimation of mortality cost in Singapore

Frequently in the economic literature, the mortality costs can be estimated using VOSL. If each of 10,000 people is willing to pay S$100 to reduce their risk of dying by 1 in 10,000, they are together willing to pay S$1,000,000 for risk reductions of that sum to one statistical life. The S$1,000,000 is the value of statistical life. In estimating the mortality costs of dengue in Singapore, we use S$2.05 million as estimated by Quah *et al.* (2009).

Estimation of cost of prevention and control

Various government agencies in Singapore provided their estimated costs incurred in dengue prevention and control in 2007. Out of 21 government agencies, 16 responded. Additionally, the NEA managed to provide estimated costs from 1999–2007. Table 8.2 summarizes the estimated costs incurred by Singapore's government agencies in combating dengue.

It is noted that total costs of prevention and control increased substantially in the high incidence year of 2005 and the subsequent years.

Results and discussion

In estimating the morbidity and mortality costs associated with dengue we calculate the costs for the four cycles of 1983–87, 1988–92, 1993–98 and 1999–2005 with special focus on the most recent cycle of 1999–2005. We also compute the morbidity and mortality costs for 2006 and 2007, respectively.

According to Ministry of Health records, 80–90 per cent of patients diagnosed with dengue were hospitalized before 2006. However, when a set of new admission criteria was implemented in 2006, only 68 per cent of patients diagnosed were hospitalized. Therefore, in estimating the economic costs associated with dengue, we take into consideration the following. First, the percentage of hospitalization varies from 80–90 per cent for the period of 1980–2005. For a more conservative estimate, 80 per cent of hospitalization is assumed for the period of 1980–2005 and 68 per cent of hospitalization is assumed for 2006–2007. Second, mortality costs are estimated using the VOSL of S$2.05 million. Third, the average number of days of hospitalization is 3.7 days. The loss of productivity days varies from three days for unreported cases, five days for reported but not hospitalized cases and ten days for reported and hospitalized cases. Fourth, since formal study focusing on the effect of dengue on lost tourism is virtually non-existent, we are aware of the potential tourism lost but do not consider it in this study.

Morbidity and mortality costs associated with dengue

Table 8.3 summarizes the total morbidity and mortality costs. Total morbidity and mortality costs increase over the cycles. For the estimation using the VOSL of S$2.05 million, the total morbidity and mortality costs for the cycles 1999–2005, 1993–98, 1988–92 and 1983–87 are S$209.15, S$75.47 million, S$57.18 million and S$25.31 million, respectively.

Based on the above, it is concluded that the total and average morbidity and mortality costs of dengue show a significant rising trend.

Morbidity and mortality costs of dengue for 1999–2005 cycle

This subsection focuses on the most recent cycle of 1999–2005. Figure 8.4 shows the number of dengue cases reported and the morbidity and mortality costs for the cycle of 1999–2005 using the VOSL of S$2.05 million.

It is noted previously from Figure 8.2, for the cycle of 1999–2005, that 2005 is identified as high incidence year where 14,209 cases were reported (with 8,525 cases unreported) compared to only 673 cases (with 404 cases unreported) in 2000. From Figure 8.4, the estimated morbidity and mortality costs increase with the number of cases reported. Using the VOSL of S$2.05 million, the costs are S$87.82 million in the high incidence year of 2005 compared to only S$5.64 million in the low incidence year of 2000. In other words, the morbidity and mortality costs of dengue in the high incidence year are approximately 15 times

Table 8.3 Total health cost of dengue

Cycle	Health cost of dengue (S$ million)
1983–1987	25.31
1988–1992	57.18
1993–1998	75.47
1999–2005	209.15
2006	27.09
2007	32.69

Source: Author's own calculations.

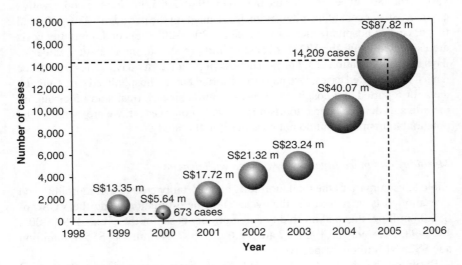

Figure 8.4 Total health cost of dengue, 1999–2005.

higher compared to the low incidence year, measured using the VOSL of S$2.05 million.

Economic cost of dengue in 2005

Based on the data provided, we estimate the overall economic cost of dengue in 2005. The costs include (1) morbidity cost, (2) mortality cost and (3) cost from prevention and control by various government agencies. Figure 8.5 shows the breakdown of costs of dengue in 2005 assuming no loss in tourism. The overall economic cost of dengue amounts to S$144.47 million. The cost of prevention and control, mortality cost and morbidity cost makes up 39.2 per cent, 38.3 per cent and 22.5 per cent of the economic cost of dengue, respectively.

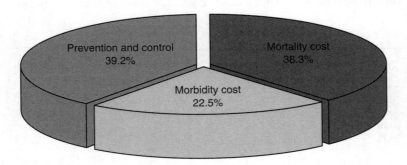

Figure 8.5 Breakdown of the economic cost of dengue in 2005.

Table 8.4 Total economic cost of dengue, 1999–2005

Cost	2005 S$	2006 S$	2007 S$
Mortality cost	55.35	20.50	14.35
Morbidity cost	32.47	6.59	18.34
Cost of prevention and control	56.65	62.30	151.89
Total economic cost (S$ million)	144.47	89.39	184.58

Source: Author's own calculations.

Table 8.4 shows the overall economic cost of dengue using a VOSL of S$2.05 million. The economic cost is S$144.47 million in 2005, S$89.39 million in 2006 and S$184.58 million in 2007.

Conclusions

Dengue virus infection is without doubt one of the most common arthropod-borne diseases worldwide, representing a major health and economic burden for many tropical countries including Singapore. This study quantifies the economic cost associated with dengue for the four cycles of 1983–87, 1988–92, 1993–98 and 1999–2005. The morbidity and mortality costs for 2006 and 2007 are also estimated. The study may serve as an important guide for policy-makers as the estimates indicate the magnitude of the problem and provide a necessary perspective, so that fighting dengue can be prioritized relative to other interventions that improve public health. Based on this study, several important findings have been identified. First, the morbidity cost per case covering the direct cost of hospitalization and medical care and the indirect cost of lost productivity is approximately S$1,495 before 2006 and S$1,380 after 2006. This is because of the observed reduction in the percentage of hospitalization from 80–90 per cent before 2006 to only 68 per cent after 2006. The mortality cost per case is estimated based on a VOSL of S$2.05 million. Second, when an estimation is made for the most recent cycle of 1999–2005, the morbidity and mortality costs of dengue in a high incidence year are approximately 15 times higher compared to a low incidence year. Third, using a VOSL of S$2.05 million, the cost of prevention and control, mortality cost and morbidity cost makes up 39.2 per cent, 38.3 per cent and 22.5 per cent of the economic cost of dengue, respectively.

The overall economic cost associated with dengue may be small in magnitude compared to Singapore's GDP but it is an increasing trend. Hopefully to some extent, it may gain sufficient attention from decision-makers in setting health priorities and making budgetary decisions. The study suggests that when resources for research and control are allocated, dengue should be given a priority equal to many other infectious diseases that are generally considered more important.

Part III

New applications in cost–benefit analysis

9 Pair-wise comparison: a novel approach

The recognition of flaws generally inspires improvement. In the same vein, the recognition of the limitations of stated and revealed preference approaches in valuation methods has spurred the development of novel techniques. The pair-wise comparison method is one such example. While the method is not entirely new, being first thought up by Thurstone in 1927 (Thurstone, 1927) to measure attitudes in psychological studies, its introduction into the valuation of non-market goods literature is considered rather novel. Peterson and Brown (1998) were the first to employ the method to compare the preferences of individuals with regard to six different public goods.

Having provided some historical background of the method, the rest of the chapter is organized as follows. We first review the main weaknesses of stated and revealed preference approaches. This is followed by an illustration of how the pair-wise comparison method may be carried out and how it avoids the problems inherent in both stated and revealed preference approaches. Finally we conclude by summarizing the main points and present cases in which the method has been applied in valuation studies.

Weaknesses of the stated and revealed preference approaches

Stated preference approaches are methods that require individuals to state explicitly what a particular item is worth to them. Revealed preference approaches, on the other hand, are methods that derive the value of items implicitly through observing the effects that the item in question has on related markets. To give examples of each approach, the contingent valuation method (CVM), discussed in Chapter 3, is a stated preference approach while hedonic pricing and the travel cost method are revealed preference approaches. Detailed explanations and evaluations of each specific method are provided in Chapter 3 on valuation issues and techniques. Nonetheless, a brief review of the main weaknesses of stated and revealed preference approaches is presented here for ease of reading.

Limitations of the stated preference approach

The key problem with stated preference approaches is that it is highly susceptible to survey and behavioural bias. This is because any method that requires individuals to state explicit amounts that they are willing to pay or accept must necessarily involve a survey of some sort. While survey bias may be eliminated or at least kept to a minimum by improving the survey technique and providing proper training for surveyors, behavioural biases prove to be difficult to eradicate.

One challenging behavioural bias stems from the observation first made by Knetsch and Sinden (1984) that the willingness-to-pay (WTP) for any item was consistently and significantly lower than the willingness-to-accept (WTA) to forgo it. Also known as the endowment effect, it presents a problem in stated preference approaches as it means that the value of any item to an individual is not unique and will depend on whether the questionnaire is phrased to put the respondent in the mind of a payer or receiver. As such, there may be multiple equally valid values of any one item, which is hardly useful when trying to calculate whether the net value of all items yield a positive figure (i.e. whether the project fulfils the Kaldor–Hicks criterion). In other words, the endowment effect is the Achilles' heel of stated preference approaches.

Limitations of the revealed preference approach

The problems with revealed preference approaches are no less thorny, the principal weakness being the assumptions regarding the market that it requires. This is because the approach generally relies on price differentials within a market (usually housing or labour) to calculate the value of certain items (e.g. measuring the value of a life through observing the wage differentials between a job that carries some mortality risk and one that does not). Hence, the accuracy of the valuations will be constrained by the degree to which price differentials reflect people's differing preferences.

Immediately, the associated problems become obvious. In order for price differentials to reflect the true marginal value of an item, the approach has to assume that, at the equilibrium set of prices, individuals are indifferent between their situation and any other alternative. This in turn requires rationality and perfect information on the part of individuals, such that at any set of prices, if a better alternative exists, rational individuals with perfect information would know of it and immediately switch to it. This then causes a change in relative prices, until eventually equilibrium can be reached in which price differentials reflect the values of differing characteristics between goods and no individual can be made better off by switching to an alternative. To enable the smooth switching between alternatives, individuals would also have to be perfectly mobile – a situation that is hardly realized in the real world. Additionally, other common market distortions such as those caused by taxes or subsidies also reduce the effectiveness of the method by altering the price signals.

As can be seen, the assumptions that have to be fulfilled before revealed preference approaches produce reliable estimates, limit the efficiency of the method.

Carrying out a pair-wise comparison study

The ingenuity of the pair-wise comparison method is in how it manages to side step the problems associated with the stated and revealed preference approaches. However, to understand how it does so, we must first understand how the method is carried out. We will illustrate the method via a hypothetical example.

Suppose a practitioner is tasked to find out the relative ranking of four items:

1   preventing the loss of 1 ha of rainforest in the Amazon rainforest;
2   a 1 per cent decrease in unemployment from 5 per cent to 4 per cent;
3   a reduction in global carbon emissions by 5 per cent;
4   a 2 per cent decrease in infant mortality rates.

The items presented are purposefully kept short for ease of presentation. However, when employing the pair-wise comparison method, it is better to describe the items in as much detail as possible to minimize the need for respondents' imagination.

The first step is to conduct a survey into which the items are presented as binary choices to individuals who have to select the option that they deem more important or valuable. If the number of combinations is not too many[1], all possible combinations of binary choices should be shown to every respondent. The possible combinations for our example are shown in 9.1. Only one pair would be presented at one time for the respondent to choose.

As can be seen from Table 9.1, for any of the four items, the maximum number of times it can be chosen over other items by a single individual would be three[2]. The number of times the item is actually chosen is also known as a preference score. For an individual in our sample, the preference scores might then be as shown in Table 9.2.

Table 9.1 Combination of items as binary choice sets

Option		Option
1 Preventing the loss of 1 ha of rainforest in the Amazon rainforest		2 A 1% decrease in unemployment from 5% to 4%
1 Preventing the loss of 1 ha of rainforest in the Amazon rainforest		3 A reduction in global carbon emissions by 5%
1 Preventing the loss of 1 ha of rainforest in the Amazon rainforest	versus	4 A 2% decrease in infant mortality rates
2 A 1% decrease in unemployment from 5% to 4%		3 A reduction in global carbon emissions by 5%
2 A 1% decrease in unemployment from 5% to 4%		4 A 2% decrease in infant mortality rates
3 A reduction in global carbon emissions by 5%		4 A 2% decrease in infant mortality rates

Table 9.2 Sample of an individual's preference score

Items	Preference score
1 Preventing the loss of 1ha of rainforest in the Amazon rainforest	1
2 A 1% decrease in unemployment from 5% to 4%	3
3 A reduction in global carbon emissions by 5%	0
4 A 2% decrease in infant mortality rates	2

The variance stable rank method may then be employed to summarize the preferences of the entire sample. This is done by summing up the preference scores of each item across all respondents in the sample and then dividing it by the maximum number of times it could have been selected[3]. The resulting figures can then be multiplied by one hundred to place them on a scale of zero to one hundred.

Going back to our example, suppose that the sample consisted of 100 individuals. After summing up the preference scores of each item, we may get values as in the first column of Table 9.3. We may then derive the variance stable rank as shown in the last column of Table 9.3.

The values obtained from the method are scale values since the figure reflects the proportion of times the item is preferred. This allows for measurements of intensity of preferences. In addition, some degree of indifference is allowed since scores of different items may be the same. In the example used above, it can be seen that individuals had a strong preference for the decrease in unemployment.

At this point, one might ponder the relevance of the above exercise with regard to deriving monetary valuations of non-market goods. The issue is easily

Table 9.3 Variance stable rank of items

Items	Sum of preference scores (x)	Maximum sum of preference scores (y), (n − 1) × 100	Variance stable rank scale, (x / y) × 100
1 Preventing the loss of 1 ha of rainforest in the Amazon rainforest	110	300	36.7
2 A 1% point decrease in unemployment from 5% to 4%	284	300	94.7
3 A reduction in global carbon emissions by 5%	67	300	22.3
4 A 2% decrease in infant mortality rates	139	300	46.3

resolved. To derive monetary valuations as opposed to simply finding out the intensity of preferences between various items, as shown in the example, one simply substitutes (or inserts) two or more of the items with monetary gains (e.g. a two percentage point decrease in infant mortality rates versus a gain of S$300). The remaining steps are the same. The ranking derived may then provide estimates for the values of the items. For example, if the ranking of a reduction in infant mortality is bracketed between that of a gain of S$300 and S$350, then the value of the reduction in infant mortality must lie somewhere between the two. Quah *et al.* (2006) provide a good example of how this may be carried out.

Strengths and limitations of the pair-wise comparison method

The advantage of the pair-wise comparison lies in how it avoids the major limitations of stated and revealed preference approaches. In using surveys like the stated preference approaches, the pair-wise comparison method easily avoids the strict assumptions mandated by the revealed preference approaches.

At the same time, through providing a third viewpoint of that of a selector, the method also circumvents the endowment effect that causes a positive divergence of WTA from WTP which plagues stated preference approaches. This is because the WTA is obtained from the viewpoint of a seller while the WTP is obtained from that of a buyer. Knetsch and Sinden (1984) observed it is the difference in the reference points that gives rise to the discrepancy. The selector's reference point that the paired comparison uses thus side steps the effect by eliminating the loss aversion caused by perceived losses when one takes the viewpoint of the seller as opposed to that of the buyer (Kahneman *et al.*, 1999). As it is the loss aversion that leads to the endowment effect in the first place, the endowment effect is avoided.

Apart from working around the major limitations of the stated and revealed preference approaches, the pair-wise comparison method has also been shown to be relatively easy and cost-effective to implement (Peterson and Brown, 1998; Rutherford *et al.*, 1998; Chuenpagdee *et al.*, 2001; Quah *et al.*, 2006; and Ong *et al.*, 2008).

As with all other techniques, the pair-wise comparison method is not perfect. The key problem a practitioner may run into when employing this method is that of survey participants having intransitive preferences (i.e. A is preferred to B; B is preferred to C; and C is preferred to A). The only two possibilities that could give rise to this observation are indifference between certain choices (the method requires participants to make a choice between two options even if they are indifferent which could give rise to seemingly intransitive preferences) and truly intransitive preferences. It is not difficult to find out which case it is. One simply has to re-present the upsetting choice to the survey respondent. If the respondent switches choices, it is probably a case of the former and the issue is resolved. If not, it is possible that the individual in question truly has intransitive preferences and the practitioner may then choose to subtract that individual from the survey sample[4].

Table 9.4 Studies using the pair-wise comparison approach

Author	Year of study	Items of study
Peterson and Brown	1998	Comparisons between: • 6 public goods (2 environmental, 4 non-environmental) • 4 private goods • 11 monetary sums
Rutherford *et al.*	1998	Comparisons between: • 4 non-pecuniary environmental losses resulting from oil spills
Chuenpagdee *et al.*	2001	(Part 1) Comparisons between: • 8 losses of economic resources (Part 2) Comparisons between: • 8 increases in economic activity
Quah *et al.*	2006	(Part 1) Comparisons between: • 8 losses related to the environment (Part 2) Comparisons between: • 10 monetary gains • 4 environmental improvements
Ong *et al.*	2008	(Part 1) Comparisons between: • 2 improvements pertaining to education • 2 reductions in losses pertaining to education (Part 2) Comparisons between: • 2 improvements pertaining to transportation • 2 reductions in losses pertaining to transportation (Part 3) Comparisons between: • 2 improvements pertaining to the environment • 2 reductions in losses pertaining to the environment

Conclusion

The growing understanding of the limitations of current valuation approaches has resulted in efforts to either refine the existing methods or to explore new (and possibly superior) techniques. Motivated by relatively recent findings from behavioural economics that highlight the weaknesses of the CVM, the pair-wise comparison method is an illustration of the latter,

The strengths of the method lie in its not requiring the strict assumptions of the revealed preference approach and in its avoidance of the behavioural bias inherent in stated preference approaches.

While still comparatively uncommon, there are a small but growing number of valuation studies that have made use of the technique. Each study illustrates the simplicity and cost effectiveness of the method. In concluding this chapter, we present a summary of these studies in Table 9.4. For each study, the author, the year of publication and the items of comparison are presented to illustrate the variety of items that the pair-wise comparison method may be applied to.

10 Behavioural effects and cost–benefit analysis: lessons from behavioural economics

Contributed by Jack L. Knetsch[1]

Three groups of people – international transportation experts attending a professional conference, senior Singaporean public servants and university students – were asked which of two transportation projects they would recommend should be built or if they saw them as equally valuable and therefore expressed no preference. One project would shorten the road distance between two destinations; the other would replace a bridge and eliminate a detour made necessary by the failure of the original bridge. The two projects would cost the same and would save equal numbers of motorists the same amount of travel time and expense. Only one could be built. The choice of people in each of the groups was, interestingly given their diverse backgrounds, nearly the same. A solid majority, of about two-thirds, in each group favoured the second project that eliminated the detour, with the remaining third nearly evenly split between favouring the road improvement and expressing no preference (Chin and Knetsch, in progress).

Most people would probably not find these results particularly surprising – in large part, because they too feel it is better to return or restore something that was enjoyed and then lost, than it is to provide a gain of something new. What would probably be a big surprise to most people, however, is that nearly all economists and policy analysts in and out of government agencies throughout the world, who evaluate and recommend possible projects and policies, along with the people who write the textbooks and manuals on which their valuations and recommendations are based, would find the choices made by the participants in this transport study completely contrary to their assumptions about people's preferences. To economic and policy analysts, whether a project provides a gain or reduces or eliminates a loss should be totally irrelevant, and therefore analysts should have no preference for either project as they cost the same and provide identical savings of time and costs to equal numbers of travellers.

The main reason the views of analysts would differ from those of other people on this choice of project, and in so many other real cases, is that their analyses and predictions of likely consequences of alternative actions are based largely on the traditional assumptions of what has become known as standard economic theory. Indeed, analysts are often reminded that 'any measurement …should be consistent with standard economic theory of individual preferences…' (Freeman,

1993, p. 285). By and large, such admonishments are well taken as far too many 'analyses' and popular discourses on the economic justification for projects and policies often reflect little more than self-serving assertions that lack much in the way of a reasonable claim as guidance to further social well-being. When employed as intended, the standard tools of traditional economic and policy analyses have, with little doubt, provided useful guidance that has led to improved policies, regulatory reform, provision of infrastructure and design of institutions in countries throughout the world. There is wide agreement that people would generally be much better served by far greater use of such analyses and more attention to the results, in coming up with proposals to deal with problems and to take advantage of opportunities.

However, what has also become increasingly clear in recent years, as a result of research by psychologists, a growing number of economists, and other decision-making scientists, is that some of the assumptions of standard economics often fail to reflect how individuals and groups actually make decisions, and value and choose among alternatives. The findings suggest, for example, that contrary to the strong assumptions of standard theory, people commonly value losses more than gains, spend or save money received from some sources differently from money received from others, have regard for the well-being of others, and adhere to norms of fairness even at the expense of maximizing their own wealth.

Testing the assumptions of standard economics against people's observed actual valuations and choices does not have a long tradition in economics. Such research has been common only in the past couple of decades, giving rise to what has become known as the sub-field of behavioural economics or economic psychology. The findings are not only providing evidence of systematic departures of actual behaviour from behaviour assumed in standard economics, but also they are bringing attention to other factors that influence people's behaviour and choices beyond those taken into account in standard economics. These behavioural findings have direct implications for public as well as private decisions. Behavioural economics is not in any way a substitute for standard economics, but is instead an increasingly useful supplement to economic analyses that can greatly improve the usefulness of economics in many areas, including applications to improve the design of policies and regulatory reform dealing with environmental matters to make them more consistent with people's real preferences.

The insights from behavioural economic findings can be applied to an extremely wide range of subject areas and problems – essentially to all of economics, decision-making and policy analysis, including environmental concerns. Specific applications are continually being made in all areas – some, such as behavioural finance, at a far faster rate than others – making it impractical to attempt a complete cataloguing in any. However, a few illustrative examples can show how behavioural findings might be used to improve how environmental problems are dealt with.

Behavioural findings

Mental accounting

A standard assertion of standard theory is that individuals treat money gained from whatever source – wages from their labours, returns from investments, inheritances, gifts or whatever – as all the same. It is all figuratively put into the same big account from which they make payments for the vast array of goods and services they want – an assumption economists refer to as fungibility. People are assumed to make choices and decisions over incomes and expenditures as if they are completely substitutable regardless of source or purpose.

Common observations, as well as the evidence from careful empirical studies, however, suggests that people treat money quite differently depending on how it is obtained and the reason for spending or saving it (an excellent review is provided by Thaler (1999)). Most people, for example, spend differently on food while on holiday than at home, they treat windfalls differently from earned cash, they increase the tax withheld from their pay-cheques to ensure a refund at the end of the year rather than a requirement to pay more, and they are willing to spend time to save money on a small purchase but not to save the same sum on a large one. Overall, they tend to organize information and make many decisions based not on one overall account of income and expenditure, but instead make many decisions based on smaller mental sub-accounts.

A fairly transparent example of mental accounting is the discounting of capital gains relative to dividends, particularly by retired people drawing on their investment accounts for living expenses. Corporations can presumably choose to transfer their earnings to shareholders by paying dividends, by buying up shares to increase the value of the remaining shares, or by retaining the earnings and have them accrue as an increase in the value of the corporation and corresponding increase in the value of individual shares. In spite of often more favourable tax treatment of capital gains in many countries, retired investors generally greatly prefer to receive the return in dividend cheques that they can spend rather than accumulate equivalent sums by periodically selling their increasingly valuable shares. Even though the balance on their account remains the same with any of the three options, having to sell portions of their holdings to capture their returns conveys an adverse feeling of 'dipping into their capital' that is absent from receiving and spending their dividend capital (Thaler, 1999). The sums may be equivalent, but the mental accounts, and choices, differ.

Forgone gains versus losses

A generally useful approach to using behavioural findings to improve outcomes can be demonstrated by the instructive example of how they were used in framing workers' decisions as to how much they would contribute to their own retirement fund (Thaler and Benartzi, 2004). While not an environmental case, it is one of the best known and most successful applications of behavioural findings that has been reported, and is also one that clearly illustrates how behavioural findings might be used in any area – environmental included.

It is a usual practice in most countries to inform new workers of not only their pay level, but of any deductions that will be made from this pay for taxes and possibly outlays for various benefits. It is common to also ask employees at that time how much the employee would like deducted as their contribution to a retirement plan (to be matched or added to by the employer in accord with the employment contract), with greater contributions resulting in higher pensions. Unfortunately, posing the contribution choice in this way has resulted in employees choosing, and keeping, very low retirement savings rates, in many cases, which are unlikely to provide a suitable or expected living standard on their retirement – a problem that has been brought to public attention particularly in the United States and Europe.

In response to a request to use behavioural economics findings to modify the information and pension contribution choice format used by a particular company, Richard Thaler and Shlomol Benartzi first noted three aspects of current procedures that actively discouraged employees from contributing more to their retirement savings (Thaler and Benartzi, 2004). The first is the well-known finding that losses are far more aversive to people than forgone gains, and contributions were in this instance framed as subtractions from their reference income. The second is that people commonly exhibit declining discount rates for things further in the future, that is, payments required at present or in the near term are much more important, and therefore aversive, than similar contributions made sometime beyond the immediate future. The third is the related finding that people find it much easier to commit to doing something in the future than to agree to doing it now.

After determining that these three characteristics of the process were probably inhibiting the choice of higher retirement contributions, Thaler and Benartzi focused their attention on the means of mitigating the impact. The result was the suggestion that instead of asking employees how much they want deducted from their present pay packet, they ask how much of future wage increases they would want to contribute. Thus, rather than the very aversive idea of giving back a portion of their present pay, the modification asked for a much less painful forgoing of a gain. It also asked for a commitment to do something in the future rather than make a sacrifice now.

The result of implementing this suggestion was very dramatic and favourably so. The average retirement savings rate was 3.4 per cent before the change and 11.6 per cent after, well over a three-fold increase! Further, the higher rate has not decreased over subsequent years, as the wage increases over time better ensure that the contributed sums also increase. This basic change in format has now been incorporated into the retirement programmes of hundreds of firms with many thousands of employees, and the results have been similar in essentially every case. Employees were, of course, free to continue choosing low savings rates under the modified procedure, but being relieved of the inhibiting framing of the choice, most did not choose to do so.

As seemingly obvious as the contribution inhibiting factors would appear to most people once they are pointed out, it is worth noting that none would be given any weight in standard economic analyses and, consequently, no change in contribution levels resulting from the modification of procedures would be anticipated by standard economics. It was only with the additional insights provided by behavioural findings that the problem could be better understood and, therefore, effective changes suggested.

Sunk cost effect

Another implication of mental accounts, and one somewhat more closely related to environmental matters, stems from the so-called fixed or sunk cost effect. The dictates of standard theory explain that once an expenditure is made, it is sunk and irretrievable and therefore decisions should be based only on gains and losses from that point on – the expenditure is equally gone whether the activity is continued or abandoned. For example, if a person pays a non-refundable deposit of US$100 towards the purchase of an automobile or household appliance, and then finds the identical model available from another dealer for US$200 less, it would make no financial sense to go through with the original purchase because of the US$100 that had already been paid. The individual may regret having paid the deposit to the first dealer, but it is now gone, sunk, and it is only comparisons with the remaining balance that determines the cheapest alternative.

The evidence of people's actual behaviour, however, suggests that most of them often take some account of their previous outlays or commitments when considering future moves. They are more likely to endure a blizzard in going to a sporting event if they have already purchased a ticket than if they have not (Thaler, 1999), and the more people have paid for a season ticket to performances of a theatre group, the more likely they are to go to every event (Arkes and Blumer, 1985). Attention to sunk costs can also give rise to more tragic consequences, as in cases when continuations of armed conflicts are supported with the persuasive emotional appeal that cessation of hostilities would mean that people killed earlier 'would have died in vain'.

The use of cars is, in most places, a major environmental issue as greater use has a direct detrimental impact on, for example, air quality, congestion and greenhouse gas emissions. Moreover, people's inclinations not to ignore sunk costs can have an impact on their use.

Many countries and cities attempt to discourage the purchase and use of cars by imposing high purchase and operating taxes, and other charges. The use of very high purchases taxes or other fixed costs – sometimes reaching levels equalling or even greatly exceeding the purchase price of the car – can, however, because of the sunk cost effect, have an impact opposite to the one of curtailing use that is intended. Having paid the high purchase costs, many people then feel that they need to drive more to justify this high outlay and rationalize their greater use by telling themselves and others that, 'I paid a lot to be able to have a car, so I am going to use it and spread this cost out over more trips'.

The opposite, and usually more socially desirable, incentive is created by imposing a high tax, not on the purchase of a car, but on its use. People would then be more transparently faced with an added cost on each trip. This might be made even more the case, and therefore more effective, if the user charges or fees are more transparently tied to the actual social costs that added use imposes on others by adding to congestion and pollution. This would not only face car owners with the costs of driving, but would also be likely to make it easier for them to self-justify using alternative transit arrangements.

Given the opposite likely impacts of purchase and user taxes or charges, if the aim is to discourage car use, especially at certain times and in particular areas, this might be best supported by reducing fixed cost taxes and increasing variable taxes or charges. The latter might be done with a fuel tax, but this would be largely insensitive to the important differing impacts of where and when the car was driven – driving late at night in remote areas generates less congestion, pollution and other external costs than driving in business districts during rush hours. A system of tolls, for example, can be made more sensitive to the actual distance travelled at particular times and places, though they too are not without problems.

Decoupling

In the normal model of a purchase transaction, a buyer pays the stated price to a seller and takes away the good. The buyer is then presumably keenly aware of the price, and sensitive to it, and makes decisions accordingly. Arrangements that 'decouple' payment from consumption usually cause potential buyers to be less sensitive to the terms of the purchase. A fixed charge for multiple items, for example, often results in consumers paying for and consuming items they would not have purchased if priced separately – a strategy often used by resorts charging an all-inclusive tariff. Credit cards are perhaps the most common decoupling device. While offering great convenience, they are also a very effective means of separating purchase from payment, thereby lessening the restraint provided by the necessity of paying cash to the seller.

Road tolls can be an effective means of facing motorists with the real costs of their driving on particular roads at particular times, and thereby promote socially efficient use of roads and other transportation options. However, their effectiveness is at least in part, and likely in large part, dependent on motorists being sensitive to the charges imposed by alternative routings and times. This is likely to be greater with the need to make a cash outlay when passing a toll point.

The desired sensitivity to the collection of tolls and their resulting effectiveness is, however, likely to be a great deal less with the use of automatic toll collection devices. A probable serious consequence of the use of such automatic collection devices is to largely decouple use of the roadways from payment, by having the toll payments almost completely unknowingly deducted from bank accounts or cash cards or by monthly billings posted to owners long after the contribution to congestion and pollution has taken place. Whatever the convenience and other benefits of automatic toll collection, they seem likely to come at a cost of reducing awareness of the link between payment and road use, and consequently of the effectiveness of the tolls.

The appeal of dedicated funds (ear-marking)

A firm principle of standard economics and of public finance is that monies collected for the use of public facilities should be put into the general public revenue accounts of the government, where they can be used for whatever purposes are deemed to be socially most desired, and not dedicated, or ear-marked, for use by agencies collecting the money or used for purposes related to the provision of the service for which the sums were collected. The reason for this policy directive is straightforward. If the money is left with the agency collecting the money, its necessarily narrower focus may well result in using it for a purpose that is less valued than if it could be allocated to some other public use. Money collected for the use of a park, for example, might be better used in providing healthcare than in expanding parks. In addition, funds from road tolls might be better used to hire more food inspectors than to build more roads. Better then to put the monies into the general fund and allocate it to healthcare and food inspectors.

Although the rationale for the standard economics principle of putting all collected sums into the most general of accounts may be clear, people's reactions have, in many cases, been found to be seriously at variance with it. Money paid in fees that are returned in some form related to the use for which the money is collected, appears to often mitigate the feeling of loss. For example, users of public parks and campsites have been found, not surprisingly, to be much more accepting of an increase in entrance or user fees if the money collected is used to maintain or improve the facilities in the area they are using rather than put into general government revenues.

The lesson for the use of money collected in pollution charges or allocation of pollution rights in a cap-and-trade scheme may be closely parallel. Using the funds for a purpose related to the reason for the payment of fees may well make the collection scheme acceptable to a large portion of the individuals affected by the requirement. An instructive example is provided by the way the government in Columbia overcame the strong resistance to a proposed financial disincentive scheme to control pollution. The objection to the proposal persisted until the government changed its policy and announced that the monies collected from the pollution charge programme would not be put in general revenue accounts, but would instead be used to fund sewage treatment plants throughout the country. Again, the more limited view of standard economics missed the real opportunity to advance environmental provision that became evident with the wider view of preferences that were more apparent with the insights provided by behavioural findings.

Valuations of gains and valuation of losses

Probably the most extensively studied of all behavioural findings – and probably, the most important – is the evidence that people frequently value losses much more than gains. This very unexpected result was first reported in 1974, in a study of people's valuation of duck habitat (Hammack and Brown, 1974). It has been replicated in a very wide array of survey studies and real exchange laboratory and natural experiments conducted over the years since (reviewed in, for example, Kahneman *et al.* (1990) and Rabin (1998), and with particular reference to environmental values in Horowitz and McConnell (2002)).

There is near-universal agreement that economic values are correctly measured by the sacrifice that people are willing to make. In the case of a gain, this measure is the maximum sacrifice that an individual is willing to make to obtain it. In practice this is taken to be the maximum amount of money that the person is willing to pay for it (commonly abbreviated as WTP). In the case of a loss, it is the minimum sacrifice the individual is willing to take to accept it – in practice the minimum sum of money to accept the loss (or WTA). While there are then these two different measures for gains and for losses, the dictates of standard economics are quite clear that there should be little or no difference between them, and consequently little or no difference in the valuations of gains and losses. That is, the amount a person is willing to pay to gain a good should be equivalent to the sum the individual will accept to give it up – 'we shall normally expect the results to be so close together that it would not matter which we choose' (Henderson, 1941, p. 121).

The assumption of equivalence between valuations using either the WTP or WTA measure has long been used to justify the overwhelming current practice of using whichever measure is most convenient. As WTP values are usually easier to estimate than WTA values, nearly all valuations are made with this measure in spite of the clear principle that losses are to be assessed in terms of people's WTA valuations – 'In practice, the WTP is generally used to value benefits because it is often easier to measure and estimate' (US Environmental Protection Agency, 2000, p. 61). The practice of estimating essentially all environmental values with the WTP measure – losses as well as gains – continues in spite of the mounting empirical evidence demonstrating that WTA values are typically much larger than WTP valuations. In their review of 45 environmental valuation studies, Horowitz and McConnell found that the median WTA/WTP ratio among them was 2.6 (the mean ratio was approximately 7).

An example of the many experimental studies that have shown the significant disparity between the measures, and one of many that was carried out with real money exchanges to help motivate the participants to give more seriously considered responses and with questions that revealed real preferences and precluded strategic behaviour, involved valuations of a 50 per cent chance to win US$20 (Kachelmeier and Shehata, 1992). One half of the individuals in a large group of people were asked the maximum sum they would pay for a ticket that gave them this chance to win US$20. The other half were given a ticket that gave them the identical chance to win the same prize and were then asked the smallest amount they would accept to give up their ticket. Then the roles of people in the two groups were reversed and the alternative valuations were obtained from each, so that in the end everyone valued the ticket two ways: by the maximum amount they would pay to get one (their WTP valuation) and by the minimum sum they would accept to give one up (their WTA valuation). Note that the item being valued – a 50 per cent chance to win US$20 – is exactly the same for both valuations, giving no reason to expect people to value the ticket differently when buying it or selling it. Indeed, this is what standard economics says, and consequently what analysts assume when they assess alternatives and make recommendations. The valuations of people in this experimental demonstration, like those in dozens of others, were sharply different from these expectations. The buy and sell valuations were not equal as standard economics assumes, they were far from it. When asked the maximum amount they would pay for a ticket, the average for all of the participants was US$5.60; when asked the minimum sum they would require to give up a ticket, these *same* people valued it at US$11.02.

The results from a series of studies of people making common choices in non-experimental settings have also been reported over the years and show similar and consistent results. For example, shoppers making routine purchases of eggs showed a much greater sensitivity to price increases, which impose losses (a price elasticity of –1.10) than to price decreases, which provide gains (elasticity of only –0.45) – here too losses were taken to be more important than gains (Putler, 1992). Similar behaviour has been observed among investors in securities who often do not sell shares that have gone down in price because they are reluctant to realize they have made a loss, a reluctance that does not influence their sell decisions on shares that have gone up in price (Odean, 1998). Consistent behaviour has also been reported among sellers of houses of the influence feelings of gain or loss have on them when selling above or below their original purchase price (Einio *et al.*, 2008).

Given the evidence of pervasive and large disparities between people's valuations of gains and losses, a failure to take this into account can lead to bad choices that can compromise public welfare and to economically unwarranted deterioration of the environment. This might be illustrated with the case of a decision to preserve an important bird habitat in the United States, or to allow it to be developed for some alternative purpose. In the study noted above, people who benefited from the natural habitat were willing to pay an average of US$247 to preserve it, but the average amount they demanded to agree to its demise was over four times larger – US$1,044 (Hammack and Brown, 1974). The valuation that should be used in this case is the latter, as the change at issue is the loss of the habitat, but the usual current practice all over the world is to use the lesser amount of what people would pay to preserve it. Consequently, alternative developments that would result in the destruction of the habitat that are worth more than the equivalent of the US$247 would be seen to be economically justified and worth doing even if they are worth less than the actual value of the loss of the equivalent of US$1,044.

The choice of measure to value changes

When there was the secure belief that there was little or no difference between people's valuation of gains and valuations of losses, the issue of which measure of value was most appropriate to use in specific cases seemed to be of little practical importance – the circumstance that has led to current practice of WTP use for all changes. The now widely observed and reported disparities between the measures changes this; the choice of measure is now an issue of substantial consequence.

The major focus of the concern over the appropriate measure is whether a negative change is best regarded as a loss, which would call for the WTA measure, or a reduction of a gain, which is best assessed with the WTP measure; and whether a positive change should be considered a gain, calling for the WTP measure or a reduction of a loss, which is most accurately assessed with the WTA measure. Current practice, to the extent that this is taken into any account, is to regard all positive changes as improvements or gains, and to consider all negative changes as losses. This is, however, unlikely to lead to a useful distinction.

A more useful discrimination might be suggested with a simple thought experiment involving a hypothetical environmental change of an oil spill. Most people seem likely to regard such a spill as imposing a loss from what would be considered the normal or expected condition of their surroundings free from the spilled oil washing up on foreshores. Given the presumption of it being a loss, the appropriate measure of its value is then the WTA of people to accept it. The value of cleaning up the spill turns on whether people regard this mitigation as being a gain or a reduction of a loss. Here it seems most likely that most people would consider the clean-up activity as a restoration of the norm of an environment free of the spilled oil – much as they would probably regard clearing a road of spilled lorry cargo to allow normal traffic to resume. To the extent that this is the case, the proper measure of the value of the clean-up is the minimum sum people would accept to forgo this action and remain with the consequences of the spill (the WTA measure), and not how much they would be willing to pay to have the clean-up proceed as is now overwhelmingly the choice in environmental (and other) valuation efforts.

While usually a less frequent issue, a similar discrimination is applicable to negative changes. The WTP to avoid a loss is only applicable to changes that would change things back to a normal or expected condition. Other negative changes are best regarded as losses from this neutral reference and are therefore more appropriately assessed with the WTA measure.

While the choice remains an empirical issue in particular cases, it is at least arguable that most environmental changes, and particularly the ones that most people are concerned with, are most likely to be best considered as losses, prevention of losses, mitigation or eliminations of losses, and are therefore in all of these cases best assessed with the WTA measure.

To the extent that valuations of losses exceed those of gains, the current practice of using the WTP measure, rather than the appropriate WTA measure, for losses and reductions of losses will in most cases give rise to systematic understatements of their value. This will likely lead to undue encouragement of activities with negative impacts, such as pollution and risks to health and safety, as such losses will be under weighted. Similarly, compensation and damage awards will be too small to provide proper restitution and deterrence, and inappropriately lax pollution and other environmental standards against further degradation will be set because assessments of added costs of further harm will be heavily biased.

Too few resources will be devoted to avoiding environmental deterioration because the determinants of allocation efficiencies will be biased against avoiding losses, and full accounting of resource values and appropriate pricing of resource services, such as environmental amenities, will be frustrated.

Opting in versus opting out and the power of the default

Recognition of the disparity between people's valuations of gains and losses also helps in explaining the difference in outcomes due to default designation of options – people are reluctant to give up an entitlement for an alternative, as the loss looms larger than the potential gain. This was quite evident in the results of an experiment in which people in one group were given a decorated mug and others in another group a 400 gram Swiss chocolate bar, and then all were given the chance of a costless exchange of whichever good they were initially randomly given, for the alternative. People in both groups had a presumably equal opportunity to end up with the good they preferred, and as there is no reason to expect more people favouring either good to be in one group or the other, the strong prediction of standard economics is that the proportions ultimately going home with each good should be about the same in both groups. The result was quite different. Ninety per cent of those given a mug kept it rather than exchange it for a chocolate bar and 89 per cent of those initially given a chocolate bar kept it (Knetsch, 1989). For most participants, whichever good they were initially given, and had in their possession at the time of deciding whether or not to exchange it for the other, was more valuable to them when facing its loss than the one they could acquire as a gain. For everyone, the good they had was the default and it mattered in terms of their final choices.

A similar influence of default positions is observed in non-experimental circumstances of people making everyday decisions. For example, car owners in two US states, New Jersey and Pennsylvania, were offered a choice of two insurance options: one was considerably less expensive but restricted recovery in the event of an accident; the other was more expensive but had fewer restrictions. Both options were nearly identical in the two states, but the default option differed. Even though the transaction costs of changing from the default to the other alternative were essentially zero and the cost differences substantial, only 20 per cent of the car owners in New Jersey and 25 per cent in Pennsylvania changed from the default. As a result of the different defaults, the more expensive but less restrictive policy was chosen by motorists in Pennsylvania, where it was the default, and 20 per cent in New Jersey, where the cheaper alternative was the default – a 55 per cent difference (Johnson *et al.*, 1993).

In countries where organ donations, usually from people killed in accidents, are made only in cases in which the donor has given *ex ante* consent, donations are typically around 20 per cent and lead to perpetual shortages of needed transplants. The default for donations differs in many European countries, Singapore and others, where people are assumed to have given consent to the taking of their organs after death unless they have made an explicit declaration to the contrary.

In these countries, the rates of donation are commonly above 80 per cent, which is more in line with the proportions of survey respondents who indicate they favour the taking of organs for this purpose.

Default positions exert a strong influence over choices in all areas, including environmental. This is evident, for example, in people's attachment to what they consider as normal conditions – often the present ones – that are free of oil spills, pollution, extinction of favoured species and the like. It is also specifically apparent in environmental impact assessments, which many countries require before permitting certain types of development or activity. The focus of such appraisals is overwhelmingly on implications of changes from the status quo, or other neutral reference, that might result from the development or change being assessed.

Mitigation versus compensation

There are two general forms of remedy that people causing injury or harm to others may be required to provide. One is to undertake mitigation measures to reduce or eliminate the harm that was caused by the person responsible. The other is to pay compensation to the victims for the harm they suffered.

Conventional economic analysis suggests that, all else being equal, compensation will normally be a more efficient and preferred means to deal with losses. Mitigation restricts the remedy to dealing only with whatever has been injured whereas compensation payments permit recipients to use the funds for whatever good or service is of most value to them – which may well be something totally unrelated to the thing that was harmed. Thus, if a negligent action causes an accident that severely damages an older car, the owner should be less satisfied with having the car repaired than with a monetary payment that can be used to either repair the car, as part payment for a newer car, or to underwrite a family holiday.

The evidence of the disparity between people's valuations of gains and losses suggests an alternative view of people's preferences over the remedies. They may well view the compensation remedy as really very much two separate issues, one that provides the gain of money, which is discounted for being a gain, and the other as leaving them with the injury, which is valued more highly for being a loss. The mitigation measure, on the other hand, will be viewed as reducing the loss and valued more because of this.

The strength of this distinction has been borne out in survey and experimental studies, as well as in the observations of reactions of injured parties. For example, upwards of 70 per cent of respondents favoured spending large sums of money on only very partially effective efforts to mitigate a minor environmental problem rather than spend the same sums on 'whatever use is decided on by local residents in a referendum' (Knetsch, 1990, p. 233).

Fairness and other regarding behaviour

The standard model of behaviour used in most analyses of issues also suggests that people seek to maximize their personal welfare, with little regard for others outside of their immediate household. Here too, the empirical evidence suggests that regard for others and feelings of what is and is not fair does in fact influence the actions and choices of most people. While standard analysis has long taken account of issues of vertical equity, that is the treatment of and consequences for poor relative to rich, there has been much less explicit regard for issues of horizontal equity, that is the like treatment of people in like circumstances. The empirical evidence that is available, however, indicates, among other things, that people do appear to care and change behaviours to accommodate others, and that some simple rules seem to dictate much of what people regard as fair dealings (Kahneman *et al.*, 1986).

For example, one rule seems to be that it is generally unfair for one party to gain at the direct expense of another party. In a random household survey of Canadians, and confirmed by later studies in other countries, a large majority of respondents judged a department store holding an auction to secure the highest profit from the sale of one remaining toy doll to be unfair, as the store would benefit at the expense of the customer. However, when the added profit went to a charity, the auction was then judged to be fair – the store was then seen not to benefit at the expense of others.

It also appears to be unfair for one party to exploit circumstances to increase profits. Very large majorities of respondents judged it very unfair for a greater than intended increase in rent to be imposed when the landlord learned that the tenant had taken a job nearby and was therefore unlikely to move.

People did feel, however, that it was fair for landlords and others to pass on cost increases. They also said it was fair to share losses with employees by cutting their wages, though this was very unfair if the firm was making profits.

While fairness motivations and regard for others are not generally considered, at least very explicitly, in policy analyses, there is considerable evidence that they influence a wide range of people's behaviours. There is also surprisingly consistent regard for fairness in judgments in common law jurisdictions, as rulings closely mirror the findings of fairness studies as to what is and is not fair (Cohen and Knetsch, 1992). Prices generally more closely reflect changes in costs than they do shifts in demand, as it is almost unquestionably fair to pass on these costs along with a fair profit. Many markets, such as resorts during holiday periods, fail to clear the fairness standards because taking too great an advantage of opportunities is regarded as unfair 'gouging'.

The evidence suggests that a greater sensitivity to fairness concerns would increase the success of policy design and result in greater support and socially useful change. For example, fees that transparently reflect costs of provision or charges that reflect recognizable environmental damages are likely to be far more acceptable than levies that are less so.

It seems also likely that the responsibility–cost link might usefully be exploited in the design of measures to deal with environmental externality costs, to the extent that if people can be explicitly shown the costs they impose on others by, for example, driving their cars at peak traffic times, there may be greater acceptance of paying this full cost for doing so and of making greater effort to use alternative transit modes or times in order to lower these costs.

Conclusion

Although there is yet much more to be done in this area, it seems already clear that the level of debate and decisions about environmental policies and regulations, like so many other areas, could be markedly improved with more attention to behavioural findings. Establishing priorities more in keeping with people's feelings of the seriousness of problems would be easier, and improved means to resolve or mitigate them might be possible.

The results from behavioural economics research have not, however, with a few notable exceptions, yet reached the mainstream of environmental economics textbooks or been used in any appreciable way in environmental decisions, despite publication of findings in *every* leading professional journal in economics, psychology and related fields, the degree to which they conform to the common sense of most people, Daniel Kahneman sharing the 2002 Nobel Prize for Economics for his work that led to the development of the field and a literature pointing to applications extending well over two decades. Analysts continue to show 'restraint' in giving up their present assumptions and procedures. There may be various reasons for this lack of more serious attention, but career incentives that reward going with the tried and tested, and censure results that depart from the norm, may well be among them (Knetsch, 2000). While care must be taken with environmental applications, as with all analyses, the case for continued lack of attention to these findings seems to lack an easy justification.

Part IV

Case studies of cost–benefit analysis

11 The Three Gorges Dam project, China

《游泳》~ 毛泽东
一桥飞架南北，天堑变通途。
更立西江石壁，截断巫山云雨，高峡出平湖。

Swimming by Mao Zedong

A bridge will fly to span the north and south,
Turning a deep chasm into a thoroughfare;
Walls of stone will stand upstream to the west
To hold back Wushan's clouds and rain
Till a smooth lake rises in the narrow gorges.

Introduction

The Yangtze River is China's longest river and it spans a length of 6,363 km (3,953 miles). Geographically, it separates China into north and south regions but the Chinese people were never divided, as the population was attracted to settle down near the river due to the rich and fertile soil. In fact, as the 'rice bowl' of China, the Yangtze basin supports some 400 million Chinese and produces nearly half of the total agricultural produce annually, including two-thirds of the rice crop. Nonetheless, this important contribution is both a blessing and a curse as heavy rains in the upper streams of the river would often cause the waters to flood the lower plains, destroying much agricultural land and many properties, and killing many people.

Such was the case in 1998, when a disastrous flood killed more than 1,500 people and destroyed about 2,400 sq.km (920 sq.miles) of farmland. Records showed that in the twentieth century alone, heavy floods were recorded in 1931, 1935, 1949 and 1954, and thousands of lives were lost, along with millions of people being affected and properties destroyed in the floods. (See Table 11.1.)

A vision was hence born to build a dam across the Yangtze River so that the waters of this raging river could be tamed and floods of such devastating consequences could be avoided. While the vision began as early as the beginning of the twentieth century and feasibility studies on suitable sites were even conducted in 1953 under the Chinese Communist leadership of Mao Zedong, the project was strongly

Table 11.1 Yangtze river flood record in the twentieth century[1]

1931	An area of 130,000 sq km, with 33,900 sq km of farmland, was flooded. It destroyed 1.8 million houses, affected 28.55 million people and killed 145,000 people.
1935	Six provinces in the middle and lower reaches of the Yangtze River (Hubei, Hunan, Jiangxi, Anhui, Jiangsu and Zhejiang) were flooded, totalling an area of 89,000 sq km (34,300 sq miles), and 15,100 sq km (5,800 sq miles) of farmland was inundated. Over 10 million people were affected with 142,000 killed.
1949	The flood inundated 18,100 sq km (7,000 sq miles) of farmland; 8.1 million people were affected and 5,699 lives were lost.
1954	The damage caused by the flood included the destruction of 31,800 sq km (12,300 sq miles) of farmland and 4.27 million houses. About 18.884 million people in 123 counties and cities were affected and 33,169 people were killed. This flood severely interrupted the Beijing–Guangzhou Railway for 100 days.
1998	The flood struck a large area of the Yangtze Valley for nearly 3 months. The flood caused damage to 2,390 sq km (920 sq miles) of farmland. It affected 2.316 million people, killing 1,526 people from four provinces of Hunan, Hubei, Jiangxi and Anhui. Although the damage was minimized, more than yuan 13 billion of flood-fighting materials were deployed to control the flood.

[1] Adapted from China Three Gorges Project (2002).

contested. It was only in 1993 that a decision was finally taken and construction on the dam was approved to begin in 1994. In 2006, after almost a century, the Three Gorges Dam finally became a reality.

The Three Gorges Dam

The Three Gorges Dam is built near the Three Gorges[1] that is found in the middle course of the Yangtze River where the waters traverse from the western Sichuan province into eastern Hubei. The massive Dam is the world's largest dam structure, about 2,335 m (7,660 feet) long and has a maximum height of 185 m (607 feet). It cost US$24 billion to build. The project consumed many resources including the employment of 60,000 workers, and used 28 million cubic metres of concrete and 463,000 metric tons of steel.

The result of the dam across the Yangtze River is the creation of a deep-water reservoir, which allows ocean-going freighters to navigate 2,250 km (1,400 miles) inland from Shanghai on the East China Sea to the inland city of Chongqing. This will greatly facilitate inland trading and bring about greater development and economic progress. However, in the midst of creating this immense reservoir, large areas of the Qutang, Wu and Xilang gorges, some 600 km (375 miles) upstream of the dam, were totally submerged. Not only did these natural sites disappear, during the construction phase, the rising water levels also flooded some 500 cities, towns and villages along the river and between 1.6 and 1.9 million people had to be displaced to accommodate the changes.

As a result of the damming, some 1,200 sites of historical and archaeological importance that were to be found in the middle sections of the Yangtze River also vanished. One of these archaeological sites is the Baiheliang, also known as the White Crane Ridge. The Baiheliang is a natural stone ridge that is 1,600 m long and 10–15 m wide, and located in the north of Fuling (Chongqing). At the site can be found 165 pieces of inscriptions with more than 30,000 characters that were written by poets and writers dating as far back as the Tang Dynasty (1,200 years ago). However, these are now submerged and an underwater museum had to be constructed so that tourists can continue to visit and gaze at these historical wonders[1]. Another example is the Zhang Fei Temple at Yungang, which had to be relocated two kilometres (1.2 miles) upstream of the Yangtze River, as a result of the rising waters[2].

It seems ironic that this mega-structure, whose original intention was to control flooding, has been responsible for the massive submerging of many parts of the basin. Arguably, this is a sacrifice due to development and progress. Furthermore, not only has the river been tamed, other tangible benefits of the dam are clear and these include the provision of drinking water to Shanghai's 13 million inhabitants and the creation of a cheap and clean source of energy that will support the industrial growth in eastern and central China, and eastern Sichuan.

With 26 hydroelectric turbines fully operational in 2009, approximately 84.7 billion kWh of hydroelectric power will be generated. As China depends on coal to provide about 66 per cent of its energy needs, the Three Gorges Dam will reduce dependency on coal and other non-renewable sources of energy (about 1.1–1.2 billion tons of coal is burned annually). This will vastly reduce the amount of carbon emissions in its energy production. There are further plans to add another six turbines by 2012, which will increase the power output to 104.2 billion kWh annually (about 10 per cent of all China's power).

However, there is much fear about other environmental issues associated with the project, such as water pollution and destruction of wildlife. According to the Chinese Academy of Sciences, the Yangtze River takes in more than one billion tons of wastewater annually. There are more than 50 types of pollutant coming from various sources such as agricultural run-off, urban sewers and residential wastewater. By damming the river, the water flow is obstructed and toxins and pollutants are concentrated behind the dam rather than being washed downstream and out to sea. Furthermore, without the annual flooding and deposition of fertile silt onto fields, chemical fertilisers are increasingly being used and associated problems of nitrate run off and groundwater pollution has resulted, causing more damage to the environment.

The impact on wildlife is also significant. Stagnation of the waters changes the water temperature and drastically affects the breeding patterns of the animals that make the river basin their habitat. It was reported that 3,000 to 4,000 of the remaining critically endangered Siberian Crane, a large number of which spent the winter in the wetlands, were destroyed by the Three Gorges Dam. The Baiji, the Yangtze river dolphin, has also been reported as extinct as a result of the damming[3].

Benefiting the economy

There is no doubt that the Three Gorges Dam generated much adverse impact on the environment and caused several natural and heritage sites to disappear forever. The lives of millions of people were impacted upon as they had to be relocated from their birth place to a new development entirely unfamiliar to them. However, the investment to the region had a much wider benefit to the economy that has to be accounted for.

For example, the building of the dam improved the lives of thousands directly through the employment opportunities created. China is a nation of 1.3 billion people and many still live in rural parts of the mainland. Those who were unemployed or working in low-paying farming jobs enjoyed better and consistent wages for the period of construction. Subsequently, they learned new skills and achieved steady employment within the construction sector. The multiplier effect of the capital investment also supported the development of many more business opportunities, creating more wealth for the nation. Local governments could also use the increased tax revenue to build more public facilities that the people could enjoy, such as new public housing, and improved transport and utility infrastructures.

The continuous benefits of the dam can be observed in the farming sector. As the dam improved the irrigation system and allowed water to be channelled to farmland further away from the Yangtze Basin, this increased the total crop yield and improved the farmers' livelihoods. This brought about an incidental benefit of reducing the wage disparity between the incomes of rural farmers and urban workers and could potentially prevent any social unrest resulting from the persistence of income disparity.

Conclusion

The Three Gorges Dam project was a massive and expensive project. The World Bank refused to support the project due to the high environmental costs attached to the price tag, besides the construction costs of US$24 billion. The potential benefits of the project however are just as significant because of the lost lives and destroyed property that have been avoided by the construction of the dam. The dam also provides a cheap source of energy that is potentially equivalent to 10 per cent of the nation's needs. With an ever expanding Chinese economy, it seems vital that China employ cleaner technology in satisfying its energy appetite.

In the long run, it seems that the Chinese government's building of the Three Gorges Dam is the right decision. What should be more prevalent are the mitigating actions that the government has taken to reduce the social costs and environmental damage that the project has brought about. Actions such as the preservation of the historical and archaeological structures, the stepping up of artificial reproduction schemes for endangered animals and proper management of the quality of water in the dam reservoir would go a long way to ensure that the project's costs are minimized and society can benefit from the invested project.

Discussion questions

1　The Three Gorges Dam brings economic development, controls flooding and provides irrigation to crops and farming to much of rural China. So why is there so much opposition to this seemingly beneficial project?
2　How can the Chinese government internalize the external social cost?

Table 11.2 Summary of cost and benefit items for the Three Gorges Dam

Private costs	Social costs	Private benefits	Social benefits
Costs that economic agents alone face when producing or consuming economic resources.	*Incidental costs created by production or consumption of goods and services. These are faced by third parties.*	*Benefits (monetary and non-monetary) accrued to economic agents alone when they produce or consume products.*	*Incidental benefits created by production or consumption of goods and services. These are faced by third parties.*
Building costs, such as raw materials, manpower, costs of machinery, amounting to US$24 billion.	Improper disposal of waste materials from the building project.	Controlled flooding, preventing the loss of lives and properties.	The investment in the area improved the lives of other residents by new businesses and new public amenities.
Relocation of towns and cities that will be affected by the rising waters.	Environmental costs – destruction of wildlife, increased soil erosion, risk of flooding and dam failure.	Increase in wages of labourers on project; long term improvement of farmers' income due to increased crop yields.	
Loss of jobs due to closure of factories.	Social costs of displaced and/or dislocated families.	Reliable source of energy and irrigation.	
	Loss of archaeological and historical sites, and artefacts.	Revenue from sale of energy for businesses, and for farmers by the sale of agricultural produce.	

12 Flue gas desulphurization in Mae Moh, Thailand

Background

Located in Lampang Province, in a town of 855 square kilometres, the Mae Moh Power Plant is Southeast Asia's largest coal-fired power plant. This power plant, which is owned and operated by the Electricity Generating Authority of Thailand (EGAT), uses lignite supplied from the nearby coal mines as the main fuel. Besides providing electricity for the region, the Mae Moh Power Plant is a support to the economy as the mining activities contribute to about 17.4 per cent of the Gross Provincial Product in 2003.

The Mae Moh Power Plant at its full installation capacity can produce 2,625 megawatts (MW) of energy. It is the largest thermal power plant in Thailand and produces about 10–12 per cent of the nation's energy requirement.

In producing the energy, about 40–50 thousand tons of lignite are consumed daily. Lignite, also known as brown coal, is the lowest quality of coal available. It has a relatively low energy content that ranges from 10 to 20 MJ per kilogram and has very high carbon emissions. According to some reports, lignite produces 1,246 kg of CO_2 per MWh[1] of energy, which is 30–40 per cent more than other types of coal and 600 times more than renewable energy generators. However, the main problem lies in its sulphur content, which, according to reports, averages about 2.5–3.0 per cent of the weight.

Sulphur pollution

The first incidence of a major emission of pollution took place on 3 October 1992 when the expansion of the plant reached the capacity of 2,025 MW and all 11 units of the power generator were in operation. A large amount of sulphur dioxide (SO_2) was emitted from the power plant and the dioxide accumulated in the air above the Mae Moh Basin. An all-time-high reading of the hourly average ground level of ambient sulphur dioxide concentration of 3,418 µm per cubic metre was recorded as compared with the hourly average of 780 µm per cubic metre, according to Thailand's standard of air pollutant control.

Within days, the high level of SO_2 concentration caused more than a thousand village people residing within several kilometres of the plant to fall ill with breathing difficulties (such as coughing, asthmatic attacks, chest tightness and wheezing), nausea, dizziness and inflammation of the eyes and nasal cavities caused by the inhalation of the sulphur dioxide gas. Within two months, more than 50 per cent of the rice fields near the plant were damaged by acid rain and at least 42,000 local people were found to be suffering from breathing ailments.

Other reported air pollution incidents occurred in April and May 1996 when six village people in the Mae Moh valley died of blood poisoning. It was reported that, in 1998, mobile clinics determined that, out of 8,214 patients they received, 3,463 were suffering from respiratory diseases. Altogether, since the plant's operation, more than 200–300 respiratory-related deaths had been registered, highlighting the extent of the health problems it brought to the population.

Acid rains continued to damage the rice and vegetable crops and destroy livestock too[2]. In May 2004, the Thai Provincial court awarded 5.7 million baht (US$142,500) to the villagers for crop damage caused by the power plant. In addition, on 4 March 2009, the Chiang Mai provincial administrative court decided that EGAT had to compensate 130 Mae Moh villagers who had suffered severe health distress due to the toxic emissions originating from the lignite-fired power plant amounting to an approximate sum of 246,900 baht per family (totalling 1.54 million baht for 64 families). EGAT was also ordered to arrange for the relocation of 400 affected families to areas at least 5 km away from the power plant, and to provide each family with a house and farmland.

Flue gas desulphurization

Sulphur oxides (SO_x) are the generic name for all oxides of sulphur which are produced when fossil fuels such as oil and coal are burned[3]. The level of emissions depends on the sulphur content of the fuel. As mentioned earlier, sulphur oxides cause acid rain when they are combined with water and such acid rains damage the crops and livestock. Inhaling sulphur oxides can also cause serious health problems for the population.

To control the level of sulphur oxides emissions, flue gas desulphurization (FGD) technology can be employed. It is a chemical process whereby raw materials (such as limestone) are used to remove the sulphur oxides from the emissions. Power plants equipped with flue gas desulphurization equipment can achieve effective control of sulphur oxides emissions with up to 95 per cent effectiveness. Usually by-products are common in such chemical processes and one useful by-product is gypsum, which is a type of usable clay. However, carbon dioxide (a greenhouse gas) is also released into the atmosphere. Therefore, in weighing the costs and benefits of such technology, these by-products have to be factored in.

Benefits

In 2002, after the completion of the desulphurization project, the sulphur oxides emissions were 67–105 parts per million (ppm). This was a vast improvement from the 352–1,919 ppm in 1998. Particulate matter (PM_{10}), another type of air pollutant, had also been reduced by more than 30 per cent as a result.

The improvement to the health conditions of the residents was clear and by far the biggest benefit of the installation of the flue desulphurization technology. One way of measuring the health benefits is by measuring the avoided cost associated with these health impacts of ambient air pollution such as mortality, respiratory hospitalizations, changes in lung function and loss of wages. However, we can also simplify the measurement by using the willingness-to-pay (WTP) to avoid morbidity risk derived through surveys. This is adequate for our purpose, as it would include the various aspects of the cost of illness, value of work and/or leisure time lost, and the pain associated with the illness or threat of the illness.

According to one cost–benefit analysis (CBA) report, it was found that, based on the WTP survey results, the health benefits for the population can be as high as 3,730 million baht (at 6 per cent discounted for 30 years), even after limiting the impact on areas to the northern region surrounding the Mae Moh power plant that are subjected to high acidic deposition (Punyawadee *et. al.*, 2006, p. 22).

Another direct benefit is the reduction of damage to crops and timber resources. In the same CBA report, the agricultural benefit, as measured by the changes in the crop yield, was approximately 80 million baht at 6 per cent discount. As for timber and non-timber forest resources, it was found that the average yield of timber stock in affected sites and the control site can differ by 30–40 per cent, depending on the proximity to the source of the air pollution. This represents an increase in teak productivity by about 706 million baht and the increase for non-timber forest products was 174 million baht at 6 per cent discount.

An indirect benefit is the sale of gypsum for commercial use. Gypsum is a by-product of the chemical process and is used in a wide variety of applications, primarily as a plaster finish for walls and ceilings. Unfortunately, the quality of the gypsum from the Mae Moh Power Plant is very low and only about 3 per cent of the gypsum produced has commercial value. With a low unit price and low output, the benefit was only about 10 million baht.

Based on all the above calculations, the total benefit is approximately 4,700 million baht.

Costs

The costs of the FGD technology are largely in the capital investment cost, operating and maintenance cost, and the economic cost of input resources (limestone, energy, water). These are the direct costs of the investment. There is also a need to calculate the indirect cost of carbon emissions in the process as it may have an impact on the environment.

The capital cost of the project was about 7,000 million baht and the operating and maintenance cost, calculated and discounted to present value, is about 2,000 million baht (15 per cent) while the present value of the input cost is about 3,700 million baht (27 per cent).

As mentioned, greenhouse gas is a by-product of the process. The social cost of CO_2 can be measured using a carbon tax. The authors of the CBA report estimated that between 1990 and 1999 the carbon tax would be about US$5.9 per ton carbon and this would rise to US$9.13 in 2005, US$12.73 in 2015 and US$16.73 in 2025. Based on such figures, the estimated greenhouse gas cost is about 900 million baht.

Therefore the total cost is about 13,800 million baht, and way above the benefit calculated, which implies that there is a net loss that has to be borne by society.

Discussion

Based on the report that calculated the benefits and costs of the flue desulphurization investment, there is a large net loss that is borne by society. This is quite apparent because of the large capital investment (7,000 million baht) involved. However, policy-makers must bear in mind some questions before concluding the appraisal of the project.

First, can the power plants continue to function without adopting the FGD technology to control the level of emissions? The answer is clearly no, as the judiciary is prepared to compensate the villages for the health and crop damages resulting from the air pollution. The power plant in Mae Moh supplies a large proportion of Thailand's energy needs. If nothing was done to control the air pollution, alternative power plants have to be built to replace the Mae Moh plant. If the replacement costs have to be considered, then the social benefit of the FGD could be much higher.

Second, as pointed out by the authors, the benefit calculation is sensitive to the methodology employed. It is good to explore alternative methods that are acceptable to estimate the value of the true benefit of any investment.

For example, the benefits can be raised if compensation payments are used as alternative measures of the benefits. Using the compensation amounts decided in lawsuits filed against the EGAT as a guide, where approximately 1.54 million baht was awarded to 64 farmers, and extrapolated to the whole affected population (present and future), there is the possibility that the benefit can grow up to 9,700 million baht.

Direct computation of the benefits may result in a low appraisal of the project, therefore it is necessary to consider alternative measures of the benefits and adopt a comprehensive approach to ensure that all the benefits of the project are properly calculated and weighed against the cost of the investment.

Discussion questions

1   Is it right for policy-makers to use alternative measurements to quantify the health benefits of the investment? Why do you think that the authors suggest using alternative measurements?
2   Why do you think that the author used 6 per cent as the discount factor? Will the appraisal result change if a different discount factor is used? What are the implications for changing the discount rate?

Table 12.1 Summary of cost and benefit items in flue gas desulphurization in Mae Moh, Thailand

Private costs	Social costs	Private benefits	Social benefits
Costs that economic agents alone face when producing or consuming economic resources.	*Incidental costs created by production or consumption of goods and services. These are faced by third parties.*	*Benefits (monetary and non-monetary) accrued to economic agents alone when they produce or consume products.*	*Incidental benefits created by production or consumption of goods and services. These are faced by third parties.*
The capital cost of the project was about 7,000 million baht. Operation and maintenance cost was about 2,000 million baht. Input cost of resources such as limestone, energy and water was about 3,700 million baht.	Greenhouse gas (CO_2) is released into the atmosphere in the desulphurization process. The social cost of CO_2 can be measured using the optimised carbon tax, totalling about 900 million baht.	Reduced mortality and morbidity of residents living near the plant. Improvement in level of SO_x concentration and PM_{10} also reduced symptoms of illness, due to inhalation of air pollutants, such as coughing, asthmatic attacks, chest tightness and wheezing, nausea, dizziness and inflamed eyes and nasal cavities. The value of health benefits was estimated to be 3,730 million baht. Increase in yield of rice and vegetable crops (80 million baht), timber production (706 million baht) and non-timber forest production (174 million baht). There was also further reduction in the destruction of livestock due to acid rains.	Usable clay, called gypsum, is created in the desulphurization process. With only about 3% of the gypsum produced having commercial value, the benefit was valued at about 10 million baht.

13 Hosting international events: cases from the Beijing Olympics 2008 and the inaugural Youth Olympics in Singapore 2010

Introduction

The year 2010 was a special sporting year – in a short span of four months, three international sporting events took place: first, the inaugural Youth Olympics was held in Singapore in August; second, in October, New Delhi, India, hosted the Commonwealth Games; and third, in November, the Asian Games were held in Guangzhou, China. Why do so many cities around the world want to host international sporting events? What are the benefits for the hosting nations and what are the associated costs? This chapter examines the costs and benefits of hosting such international events by analysing two cost–benefit analysis (CBA) case studies from the Beijing Olympics in 2008 and Singapore's Youth Olympics in 2010.

Beijing summer Olympics 2008

The modern Olympics can trace its roots from the ancient Olympic Games that were held in Olympia, Greece, from the eighth century BC to the fifth century AD. The games included athletic sports, combat and chariot racing events. They were well represented by athletes from the city-states in Ancient Greece, competing for the glory and honour of being crowned an Olympic Champion. Now, the Olympics Games consist of 26 sports, 30 disciplines and over 300 events including traditional athletic sporting events such as swimming, track and field, and gymnastics. Yet the glory for individual athletes winning the gold medal in such games is not diminished.

While individuals compete for medals in the games, cities compete with one another to win the right to host the Olympic Games held every four years. Beijing was awarded the right to host the Olympic Games on 13 July 2001 after defeating Toronto, Paris, Istanbul and Osaka in the voting by members of the International Olympic Committee (IOC). Since then, China began the work to put the infrastructural development plans into action. A total of 17.4 billion yuan was invested to build the various sporting halls (such as the Beijing National Aquatics Centre, Beijing Wukesong Culture and Sports Centre), sporting stadiums (such as the Beijing National Stadium and Beijing National Indoor Stadium) and also the Olympic Village and the Olympic Convention Centre, in various parts of Beijing.

Over 100 Olympic projects in Beijing city and the five other cities that co-hosted the Games were undertaken, of which 36 were competition venues while the rest were used for training. The centrepiece of the 2008 Olympics was the Beijing National Stadium, nicknamed 'The Bird's Nest' because of its nest-like skeletal structure. This stadium hosted both the opening and closing ceremonies as well as several athletics competitions.

As part of the master plan to host the large number of visitors to Beijing during the Games, Beijing's transportation infrastructure expanded significantly. Beijing's airport underwent a major renovation and added a new airport terminal. Beijing's Terminal 3 became one of the world's largest airport terminals and cost more than 4 billion yuan. Beijing's subway also saw a doubling of its capacity and overall size with the addition of seven new lines (including one direct link between the city centre and the airport) and 80 stations to the previously existing four lines and 64 stations. Altogether, there were great improvements to the transport network of Beijing.

The Beijing organizing committee for the Olympic Games reported that the total spending on the games was about 19.3 billion yuan and 'generally as much as that of the Athens 2004 Olympic Games' (Xinhau News Agency, 6 March 2009). The revenues from the Olympic Games was reportedly 20.5 billion yuan, generating a surplus of about 1 billion yuan. However, the report failed to give the exact amount spent and according to other sources, it was estimated that approximately US$40 billion had been spent on the Games, making it the most expensive Olympic Games ever.

The operating expenses for the Games included 5.1 billion yuan on broad-casting, accommodation, transport and medical services; while another 1.3 billion yuan was spent on the opening and closing ceremonies, torch relay and other promotional activities. Another 1.4 billion yuan was spent on manpower expenses. On the other hand, the operating revenue came mainly from broadcasting rights and marketing programmes and according to the National Audit Office of China, ticket sales brought in 1.3 billion yuan and assets sales 240 million yuan.

A key social benefit of hosting such an international event in Beijing is that China viewed the 2008 Olympics as a showcase for its modern economy and a springboard for future economic growth. To the Chinese government, hosting the Olympics signified a turning point in its economic development and provided an opportunity to make the shift from a manufacturing based economy to one that is geared to providing goods and services for China's growing middle class and international visitors.

In addition, the Olympics sped up both the economic and infrastructural development in Beijing. Since winning the bid to host the 2008 Olympic Games, Beijing experienced an annual growth rate of 12.1 per cent according to statistics available between 2002 and 2007. This represents an increase of about 1.8 per cent from the previous period and, according to studies conducted by the Beijing Olympic Economy Research Association (BOERA), 1 per cent of the additional growth rate was directly related to the Olympics. Similar comparative statistics also show that Beijing's GDP per capita had doubled from US$3,262 in 2001 to

US$7,654 in 2007[1]. Without a doubt, a portion of the increase in the GDP per capital was a direct result of the investment for the preparation of the Olympic Games.

Many Chinese enterprises also benefited from the increased exposure of China. For example, Li Ning Company and China Hong Xing Sports are two sporting enterprises that took advantage of the Games to publish and promote the culture of the Games as well as their own brand name. These brands gained significant market share around the world through their participation during and sponsorship of the Games.

While it is recognized that the economy benefited greatly from the capital investment and financially the event broke even, what was left unmentioned in official reports were the indirect costs of the event which had to be accounted for in a CBA. Among the indirect economic costs was the social cost to the hosting city. It was reported that in preparation for the Beijing Olympic Games, some 1.5 million residents of Beijing had been displaced by the time of the 2008 Olympics and many of them were evicted against their will. According to reports from human rights groups, residents were often relocated to places far from their communities and workplaces and they were saddled with using inadequate transportation networks that added to their cost of living significantly. However, the authorities denied such claims and reported that only 6,037 people had been displaced since 2002 for the construction of Olympic stadiums and added that the citizens were properly compensated and no one was forced to move out of Beijing[2].

Many of the opportunity costs were also ignored. For example, it was reported in *The Economist* that some of the Beijing markets were less bustling than usual because Russian traders could not come to the usual trading markets to make bulk purchases for winter clothing and other cheap goods due to the tighter visa requirements introduced by China in the build-up to the games. The cost of transporting such goods also increased as police checkpoints ring-fenced the city and restricted lorry traffic from entering Beijing.

Manufacturers also suffered as they were instructed to shut down during the games to reduce air pollution in the city. The authorities also closed all construction sites in Beijing as well as dozens of factories and quarries in and around the city for two months. Others were ordered to cut production and workers were diverted to work in non-productive work or sent home with basic pay. Some factories chose to shut down voluntarily because of the transport problems caused by the Games.

Therefore, if these indirect economic costs had also been accounted for, the CBA of the Games might not look as rosy as one initially envisaged it to be.

Inaugural Youth Olympics in Singapore 2010

The first ever Youth Olympic Games (YOG) was held from 14–26 August 2010 in Singapore. A total of 3,531 athletes aged 14–18 years from 204 countries gathered in Singapore to compete in 201 sporting events in 26 sports. It was a significant event as it was the first ever major sports and cultural festival celebrated in the tradition of the Olympic Games for youths 14–18 years of age, with the aim of promoting sportsmanship among them. Singapore won the right to host the event on 21 February 2008, defeating Moscow as a contender for this inaugural Games.

Singapore's YOG differed from China's Olympic Games as Singapore did not embark on extensive and expensive construction to get the event going. It used much of its existing infrastructure, such as the Singapore indoor stadium, Bishan Stadium, to host these sporting events. There were also plans to ride on existing development projects (such as using the new University campus as the Olympic Village) to save cost. However, the plan fell through when construction was delayed and alternative sites had to be found. Altogether, the only new venue that was built was the Singapore Turf Club Riding Centre while other sporting venues were temporary ones that were removed immediately after the Games.

Singapore made quite substantial savings from not building and constructing new infrastructures, but it also implies Singapore did not enjoy much of the economic growth benefits that Beijing experienced. Instead, the observation was that Singapore had sustained substantial economic costs, for example, a large operating expense in logistics and manpower was incurred. There was some cost incurred in upgrading the sport venues too. Singapore also had to purchase costly world-class timing and information systems so that the sports venues could achieve international standards for the hosting of the sporting events. Putting these costs together, according to the Singapore government, the total cost of the event was S$387 million, about three times the original budgeted sum that Singapore submitted during the bid. Among these, S$173 million was spent on technology and upgrading of sports venues alone. As most of the items had to be imported from overseas suppliers, this meant that a large part of the investment flowed out of Singapore and did not benefit Singapore society. Nonetheless, according to the Government, local companies received about S$260 million worth of contracts from the Games.

The YOG also caused much inconvenience to those who did not directly participate in the Games. Local traffic was affected as some roads were closed off and traffic was diverted away causing loss of time and productivity for those working near the sporting venues. Additional traffic was generated as the athletes had to be ferried from the Olympic village at Nanyang Technological University (NTU) at the western end of Singapore to the various sporting venues located around the island. Students who studied in NTU also saw their university schedule affected due to the YOG as the university had to shift its timetable to start a month later than usual and residential students had very little time to settle down in their hostel before term began.

Nonetheless, some groups of people benefited from the YOG. The additional tourists brought in additional tourist expenditure and merchants saw additional revenue during this period. The official statistics in the increase in tourism receipts due to the YOG was reported to be S$57 million. This was not significant as most of the athletes were youths with little spending power. Further financial gains came from the sale of merchandise and tickets from the YOG that amounted to S$7 million and S$60 million worth of sponsored products and services and S$7.6 million in cash sponsorship. However, since the last two items were mere transfers, they could not be counted as part of the benefits to the project.

The Ministry for Community Development, Youth and Sports, which was primarily responsible for the Games, argued that the most important benefit was the gain in mind share at the international arena. Singapore was in the limelight for hosting such an international event, highlighting that even as a small nation, Singapore could pull off such a feat. Furthermore, being the inaugural city hosting the YOG, all subsequent Olympic flags will have a logo of 'Singapore 2010' and the world will continue to remember Singapore as the host nation. Other benefits, according to the Government, also include the lasting impact on Singapore society as the YOG laid down a strong foundation for Singapore's sporting culture, especially in spectatorship, community involvement and volunteer engagement. These are intangible benefits for Singapore which could not be measured in monetary or financial terms.

Discussion questions

1   Should governments spend vast amounts of money on building sporting venues that would only have occasional uses? How is the construction of such infrastructures justified?
2   Why do nations compete to host international events despite the inconvenience and high social costs? Are there intangible benefits that have not been considered?
3   When a country imports goods and services from another country, capital investment flows out and reduces the benefit to the economy. Will these payments affect the CBA if the goods and services are produced locally?

Table 13.1 Summary of cost and benefit items for the Beijing Olympics, 2008

Private costs	Social costs	Private benefits	Social benefits
Costs that economic agents alone face when producing or consuming economic resources.	*Incidental costs created by production or consumption of goods and services. These are faced by third parties.*	*Benefits (monetary and non-monetary) accrued to economic agents alone when they produce or consume products.*	*Incidental benefits created by production or consumption of goods and services. These are faced by third parties.*
17.4 billion yuan invested to build various sports halls, stadiums, an Olympic Village and an Olympic Convention Centre in the northern part of Beijing. Operating expenses totalling up to 7.8 billion yuan spent on broadcasting, accommodation, transport and medical services, opening and closing ceremonies, torch relays and other promotional activities, and wages. It was reported that total expenses were 19.3 billion yuan.	Some 1.5 million Beijing residents were displaced by the 2008 Olympics, many evicted against their will. Residents relocated far from their communities and workplaces, with inadequate transportation networks adding significantly to living costs. Beijing residents experience more noise pollution and congestion of human and vehicular traffic. Opportunity costs arose from loss of trade sales due to tighter visa requirement causing some traders to be denied entry and shut down many manufacturing plants during the Games to reduce air pollution. In general, industries experienced higher cost of production, especially in transportation.	Revenues from broadcasting rights and marketing programmes and from ticket sales and sale of assets. Ticket sales were reported as 1.3 billion yuan and about 0.2 billion yuan of assets were sold. Influx of tourists to Beijing for the games resulted in higher tourist receipts from retail and hotel expenses.	Infrastructural improvement to Beijing, including addition of new Terminal 3, the world's largest airport terminal; doubling of the subway capacity and a direct line from the city centre to the airport. Beijing economy grew at an annual growth rate of 12.1% between 2002 and 2007 – this is 1.8% higher than previous years. GDP per capita also doubled during this period. Chinese enterprises took advantage of the Games to promote their own brand names, gaining significant market share after the Games.

Table 13.2 Summary of cost and benefit items in inaugural Youth Olympics in Singapore 2010

Private costs	Social costs	Private benefits	Social benefits
Costs that economic agents alone face when producing or consuming economic resources.	*Incidental costs created by production or consumption of goods and services. These are faced by third parties.*	*Benefits (monetary and non-monetary) accrued to economic agents alone when they produce or consume products.*	*Incidental benefits created by production or consumption of goods and services. These are faced by third parties.*
Singapore had to build new and temporary sporting venues, e.g. the Singapore Turf Club Riding Centre. Singapore had to purchase very costly timing and information systems so that the sports venues were suitable for international events. Other expenses such as logistics, manpower and upgrading of the sports venues. Total cost of the event was S$387 million.	Inconvenience costs to those who did not participate in the Games directly, from loss of time and productivity for those working near the sporting venues. Traffic congestion and pollution created from the transport of athletes from the Olympic village at NTU to the various sporting venues. Students of NTU had to start a month later than usual and residential students had very little time to settle down before term began.	Increase in tourism receipts due to the YOG was $57 million. $7 million from the sale of merchandise, tickets and broadcasting rights.	Local companies benefited from the additional contracts for services. Altogether S$260 million (70%) worth of contracts from the Games were awarded to local companies. There is gain in mind share in the international arena for Singapore, as Singapore earned a reputation of being able to host international events, giving rise to future opportunities. The YOG laid down a strong foundation for Singapore's sporting culture, especially in spectatorship, community involvement and volunteer engagement.

14 Human capital investment programmes in Singapore

Introduction

To some nations with a huge resource base, human capital is just one of the resources available for the nation to employ for economic development. However, for a small nation like Singapore, which has no natural resources, she has to depend on her population to work hard and achieve high productivity to sustain economic growth. Therefore investing in human capital development, in terms of education and skills training and upgrading, is vital for the Singapore government. The debate hence turns to how the government implements programmes to keep Singapore competitive in the world economy so that the economy can continue to grow and the living standards of workers can improve.

Education and the Workfare programme

Singapore depends heavily on its workforce to be productive. Economic theory states that a wage is a reflection of the marginal product revenue of the worker and so having high productivity is the key to having sustainable wage growth. To achieve this result, Singapore spends around five per cent every year on education itself. The education budget grew from S$6.1 billion in 2005 to S$8.7 billion in 2009 and in 2010 that amount was around S$10 billion. This represents a 40 per cent growth in expenses. The budget is mainly used to provide education for the young at various levels – primary, secondary, post-secondary and tertiary. However, as more people enter the tertiary education system, a large part of the expense now goes to the tertiary education sector and this will continue to expand as Singapore increases the number of tertiary education institutes.

Singapore already has three national universities, the National University of Singapore, Nanyang Technology University and Singapore Management University. Two of the universities are comprehensive universities, teaching subjects ranging from arts and humanities to engineering and science. A fourth, Singapore University of Technology and Design (SUTD), will be enrolling students from 2011 onwards. This university is a tie-up with the Massachusetts Institute of Technology and Zhejiang University and will marry engineering, architecture and design training in both curriculum and research. A multi-campus fifth university is also planned to be opened by 2014 with the purpose of upgrading polytechnic diploma holders' qualification to a degree and thereby improving the human capital further.

Singapore can also boast that she has five polytechnics providing post-secondary diploma education for those who want to enter the workforce earlier. A wide range of courses in various fields is offered, including engineering, business studies, accountancy, tourism and hospitality management, mass communications, digital media and biotechnology. Specialized courses such as marine engineering, nautical studies, nursing and optometry are also offered to students leaving secondary school or working adults who wish to gain a diploma qualification.

For those who are working, the government has emphasized training, upgrading and continued employment for the workforce and has implemented the Workfare programme. By providing the right incentives for employees to seek individual training, the aim of the programme is to preserve the work ethic and encourage personal responsibilities.

The Workfare programme has two aspects. First, the Workfare Training Support (WTS) Scheme encourages employees to upgrade their skills through training so that they can improve their employment opportunities, allowing them to upgrade to better jobs and earn better incomes. Meanwhile, the framework provides incentives for employers to allow their workers to seek better skill sets and improve productivity as the government provides training grants for certain approved courses and absentee payroll funding for employees who desire to improve themselves.

Second, the Workfare Income Supplement (WIS) encourages older low-wage workers to work by supplementing their income and retirement savings. As long as they continue to work, they will be able to enjoy the WIS top up on their monthly income and their retirement account. Such a scheme aims to create employment for the older and lower-wage workers and encourage them to continue to work and not look for welfare income from the government.

Together, the Workfare programme is a key pillar of Singapore's social security landscape to provide support for low-wage workers so they have the best chance to progress and achieve higher living standards.

Results

The problem with education and training is that, when left to individuals to pursue, these beneficial activities are under-consumed. Individuals benefit through an improvement in their lifetime income but, in the short-term, high expenses and opportunity costs prevent them from consuming more than what is socially desirable. This is the definition of a merit good. What the government can do in such a case is to intervene by providing some form of subsidy to encourage individuals to consume more education and training. The cost will be internalized by society, through the government, but the benefit is widespread as the economy grows with a highly educated and productive workforce.

It was reported in 2010 that Singapore's intensified efforts in improving the skills of workers despite the global recession had paid good dividends. INSEAD, an international business school, reported in a study that Singapore was the most 'skills-competitive' in the Asia-Pacific region, ranking first as an economy that is most competitive based on the skill level of the workforce (reported in *Straits Times*, 13 November 2010). Singapore was ranked ahead of regional economies such as Taiwan, Japan, South Korea, China, India and Hong Kong but ranked behind Finland, Denmark, Sweden, Switzerland and the United States.

The survey showed that employers recognized that better skills would attract investments and better jobs for their workers. This is evidence for the government that the strategy will continue to work. Hence Singapore is committed to spend another S$2.5 billion between 2011 and 2015 to invest in human capital so as to boost the annual productivity growth from a dismal 1 per cent to a target of 2–3 per cent over the next decade from 2010. This spending will be on top of the education budget that is spent annually on educating the young.

Leaving economic benefits aside, better education of the population is beneficial to society too. People can thus better appreciate public policies and give support to initiatives. People with higher education also demand a higher quality of living and exhibit socially acceptable behaviours, all of which are benefits that accrue to society.

Conclusion

Therefore, when it comes to human capital investment, the cost of educating and training the workforce may be high, but the benefits of having a productive and competitive workforce and a population earning good income to sustain high living standards are certainly overwhelming from the government's perspective. Therefore, it is in this light that the government continues to make such investments in its people.

Discussion questions

1   Human capital investment has a long lasting impact on individuals and benefits the wider society. Distinguish the two types of benefits.
2   Is there a difference between a government providing the training programme and a private firm providing such services?

Table 14.1 Summary of cost and benefit items of human capital investment programmes in Singapore

Private costs	Social costs	Private benefits	Social benefits
Costs that economic agents alone face when producing or consuming economic resources.	*Incidental costs created by production or consumption of goods and services. These are faced by third parties.*	*Benefits (monetary and non-monetary) accrued to economic agents alone when they produce or consume products.*	*Incidental benefits created by production or consumption of goods and services. These are faced by third parties.*
Government spends up to S$8.7 billion in 2009 and S$10 billion in 2010 to educate the young. A further S$2.5 billion on human capital investment between 2011 and 2015 will be spent annually to boost productivity through various Workfare and training schemes.	Firms and employers have to ensure productivity is unaffected as a greater proportion of the workforce undergoes training and skills upgrade. Overall, trainees incur opportunity cost of time and effort in undergoing training, which can be put to other use.	There is an increase in tax revenue for the government, as firms increase in profitability and individuals' wages increase.	Skills upgrading will boost annual productivity growth to 2–3% over the next decade from 2010. With higher education, society is able to be more productive and lifetime income of individuals increases for workers, leading to greater consumption. Being more learned and cultured, the public is better able to understand and appreciate public policy and exhibits more socially acceptable behaviours.

15 Qinghai–Tibet railway: investment to improve travel time, promote tourism and economic growth

The Qinghai–Tibet Railway began construction in June 2001 and was operational by July 2006 in a period of less than 5 years. It is the world's highest railway, which starts from an altitude of more than 4,000 m above sea level and rises to 5,072 m at the highest point. At a distance of 1,956 km, it effectively links Tibet to the whole of China, and brings with it many economic benefits.

The Qinghai–Tibet Railway travels between Xining city in Qinghai province to Lhasa in Tibet. It is the first railway to connect the Himalayan territory with the rest of China and is the highest and longest plateau railroad in the world. The railway cost 34 billion yuan to build and was completed a year ahead of schedule. Before construction of the railway, Tibet was linked to the rest of China by several highways and air routes, but travelling by road could take an extremely long time and air travel was expensive. Many people were unable to travel to this remote part of the world. With the railway, a cost-effective alternative finally became available and the world, as well as Tibetans, have benefited from it.

Building a railway to Tibet was originally the dream of Dr Sun Yat-sen, the founding father of modern China. However, the dream did not come to fulfilment until the New China was founded in 1949. Construction of the first phase of the Qinghai–Tibet Railway, a section from Qinghai's provincial capital city of Xining to Golmud, started in 1958 and became operational in 1984. However, construction of the more challenging second phase from Golmud to Lhasa did not start until June 2001 because of technical and financial reasons.

The cost savings to travellers resulting from the railway are tremendous. According to the official website (www.chinatibettrain.com), a typical train fare between Beijing and Lhasa costs only 389 yuan (US$49) or 813 yuan (US$102) for a sleeper berth[1], while typical fares for direct air travel can be as high as 2,430 yuan, yielding net savings of 1,000–1,500 yuan per person. Of course, the flight time of six hours is much more preferable to a 48-hour journey by train. Nonetheless, tourists are generally more price sensitive and may have a lower value of travel time, such that the net benefit for train travel is most likely to be positive. Furthermore, they get to enjoy the beautiful sights and scenery along the way, making the long trip worthwhile. The capacity for rail is higher than other forms of transport to Tibet currently available, and thus more visitors are able to visit Tibet using the railway as a cost-effective travel option. In the opening year of 2007 alone, 1.5 million passengers benefited from this form of travel (Xinhua News Agency, December 2007)[2]. According to reports, by its third anniversary, the railway had delivered 8.3 million passengers and 62.21 million tons of cargo (Xinhua News Agency, 30 June 2009).

The reduction in the cost of freight has also benefited the economy and given rise to higher profit margins. According to the Xinhua News Agency, the railway transportation cost is 0.12 yuan per tonne-kilometre, much lower than the 0.27 yuan road transportation cost. The transportation of cargo from Xining to Lhasa thus saves 500 yuan per tonne[3].

With the successful opening of the complete Qinghai–Tibet railway, the Chinese government plans to build three more railway lines in Tibet as extensions of the current railway. This would link the Tibetan capital, Lhasa, with Nyingchi to the east and Xigaze to the west, and a third extension will link Xigaze with Yadong, a major trading town on the China–India border. Altogether, the total rail length in Tibet is planned to be more than 2,000 km.

With better linkage to the world, the tourism industry plays an increasingly important role in Tibet's economy. Although Tibet has unique natural, cultural and tourism resources, Tibet did not develop its tourism sector before the development of the railway. In fact, before 1978, there was almost no tourism in Tibet and according to some reports, in 1980, there was only one hotel for overseas tourists and it had fewer than 100 beds. Tourism was practically non-existent.

However, the completion and operation of the Qinghai–Tibet railway changed everything and Tibet's tourism entered a period of rapid development. In 2006, the influx of tourists was more than 2.5 million, including 154,800 from overseas and a total tourist expenditure of about 2.8 billion yuan in the region was estimated. In 2007, according to the Development and Reform Commission of the Tibet Autonomous Regional Government, Tibet reportedly hosted 3 million tourists, bringing in a total of 3.4 billion yuan (as reported by Xinhau News Agency, June 2007). It was expected that the visitor numbers would grow by 30 per cent every year until 2010. By then, Tibet's tourism revenue was forecast to hit US$250 million, as more than 5 million tourists would visit this region annually, representing a huge change from the 1.2 million visitors in 2004.

Tibet's tourism plays a significant role in increasing employment and tax revenues, and raising the living standards of both urban and rural residents. Tourism is a major channel for creating job opportunities and increasing people's incomes as more investments are poured into the development of hotels and the food and beverage industries. This has helped to improve the employment prospects of Tibetans and has resulted in drastic improvements in the living standards of local Tibetans. Many of them were lifted out of abject poverty as their income grew.

Investment into the region in sectors other than tourism also grew with the opening of the railway. According to Tibet's Regional Development and Reform Commission, Tibet received 4 billion yuan of domestic and overseas investment in 2006 alone. The amount was close to the total of the previous five years, which amounted to 5.1 billion yuan between 2001 and 2005.

The railway development was not without its costs. The potential environmental damage caused by the railway construction and increased human activities was a worry to both the government and nature groups. Accordingly, the Central Government invested 38.7 billion yuan to build nature reserves, protect forests and prevent soil erosion. Continual monitoring of the environment did not reveal any signs of extensive damage to the environment during the construction period. According to a panel of officials and experts from the State Environmental Protection Agency and the Ministry of Railway from Tibet and Qinghai Province, a field investigation along the route found no evidence of damage to the local environment. The landscape, lakes and the frozen earth are well preserved and wildlife migration patterns have not changed. It was also reported that a poll on the environmental protection was carried out and 96.9 per cent of the Tibetan residents surveyed said they were satisfied with the environmental protection along the Qinghai–Tibet railway, highlighting the efforts that the government took to preserve and protect the natural environment, Tibet's most precious tourism capital.

Discussion questions

1   Time-saving is one of the key benefits of any transport project. Discuss the various ways to measure the value of time-saving. How do the different types of measurement affect the cost–benefit analysis (CBA) of a transport project?
2   How should policy-makers treat economy-wide benefits, such as economic growth and the increased employment of workers, in CBA?

Table 15.1 Summary of cost and benefit items of Qinghai–Tibet Railway: investment to improve travel time, promote tourism and economic growth

Private costs	Social costs	Private benefits	Social benefits
Costs that economic agents alone face when producing or consuming economic resources.	*Incidental costs created by production or consumption of goods and services. These are faced by third parties.*	*Benefits (monetary and non-monetary) accrued to economic agents alone when they produce or consume products.*	*Incidental benefits created by production or consumption of goods and services. These are faced by third parties.*
The railway cost 34 billion yuan to build.	Potential environmental damage due to the railway construction and increased human activities worries both government and nature groups.

Central government is spending 38.7 billion yuan to build nature reserves, protect forests and prevent soil erosion. | Reduction in travel time by highway and travel cost by air. This cost saving is reportedly at least 1,000–1,500 yuan per person for a travel pass, and 2.5 million passengers stand to benefit annually.

Business cost is reduced as cost of transportation of cargo from Xining to Lhasa is reduced by 500 yuan per tonne.

The influx of tourists was more than 2.5 million in 2006, which is expected to grow by 30% every year until 2010. Total tourist expenditure in the region was estimated to be about 2.8 billion yuan in 2006 and 3.4 billion yuan in 2007. | With greater access via the railway, the tourism industry expanded rapidly. The increase in tourism increased employment and tax revenues, and raised the standards of living of both urban and rural residents.

Greater access to external economies brought investment into the region. According to some reports, the Tibet region received 4 billion yuan of domestic and overseas investment in 2006. |

16 Proliferation of nuclear power plants in Asia: examples from Malaysia and Singapore

Introduction

When the price of crude oil spiked at US$147 per barrel in July 2008, many countries began to examine whether there were alternative sources of energy that could be cheaper, more efficient and less polluting than fossil-based fuel. For many years since the oil crisis in the 1970s, many developing nations enjoyed cheap and stable energy prices. This propelled the development of manufacturing industries and helped these economies to stay productive and competitive in international trade. However, over-reliance on fossil-based fuel to power the advancement of their economies made them a hostage to increasing oil prices. In order to overcome this, many nations sought alternative energy sources so that they could be self-sufficient in the production of energy. Nuclear power plants thus become an increasingly attractive option; furthermore, the desire to be environmentally friendly by reducing carbon emissions was an added advantage.

Nuclear power generation in Asia

The mood in Asia towards nuclear power is softening. In the past, a tough stance against nuclear power was adopted due to the fear of nuclear disaster. However, nowadays, many nations are planning to build several nuclear power generators within the next ten years to satisfy their growing demand. Some Asian countries, such as Malaysia, Singapore, China and Vietnam, have already committed to building plans or are commissioning studies on the feasibility of nuclear power plants. For example, according to reports, Malaysia has announced that it aims to get its first nuclear power plant operational by 2021 and a second plant in 2022; Singapore, on the other hand, has few renewable energy options and will be studying and evaluating the available options, including the possibility of a nuclear plant.

Both Malaysia and Singapore traditionally depended on fossil-based fuels (such as oil and natural gas) as their primary energy source. Although Malaysia has some form of renewable energy, such as hydroelectric generators, less than 10 per cent of its energy consumption is from renewable sources. As for Singapore, all its energy is imported and about 76 per cent of Singapore's electricity is generated using piped natural gas (PNG) and this proportion is likely to grow to 80 per cent by 2020.

While Malaysia is currently a net exporter of energy, Singapore imports natural gas from its neighbouring countries, Indonesia and Malaysia. As this resource becomes rare and domestic consumption increases, Malaysia is likely to reduce its export of oil and gas overseas. This could potentially create political tension between the two neighbouring countries. Therefore, as both nations aim to continue in their rapid economic development, the imperative is to diversify their energy sources and find cheaper energy sources.

What is nuclear power generation?

A nuclear reaction (usually nuclear fission) is a chemical process that releases huge amounts of thermal energy and leaves behind a small amount of radioactive residue or spent fuel. Nuclear reactors harness the heat generated by nuclear fission reactions to drive a turbine-powered generator, thus creating electricity.

Nuclear power is extremely efficient because the nuclear material has a very high energy density. It is also extremely clean because it does not produce carbon in the process. According to the International Energy Agency (IEA), a 1-GW nuclear power plant can avoid emissions of some 6–7 million tonnes of CO_2 each year when replacing coal-fired power generators.

Currently, more than 400 nuclear power plants are in operation worldwide, producing about 370 GW of energy. This represents about 16 per cent of the global energy supply. The United States has about 85 per cent of the total capacity with 104 plants. France, with 59 nuclear power plants, is another country with a very high nuclear presence. Japan, Russia, the United Kingdom, Korea and India also have several nuclear plants. As mentioned, Asia is catching up with the demand for nuclear power plants. It was reported in 2010 that more than 60 new reactors were under construction worldwide and two-thirds of them were being built in Asia. This shows the rapid development of nuclear power plants worldwide and in Asia.

Building a nuclear power plant is expensive and capital intensive. A typical nuclear plant can cost US$6–$8 billion to build but it has an economic lifespan of 40–60 years for the newest type of nuclear plants (Gen-3 power plants). On top of the construction cost, it is necessary to account for the decommissioning cost at the end of the nuclear plant's useful life. The on-going operating expenses are quite substantial too as they include the costs to purchase fuel, manage the nuclear waste, purchase insurance and hire expertise to maintain the nuclear plant and manage the associated security and risk.

One particular issue in the operation of a nuclear power plant is the management of spent nuclear fuel. The usual method of disposing of the spent fuel is to bury the nuclear waste in the ground and allow the radioactivity to decay over time until it is no longer a hazard to the environment. The land around the burial site will hence become unusable for any developments due to the potential risk of a radiation leakage. If Singapore exports the nuclear waste and pays the receiving country to accept the spent fuel as a form of compensation for the loss of use of the land, then the associated economic cost will be internalized. A larger nation like Malaysia, which has sufficient land mass, will probably site its nuclear waste dump within its boundaries. The parcel of land will be sterilized for many years to come and it will not be available for use by many generations to come. Hence, the economic cost will be borne by the future generation living on that land. Furthermore, if the amount of compensation to the affected communities is insufficient because of national interests, there will be some spillover social cost.

Despite the large capital and social costs of the project, it is estimated by the IEA that given the project timeframe of 40 years, nuclear is the cheapest form of energy compared to other sources. The IEA study reported that the cost of electricity is US$30–57/MWh at 10–15 per cent discount rate; about 65–70 per cent is the cost of the initial investment and the nuclear fuel is only 10 per cent of the cost of energy. The rest of the cost is in the operation and maintenance of the nuclear plant (OECD and IEA, 2007, p. 4).

Dangers of nuclear power

For countries like Singapore and Malaysia in deciding whether to adopt nuclear energy, the paramount concerns regard the safety and security of their populations, especially the community living around the planned nuclear power plant. This is especially pertinent since the memories of Chernobyl and Three Mile Island remain in the public consciousness even though the incidents took place several decades ago. However, as the Chernobyl nuclear accident in 1986 caused thousands of radiation deaths, while the Three Mile Island incident in 1979 caused a major scare to the people living on Three Mile Island with a partial nuclear core meltdown, these incidents remind the world that nuclear power plants are very dangerous and can potentially be very harmful.

In fact, the risk of a nuclear meltdown weighed heavily on the minds of those living in Asia as events unfolded following the Sendai earthquake in Japan on 11 March 2011. A powerful earthquake measuring 8.9 on the Richter scale caused a tsunami to hit Sendai, destroying the homes of many. While nuclear plants in Japan were generally well equipped to deal with natural disasters, such as earthquakes, the tsunami unfortunately caused the power supply to the Fukushima Dai-ichi nuclear complex to be completely cut off and the whole power plant had to shut down from operations entirely. Without any power supply to circulate water to cool down the reactor cores where the nuclear fuel was stored, several of the reactors became severely overheated. Within hours of the disaster, a hydrogen explosion took place causing severe damage to the power plant building. Several hydrogen explosions followed with some of them so powerful that the containment vessels of the reactor were destroyed, exposing the nuclear fuel rods to the environment. It was recorded that at least four of six of the nuclear reactors showed critical signs of meltdown as a result of the tsunami and overheated reactor cores.

While the Japanese government battled to contain the damage and to restore the power supply to the reactors, the population within 20 km of the power plant were evacuated and those living within 30 km were advised to stay indoors to reduce the risk of over-exposure to the radiation. However, the impact could not be easily mitigated as the food supply was also affected, with high levels of radioactive materials being detected in vegetables and water. Besides the localized impact, the explosions also caused radioactive particles to enter the atmosphere, which were carried by the wind to different parts of the world, and there was fear that the nuclear impact could be widespread and that a nuclear meltdown was imminent.

This incident and the fear of a potential nuclear plant meltdown raised the debate again over whether the risk of a nuclear disaster, which could potentially destroy the lives of thousands, if not millions, is worth more than the benefits. Many countries with nuclear plant development plans, such as China and Germany, reconsidered their energy needs and even suspended their expansion plans.

However, nuclear power plant experts still felt that the risk of such major nuclear incidents is very small. There have been substantial improvements in nuclear power plant design and technology making them very safe to operate. Furthermore, with proper procedures and containment strategies, nuclear meltdown is not a likely outcome. Accidents, however, can still occur caused by human error; for example, the human lapses at the Forsmark nuclear facility in Sweden on 25 July 2006 almost caused a nuclear plant meltdown. Accordingly, this was reported as the most serious incident since Chernobyl. Fortunately, the damage was contained and there was no radiation leakage.

According to the IEA in 2004, since the beginning of commercial nuclear power in 1957, more than a hundred Light Water Reactors (a type of nuclear technology) have been built and operated in the United States and this amounted to a total experience of 2,679 reactor-years up to 2002. During this time, there has only been one reactor core damage accident, which was the Three Mile Island incident. The frequency of core damage to reactors in the United States was therefore one in 2,679 reactor-years on average, implying that nuclear power plants are very safe. Other expert opinions used the probability risk assessment (PRA) methodology and concluded that the best estimate of core damage frequency to be about one in 10,000 reactor-years for nuclear plants in the United States. In short, the risk of a nuclear disaster is still extremely low. Even if the Fukushima nuclear disaster were to be factored in, the fact that the risk can be mitigated and damage successfully contained should assure the public that nuclear power plants are on the whole beneficial to society.

Often, the reasons relating to the dangers of exposure to radiation have also been raised to argue against the development of nuclear plants. International standards require a safety distance of 30 km around a nuclear facility to be established so that the community can be safe from potential radiation exposure and leakage. This buffer zone means that very little development can take place and the whole land mass will be sterilized. In a small country like Singapore, it may not be possible to establish such a safety zone, which thus diminishes the chances of building such facilities. However, experts argue that nuclear facilities can possibly be sited near urban areas safely as long as sufficient mitigation measures are put in place.

Furthermore, and arguably, there is no need to worry about the exposure to radiation as it is already a natural occurrence in everyday environments and nuclear radiation is no different from any other form of radiation. Natural sources, such as radon in rocks, account for most of the radiation we all receive every year. Accordingly, a person receives about 300 millirem of radiation per year from natural sources like the earth, radon, food and water. A person living within 80 km of a nuclear power plant will receive an additional 0.009 millirem of radiation per year on average. Comparatively, an average person receives 0.1 millirem of radiation each year from their computer screen. Therefore, it is possible that the likelihood of an increased risk to a person's health is not substantially higher.

Key benefits – energy cost savings and carbon reduction

The benefit of nuclear power plants amid rising energy use worldwide is that nuclear energy can potentially ensure a constant supply of electricity and cause energy prices to remain stable. The supply of fossil-based fuel will dwindle and the trend for electricity prices is upwards. With high capacity nuclear power, developing nations that depend heavily on energy for economic growth will be able to continue to grow and enjoy substantial savings from their energy consumption. With sufficient capacity, it is even possible for a consumer of energy, such as Singapore, to be a producer of energy for the region.

Furthermore, in a world confronting climate change, nuclear is a carbon-free alternative to fossil fuels. When computing the benefits of nuclear energy, it is vital to include the reduction in carbon emissions through some form of carbon tax or carbon pricing. According to the same report by the IEA, if carbon is taxed at US$100 per tonne, the electricity price will increase by at least 5 cents per unit, and this will make nuclear energy the cheapest form of energy available, even after taking into account the initial capital outlay.

NIMBY (not in my backyard)

Due to the high risk associated with nuclear power plants, even with a positive CBA, governments often have difficulties in siting them. While it is possible for the population to accept the proposal as beneficial for the nation because of the positive net economic benefits, when deciding on the location for the development, residents of the proposed site will typically be opposed to the facility being sited near them. It is felt that the burden of the high risk and economic cost is unevenly distributed, mostly borne by the community that hosts the facilities while there is only marginal benefit to them because the benefits accrue to the whole population. Such a phenomenon is called not-in-my-backyard (NIMBY) syndrome, which is particularly difficult to deal with when the country depends on such facilities for its economic development. Typically, governments can compensate the community to encourage them to accept the proposal but such a move may be seen as a bribe and thus 'crowd-out' public-spiritedness, reducing their support instead. Other ways to increase the support rate is to promise more efforts in mitigating the risk and reducing the associated social costs of the proposed project. Otherwise, it is vital to transfer more economic benefits to residents by using the proceeds to provide more public goods and services or building more communal facilities, such as parks, to improve the living environment.

Conclusion

As the world becomes more carbon conscious and energy prices from fossil-based fuel increase, the nuclear option becomes more viable. Despite the high capital cost and potential dangers associated with nuclear power generators, countries will continue to explore this option for their developing economies. Continual improvement in technology and reactor design will increase the efficiency of nuclear power generation and ensure better safety for the communities living near the power plants. When the cost–benefit analysis makes economic sense, then society will stand to benefit from having a nuclear power plant despite the potential social costs and risks.

Discussion questions

1   How do policy-makers internalize the external social cost of nuclear power plants, such as the disposal of nuclear waste? Is it possible to completely internalize the external social costs?
2   Policy-makers have to mitigate the associated risks of nuclear power plants. How do policy-makers account for risk in a project?

Table 16.1 Summary of cost and benefit items in the proliferation of nuclear power plants in Asia with examples from Malaysia and Singapore

Private costs	Social costs	Private benefits	Social benefits
Costs that economic agents alone face when producing or consuming economic resources.	Incidental costs created by production or consumption of goods and services. These are faced by third parties.	Benefits (monetary and non-monetary) accrued to economic agents alone when they produce or consume products.	Incidental benefits created by production or consumption of goods and services. These are faced by third parties.
Capital investment in the building of nuclear power plants, including land acquisition cost.	Risk of nuclear disasters causing radiation deaths will increase for the community living near the nuclear plant.	Revenue generated from the sale of electricity.	Less dependent on fossil-based fuels, resulting in energy security.
Examples of recurring cost items include operating and maintenance costs and insurance.	Up to 30 km of buffer zone may be required, creating high opportunity cost due to the loss of use of the land around the plant.	Nuclear energy will be the cheapest form of energy in the future as fossil-based fuel depletes so there are savings associated with stable electricity prices.	Sustainable supply of electricity leads to stable prices for the community.
Management of spent nuclear fuel – if they are exported to another place, the cost is internalized as an export cost.	If the spent fuel is buried within or near the community, future generations may have to bear the potential economic cost (such as loss of land use and health risks) and this can be regarded as social cost.	If there are carbon taxes, there can be savings associated with the reduction in carbon emissions.	Instead of importing fuel, if the capacity of the nuclear plant exceeds local consumption, the excess energy can be exported to the region.
One-time cost of decommissioning plant at end of its useful life.			If there is no carbon tax to internalize the emission cost, then the reduction in carbon emissions is a social benefit.
Higher risk of exposure to radiation, increasing the incidence of cancer for the people working in the nuclear plant.			

17 Preservation of the Amazon rainforest

The Amazon Basin is home to the largest natural rainforest in the world and its survival is under threat if the current trend of deforestation continues. According to the United Nations Food and Agriculture Organization (FAO) which compiles data on forests, although there are 4 billion hectares (10 billion acres) of forest covering the earth (that is, about 31 per cent of the Earth's land surface is forested land), only one-third of the forested area remains as primary or virgin forest (FAO, 2010, pp. 3 and 5). Brazil has the highest rate of deforestation in the world, at an average rate of 3 million hectares per year. With the world's forests disappearing at an average deforestation rate of about 8 to 10 million hectares per year, the whole earth could be completely without any forests in 10 to 20 generations time.

According to the FAO's statistics, over 60 per cent of the rainforest has disappeared in the past 60 years and two-thirds of the remaining rainforests are scattered and fragmented, making them very likely to be cleared for development. The pressures of growing populations with increasing demand for food and usage of natural resources have caused the rapid deforestation in many parts of the world. Illegal practices of excessive logging for timber, indiscriminate mining for natural resources and uncontrolled clearing of forests using slash-and-burn methods to create land for agriculture only worsen the situation.

There is a clear danger that these 'lungs of the earth' will disappear unless something is done to preserve the forest. The crux of the problem is that there is no proper way to value the use of these forests. Clearly, these forests have economic values that will enrich present generation users and there are many other benefits that do not have direct, measureable economic value. Furthermore, even for those benefits that can be quantified and measured, often they are generally long-term ones that benefit future generations and the discounted value to present value could be low. Therefore, it is vital to establish the value of a forest and recognize the full benefits of forest preservation programmes, so that natural forests, such as the one in the Amazon Basin, can survive for generations to come.

Point of reference in cost–benefit analysis

Whenever a cost–benefit analysis is being done, it is important to adopt a consistent point of reference so that the costs and benefits can be accounted for properly.

In the case of a programme to preserve the rainforests, it is easy to see that all the costs of preserving the forested land fall on the society which owns that land. However, not all the benefits can be accounted for by the community as some of the benefits flow out from the local community. For example, it is a well-known fact that trees absorb atmospheric carbon dioxide and convert it into oxygen via the photosynthesis process. Since all living things on earth depend on oxygen to live, this exchange of gases is extremely vital. Furthermore, through this process, the forest acts as a carbon sink, sequestrating (that is capturing and storing) the carbon dioxide and reducing its build-up in the atmosphere. Heat can escape from the earth's atmosphere, as it is no longer trapped by the greenhouse gas. Forests thus play a vital role in preventing global warming and climate change. However, Brazil will not benefit fully from the fresh oxygen produced from the Amazon forests it preserves and the cooler atmospheric temperature resulting from the carbon sink, as the constant movement of the air transfers some, if not all, of the benefits to its neighbouring countries. Adopting a consistent reference point means that policy-makers should only recognize the amount of benefits that affect Brazilian society and not the rest of the world.

To some extent, the problem of externalities, as described above, forces policy-makers to account only for the direct benefits for the community, in accordance with sound cost–benefit analysis. On the other hand, it results in underestimation of the total benefit of the programme. Local policy-makers may have to reduce the scope of the programme or even shelve such programmes because the cost–benefit analysis (CBA) is not viable from the local community's perspective. In the end, the community at large does not benefit from such decisions.

There is also the free-rider problem where some countries enjoy the results of another's efforts in reducing carbon emissions and preserving the forest without any expenditure. Without participation of all countries, the impact of Brazil's lone efforts to help fight climate change will be minimal. This reinforces the disincentives to spend money and sacrifice economic growth and development to preserve the forests. Therefore, for such programmes to work and be effective, a co-operative framework between nations is needed.

Valuation methodology

The concept of Total Economic Value (TEV) is relevant when considering the valuation of the benefits of a standing forest. The TEV captures the full economic value that people attach to each type of land use and requires policy-makers to put a monetary value on non-market goods so that they can make proper economic decisions based on rational economic principles. Many of the techniques used to quantify the value of non-market goods have been discussed in earlier chapters and are applicable here. The following sections will discuss each type of benefits (and costs) in detail but, in summary, the TEV of the forest is simply the sum of the direct value, indirect use value, option–bequest value and existence value.

Direct use value

For an existing or standing forest, the '*direct use value*' would be to value the product directly obtained from the forest, for example, the harvesting of timber and non-timber products such as nuts, fruits and latex from the forest. We can also consider the tourism value and the value derived from other genetic material. The creation of jobs associated with the agriculture and timber industries should also be counted towards the direct benefits.

In measuring the direct values, the policy-maker must work out the values by examining the current or potential use of the land, the characteristics of the forests such as the land and soil conditions, flora, fauna, access and facilities available. In the Amazon Basin, approximately 14 per cent of the Amazon rainforest has been converted to agricultural land with the remainder being left as forested area. Of the converted area, 63 per cent is used for pasturing, 7 per cent for annual crops, 2 per cent for perennial crops and planted forest and the rest, 28 per cent, is fallow land. Based on the yield of the land and the value of the outputs, we can estimate the direct use value of the land if the rest of the forested land is converted to agricultural use. According to reports, the agricultural land value was estimated to be US$41 per hectare in 1985 prices[1] (Anderson, 1997, p. 4).

Besides agricultural output, it is possible to have alternative benefits from converting the forested land to urban use. Urban benefits include the value-added to the service sector, to agro-processing industries, to timber-processing industries and to mining industries. This benefit can be calculated by estimating the amount of land cleared for urban production multiplied by the productivity of such industry.

Another direct use benefit of the forests is the production of timber products and non-timber products, such as the extraction of plant nutrients as in rubber latex, palm oil and Brazil nuts, and converting them into commercial products. Policy-makers will need to survey the land to determine the availability of such plants and trees in the area and the value of these commercial products.

Tourism value is known to be generally derived from recreational benefits. This is measured using the travel cost method that depends on the forests' accessibility. Since the Amazon forest is mostly virgin forest, it remains very inaccessible and this method is likely to yield a very small value. Alternatively, we can use the willingness-to-pay approach to establish the economic benefits of recreation. Multiply this by the number of expected tourists making such eco-tours, and we can expect the value of the benefit to be rather substantial.

However, it should be noted that over-consumption of tourism can bring harm to the environment if the intensity is greater than the carrying capacity of the ecosystem. The tourism figures used must be at a sustainable rate otherwise unreasonable estimation will lead to an overestimation of the net benefit. The fortunate thing is that tourism in the Amazon region has been extremely modest. According to statistics (SUDAM, 1992, p. 37), about half a million tourists visit the Brazilian Amazon annually, implying that there could be a huge growth in the tourism value without significant harm to the ecosystem, thus reaping the greatest net benefit for Brazil.

It ought to be clear that there are some conflicts between the different direct uses of forests – if the standing forests are cleared for development, be it for agricultural or urban use, or for production of timber products – the economic values for tourism and non-timber output will be very much reduced. Therefore, from the perspective of preserving the forest, the former category of benefits will be considered as a cost to the local community while the avoided costs associated with the transportation and conversion of the raw materials into finished commercial products will thus be counted as benefits. The associated operating costs of tourism and harvesting of non-timber products will be counted as costs.

Indirect use value

The indirect use value refers to the ecological functions performed by the forest, which include soil and watershed protection, fire prevention, water recycling and carbon storage within the forest. As many living creatures, including humans, depend on the forest for their source of food and the ecosystem cannot exist without the natural forests, this importance cannot be undermined.

The value of the ecological services of a forest is often underestimated. They include water recycling, fire prevention, erosion control and watershed protection. The reason for underestimation is a lack of quantitative studies to provide estimates of the value of these services. For example, it is difficult to quantify the exact impact on the water cycle of the removal of a forest. It could prolong a dry season or increase the severity of the dry season, and eventually there could be an impact on the yield of the agricultural products. As for the fire control service performed by an intact forest, the value is also difficult to determine even though it is known that fire damage could be catastrophic during droughts aggravated by deforestation. Deforestation can also cause an increase in siltation and sedimentation, which may create serious problems for fisheries and affect the capacity of dams and reservoirs downstream. However, to quantify the impact will be hard. Therefore, while these benefits of a forest preservation programme are recognized, it is not easy to determine a value for them.

Perhaps the most assessable and quantifiable indirect value of a standing forest is the role of carbon sink. As described earlier, trees naturally capture and store the carbon from the atmosphere within them. However, when the forests are converted to cropland or pasture, the carbon is released back into the atmosphere. It is estimated that converting one hectare of rainforest will release 100–200 tonnes of carbon (Brown and Pearce, 1994, p.5) and this will worsen the climate change and global warming situation. We can determine the value of this benefit by measuring the direct impact of a higher concentration of carbon, such as the destruction of agriculture, rising sea levels, reduction in water resources and increased intensity of natural disasters. Alternatively, we can use some implied values by examining how much society is willing to pay to abate the carbon emission, that is, carbon taxing or pricing. In the light of the awareness of carbon pricing, the latter method is preferred and will yield a significant value.

Option–bequest value

The option–bequest value represents the price that the community involved is willing to pay to preserve the forest and protect its biodiversity and its ecological services which may become available for the future in the event that something useful is found (e.g. medicinally) or for future generations to enjoy. These quasi-option values may come into play.

A much undervalued benefit is probably in the area of biodiversity. Biodiversity has both aesthetic and scientific benefits. The aesthetic benefit can be expressed in the marketplace in the form of eco-tourism, which was discussed earlier. The scientific benefit of biodiversity arises from the use of genetic material for medical purposes or for genetic engineering. It was reported that between 1999 and 2009, more than 1,200 new species of plants and animals were discovered in the Amazon Basin, almost one every three days[2]. The Amazon forest still hides mysteries that are yet to be discovered and the preservation of these forests will allow for more such discoveries.

The scientific value of biodiversity contains both a direct use value component and an option value component. The direct use value includes the use of plant and animal species in the production of medicine. About 2,000 plant and animal species from the Amazon Basin can be found in modern medicines. In other countries, such as China, there is a greater dependence on plant and animal species for traditional and modern medicine and about 5,000 species are found to have medicinal properties.

According to some reports, in the United States about 40 plant species accounted for plant-based prescription sales, amounting to US$10–15 billion per year (Pearce, 1993, p. 87). This is about 20 per cent of the estimated prescription value of the whole of the United States. It is a very small direct use value since it ignores the value of the lives that can potentially be saved. Hence, if we include such values, the economic benefit will be greater.

Measuring the option value of the scientific value is less straightforward. Accordingly, the deforestation of the Amazon forest will lead to the extinction of many plant species, making them unavailable for medical research. With less than 1 per cent of all the tropical plant species having been screened for potentially useful medical properties, the option value is significant. It is possible to quantify this with a willingness-to-pay survey.

Existence value

Finally, the existence value arises from people's willingness-to-pay for the existence of environmental assets without having direct use of the assets. It may also include the value that the community is willing to pay to secure the survival and well-being of other species.

People can reveal a willingness-to-pay for the mere existence of environmental assets by contributing to wildlife and other environmental charities without any direct use of forests or wildlife or through recreation. Existence value is likely to be an important component of the total economic value if the environmental asset is unique and/or many people recognize the features or attributes of the assets to be valued. The Amazon rainforest is certainly unique and the amount of biodiversity is astonishing. Many people know that there is an abundance of plant and animal species in the intricate and delicate ecosystems within the Amazon Basin. Therefore, the Amazon rainforest may have quite a high existence value overall.

Discussion questions

1   How do we strike a balance between urban development and economic growth for the current generation and the preservation of natural assets for future generations?
2   Option values for biodiversity have a use value, such as medical discovery, and a non-use value (also called passive value), such as preservation for future generations. Suggest some ways that policy-makers could measure some of these values properly.

Table 17.1 Summary of cost and benefit items in the preservation of the Amazon rainforest

Private costs	Social costs	Private benefits	Social benefits
Costs that economic agents alone face when producing or consuming economic resources.	*Incidental costs created by production or consumption of goods and services. These are faced by third parties.*	*Benefits (monetary and non-monetary) accrued to economic agents alone when they produce or consume products.*	*Incidental benefits created by production or consumption of goods and services. These are faced by third parties.*
Direct use – the value of the product directly obtained from the forest, such as the harvesting of timber and non-timber products (e.g. nuts, fruits, latex) from the forest (net of the production cost). These activities will lead to destruction of the forests.	None	Direct use – there are net economic benefits of tourism if the tourism rate of arrival does not exceed the capacity or cause substantial harm to the environment.	Indirect use – water recycling and carbon storage benefit society other than the community that preserves the forested area.
Direct cost of preserving the forests include policing and enforcement costs in preventing illegal logging and illegal dumping.		Indirect use – ecological functions such as soil and watershed protection, and fire prevention.	The option – bequest value of protecting the biodiversity and its ecological services for future generations. This includes the discovery of plant species with medicinal properties that could potentially save lives.
Preservation of forested areas reduces the availability of agricultural land, which may lead to higher prices of agricultural products.		Existence benefit – the existence of the environmental assets themselves may be a benefit for the community even though they may not have direct use of these assets.	

18 Wastewater management project in Sri Lanka

Sri Lanka is an island country located in the Indian Ocean, south of India. It has a population of 19.4 million in 2006, of which 80 per cent live in rural areas and the rest (about 4 million people) live in the urban areas. Sri Lanka's capital city is Colombo, which is part of the Colombo Metropolitan Area (or Greater Colombo) and its estimated population is 2.2 million. Being a capital city, it is well served by good transportation, medical facilities, communications and other community facilities.

The urban population in the Colombo area has increased rapidly with an annual growth rate of 1.35 per cent between 1981 and 2001. Colombo enjoyed a much faster growth rate, compared with the rest of Sri Lanka, which grew only at an average rate of 1.14 per cent each year. The increase in urban population has created immense pressures on the city in terms of the infrastructural services and supply of utilities. One case in point is the sewerage system, which was built many years ago. Deterioration and overuse have caused disruption to the wastewater management system. With the pressures of an increasing population that is projected to grow by 1 million by 2030, it is an urgent task for the Greater Colombo authorities to improve on the wastewater management infrastructure.

The aged sewage system brings with it many problems, among which is a very low geographic coverage. Currently, the sewerage network only serves approximately 25 per cent of the population of the urban area; this means that three-quarters of the population have never enjoyed modern sanitation facilities. Furthermore, many of the old pump stations are in poor condition and can no longer function effectively. The waste effluent is not properly discharged because of damaged sea outfalls, and there is a lack of filtering and treatment of effluent before discharge into the sea, leading to serious damage to the environment and to human lives. Therefore, major investment and overhaul of the sewage system will rectify most of these problems and bring about significant benefits.

The cost of the project consisting mainly of the capital investment is estimated to be US$134 million. Beside the operating and maintenance costs for the project's entire life cycle, other costs such as the impact of noise and air pollution and the disruption to traffic and economic activities should be included into the cost analysis. However, it is not expected to be a large amount since the impact is primarily on the rural population.

The direct benefits of the sewerage project are mostly derived from the improvement in the sanitation services and in general health. The value of improving the wastewater services can be determined by how much people are willing to pay for such services. According to a report, which used surveys and contingent valuation methods, the population sampled in the affected region are willing to pay 70 SLRs per month for such improvement to the sanitation services (quoted by Asian Development Bank, 2007). For those who do not currently have access to the existing system, they are willing to pay more in terms of connection fees to the main sewage system and ongoing fees for sanitation services. This was found to be 3,225–4,941 SLRs (for connection) and 209–366 SLRs per month for sewerage.

Health benefits, in general, are one of the largest components of the economic benefits. The reduction in morbidity rates for the affected population can be substantial, especially for areas that have not previously had access to the sewage system. The sewage project is aimed at reducing the incidence of diseases relating to diarrhoea to 622.5 cases per 100,000 persons, which was the level of incident rate in 2003. By measuring the reduction in the lives lost and hospitalization rates due to illness associated with water-borne diseases, multiplied by people's willingness-to-pay to reduce such illnesses, we should be able to obtain the total economic health benefit. However, limited data on the rates of diarrhoea incidents and morbidity and the fact that those who stand to benefit from this project are generally low-income households (that is, they have limited ability to pay) mean that the estimated value of health benefits is found to be rather low.

There are also cost savings in the operations and maintenance when changing over from the current sewage system to a new one. The reduction in the operating and maintenance costs requires the assessment of both the operating and maintenance costs of the existing facilities and the planned facilities. As the current system is very run down, the cost savings can be substantial.

Finally, the impact on property prices is found to be most significant in areas that do not have access to the sewage system. It is possible to estimate the increase in property value by asking professional surveyors and valuers about the change in property prices. However, it should be noted that there is a possibility of double counting of benefits, if the willingness-to-pay for the sewage connection covers the expected increase in property values. In this case, the low incomes of the affected population may limit their willingness-to-pay and thereby circumvent the issue of double counting. Nonetheless, when considering the increase in property value, policy-makers should be careful to count only the incremental benefit.

With the improvements in sewage and sanitation, affected areas are more attractive to investments and development – they offer a healthier workforce with higher labour productivity and a cleaner working environment. Therefore, local and foreign investments will be attracted to these affected areas leading to other economic activities and an improvement in the livelihoods of the population.

Overall, an evaluating report of the project concluded that the internal rate of return (IRR) is 19.6 per cent and the net present value (NPV) is 1,314 million SLRs, exceeding the benchmark by a considerable margin quoted by Asian Development

Bank (2007). Sensitivity testing of key variables suggests that changes in the investment costs and the impact on property prices generated by the project may result in significant changes in the NPV but not enough to affect the decision. Therefore, the sewerage project is a significant investment for the government with overall benefits for the Greater Colombo area. It allows people to improve their lives by raising their living standards and improving their incomes, through greater economic opportunities, thereby increasing the wealth of the people.

Discussion questions

1   Discuss the various ways to measure health benefits of a sanitation project.
2   Examine the sources of double counting in this project and discuss how policy-makers can avoid them.

Table 18.1 Summary of cost and benefit items of the wastewater management project in Sri Lanka

Private costs	*Social costs*	*Private benefits*	*Social benefits*
Costs that economic agents alone face when producing or consuming economic resources.	*Incidental costs created by production or consumption of goods and services. These are faced by third parties.*	*Benefits (monetary and non-monetary) accrued to economic agents alone when they produce or consume products.*	*Incidental benefits created by production or consumption of goods and services. These are faced by third parties.*
Construction cost of the sewage system of up to US$134 million. Lifetime operating and maintenance costs of the sewage system.	Externalities associated with the construction, such as noise, air pollution and disruption of traffic and other economic activities.	Improvement in sanitation. Health benefits – lower rate of contracting water-borne diseases and morbidity. Increase in property value, noting that this could be a double count if there is willingness-to-pay for the sanitation. Improvement in productivity leading to improvement in wages.	Improvement in economic activities as the affected areas become more attractive to local and foreign investments. Livelihoods of the general population improve with better incomes.

19 Nairobi–Thika highway in Kenya

Kenya is a thriving nation in the east of Africa with a land mass of 580,000 square kilometres. It has a population of 40 million of which 3 million live in Nairobi, the capital city. Even though Nairobi is only the second most populous city of Kenya and has a small land mass of around 600 square kilometres, it is regarded as Kenya's key economic powerhouse, responsible for more than 30 per cent of the national GDP. Nairobi is the engine of the nation's economic development and the centre of employment for Kenya.

As the economy develops, the city has to cope with the fast pace of development and the needs of a growing population. Many of its infrastructures were built during the pre-independence era and some are showing signs of inadequacy and deterioration. It is therefore necessary for the Kenyan government to invest further in building more infrastructures to replace some of the old ones and to upgrade the capacities of the existing ones so that the city can continue to thrive and expand.

One area that urgently requires investment is transportation. The urban motor vehicle population has grown rapidly with urbanization of the population and fast economic development. Not only is congestion a daily occurrence, causing delays to traffic movement, the terrible traffic conditions have deteriorated the living standards of the population as they limit people's access to job opportunities, education and recreation. Economic growth of the city has been constrained because goods and services are no longer free-flowing. New highways are needed so that more people and goods can move within the country in a timely, efficient and safe manner and the Nairobi–Thika highway project is designed to fulfil this objective.

Nairobi–Thika highway

The Nairobi–Thika highway is a dual-carriageway road of about 45 km linking the Central Business District (CBD) in Nairobi to the suburbs and satellite towns. It is one of only three major transport corridors, and forms part of the international trunk road that extends to Moyale at the Ethiopian border from downtown Nairobi.

The main project benefit in the economic evaluation is the time saved in the movement of passengers and goods. The Nairobi–Thika highway will improve transport services along this corridor and enhance urban mobility within the Nairobi Metropolitan Area, reducing traffic congestion and improving travel time.

The people living along the route already engaged in various economic activities, especially commuters working in secondary and tertiary sectors in the CBD, will stand to benefit most significantly and it is estimated that more than 200,000 people are affected as they commute to Nairobi daily for employment purposes. Other groups of commuters that will benefit include students, health patients, shoppers and traders as they gain access to the services they require that are only available in the city.

The highway will also improve safety for all road users. Unsafe driving behaviours and unacceptable road conditions have increased the level of accident rates. It is estimated that only about 18 per cent of the classified roads are in excellent or good condition, 49 per cent of the roads are in fair condition and 33 per cent are in poor or very poor condition. Accident data from the past five years also reveals that more than 700 accidents occurred on the road between Nairobi and Thika and about 30 per cent (or 227) were fatal (quoted in Africa Development Fund, 2007). Therefore, with the upgrading of the highway and the separation of service roads for local and non-motorized traffic, accident rates will decrease considerably and many lives will be saved.

Finally, another direct benefit is the saving in vehicle operating costs and road maintenance. As vehicles spend less time on the roads, the wear and tear of vehicle engines and roads will be reduced.

Putting together all the direct benefits, it is estimated over the project's operating life between 2011 and 2030 that the savings in passenger and cargo travel time costs will be KES 57.571 billion and the savings in motorized vehicle operating costs will be KES 27.055 billion. It is possible to value the benefits due to a reduction in the risk of accidents through willingness-to-pay surveys or using the value of statistical life to estimate the benefits; however, in this instance, accident costs savings have not been quantified.

Other social benefits

It is also possible to consider other social benefits such as improvements to the environment. Vehicles spend less time idling in the congestion and the amount of excessive emissions of air pollutants such as carbon dioxides and particulate matters is reduced. Employment may also increase as the road project brings about employment opportunities for the people living along the road corridor. It is estimated that approximately 1,200 people will be directly employed in the project and others can gain indirect employment by providing food and other supplies. Furthermore, the road will also attract the establishment of new businesses such as manufacturing, food processing and other small and medium enterprises to the relatively undeveloped areas along the road corridor.

Economic costs

Estimating the costs of the project is relatively straightforward. From the construction budget, the construction costs are obtained and life cycle costing, which includes the cost of maintenance and the investment costs of upgrading the project road to a higher standard, can be estimated based on the scope of the work.

In considering the economic cost of the project, it is necessary to be aware that there are high environmental costs due to the magnitude of civil works. There is also the significant displacement of micro and small business activities, notably hawkers, open-air markets, and tree and flower nurseries, along the road. Effective management of the environmental and social impacts during construction and operation, including control of environmental pollution and degradation, should prevent the construction from excessively damaging the environment and reduce the need to resettle and compensate affected people. An Environmental and Social Management Plan (ESMP) has been set up to deal with all the mitigation measures, the rehabilitation of all sites disturbed by construction activities and to monitor air quality over the life of the project (quoted in Africa Development Fund, 2007). The cost for implementing the ESMP will be included in the project cost as it internalizes some of the social costs mentioned. Overall, it is estimated that US$5 million is needed to implement the ESMP, of which 60 per cent is budgeted for compensation and acquisition.

The project would be implemented over a period of 36 months starting from January 2008. The estimated cost of the project is US$175.1 million (net of taxes) or equivalent to KES 18.1 billion. The internal rate of return (IRR) of the project has been estimated at 30.4 per cent based on the costs and the assumption that the residual value at the end of project life is about 10 per cent of the original economic investment cost. This is far greater than the 12 per cent opportunity cost of capital in Kenya and therefore this project is worth embarking on.

Discussion questions

1 Discuss how to quantify the environmental benefits associated with the highway project.
2 In the evaluation of the highway project, only the internal rate of return (IRR) is used as the benchmark to compare with the social discount rate (opportunity cost of capital). Discuss other investment decision criteria to decide whether this project is economically viable.

Table 19.1 Summary of cost and benefit items for Nairobi–Thika highway in Kenya

Private costs	Social costs	Private benefits	Social benefits
Costs that economic agents alone face when producing or consuming economic resources.	*Incidental costs created by production or consumption of goods and services. These are faced by third parties.*	*Benefits (monetary and non-monetary) accrued to economic agents alone when they produce or consume products.*	*Incidental benefits created by production or consumption of goods and services. These are faced by third parties.*
Cost of civil works in constructing the highway. Compensation of displaced small and micro business activities along the development corridor.	Environmental pollution and degradation of water sources, land and vegetation affecting communities that do not have access to the highway.	Time saving of vehicle users in movement of passengers and goods. Greater access to other services available in the city. Improvement in road safety reducing the number of deaths due to road accidents. Reduction in vehicle operating costs due to reduced time spent on the roads. Increase in direct employment, which increases consumption.	Increase in social and urban mobility. Reduction in air pollution. Indirect employment created by more opportunities for small and medium enterprises.

20 Southeast Asian haze of 1997

The haze is not a new phenomenon for Southeast Asia or for Singapore. It has been a yearly occurrence since 1994, though it has varied in severity and duration. During that time, most people saw the haze as an inconvenience, and a 'passing event', lasting for about a fortnight at the most. The 1997 haze, however, changed these perceptions. The haze stayed for more than two months, and occupied the headlines attracting both government and public attention.[1]

Introduction

Between April and November in 1997, a widespread series of forest fires in Indonesia threw a blanket of thick, smoky haze over a large portion of Southeast Asia. The smoke covered Indonesia, Malaysia, Singapore and Brunei, as well as southern Thailand and the Philippines, and persisted for several months. The fires and smoke represented a major environmental disaster. The fires destroyed a large amount of rainforest, contributed to a significant release of greenhouse gases and resulted in the loss of habitat for threatened or endangered species of plants and animals. They also had adverse economic impacts through the destruction of commercial timber plantations and farmland; a reduction in tourism; the temporary shutdown of commerce, industry and travel; and an increase in healthcare costs.

The 1997 Southeast Asian forest fires were unprecedented in terms of the area of land burned, the amount of smoke generated and the size of the population living in areas affected by the smoke.

Causal factors

The forest fires in Southeast Asia in 1997 were entirely man-made. The main reason for setting the fires was to clear the land of vegetation for shifting agriculture, plantations or transmigration-programme settlers. Fires were often used to resolve land disputes and, in particular, to drive off settlers. Although the fires were originally blamed on slash-and-burn farmers, examinations of satellite images have shown that large plantation companies, many with ties to the Suharto government, used the fires to clear vast areas of land. The land was then planted with trees for rubber, timber (for pulp and paper) and palm oil. Plantations generally burned marginal land that had already been logged, whereas slash-and-burn farmers and the transmigration-programme settlers often burned primary forest. Burning is a cheap, fast and efficient method for clearing land.

The management of natural resources is another important causal factor that reflects the role of governmental policy. In Indonesia, the central government owns and manages all the country's forests. Management occurs through the design and enforcement of specific policies and regulations, such as logging concessions, property rights, land tenure and the use of fires to clear land. Political factors are potentially important in this regard, as is demonstrated by concessionaires' ties to the former president, Suharto. Although the use of fire was banned in 1995 (as a result of the 1994 fires), this law has not been widely enforced and hence has had little effect. Technology may play a role in the effective use of natural resources; especially relevant are technological alternatives to fires for converting marginal land to agricultural or plantation use.

Other potentially important factors include political, social and legal institutions. Forest fires represent a failure of these institutions. An institution that is of particular importance is land tenure. Most fires occurred in areas with joint landownership. The lack of clear land-tenure laws, uncertain land status and poor relationships among concessionaires, migrants and local people all contributed to the intentional starting of fires. In Indonesia, although the forests are government owned, local people have easy access to forests and use forests as their own resource.

Traditional *adat* law, which governed the use of forestland until the past few decades, has clashed with more recent logging concessions handed out by the government. The arrival of concessionaires has been associated with restrictions on local people's use of the forests, with little attention paid to traditional, albeit informal, land rights. Burning is used as a weapon by both sets of claimants. Owners of small farms sometimes burn trees planted by big forestry companies and, in turn, large firms have burned land to drive out small landholders.

Physical factors

Three important contributing factors affected the severity and duration of the fires in 1997. The first was the presence of the El Nino-Southern Oscillation (ENSO) phenomenon, associated with the warming of the waters of the equatorial Pacific Ocean. ENSO led to unusual weather patterns around the world and, in particular, to a severe drought in Southeast Asia. ENSO delayed the northeast monsoonal weather pattern, which let the fires burn for several months longer than usual. The drought in 1997 was said to have been the worst in 50 years. The effect of ENSO, however, was to exacerbate the fires that were being set, not to cause the fires themselves.

A second contributing factor was the peat deposits that cover the topsoil in parts of Sumatra and Kalimantan, which can be as deep as two to three metres. Peat is a mixture of decaying organic matter, such as roots, tree branches and leaves. During periods of prolonged drought, the peat dries out and can combust readily.

It burns easily and spreads fire quickly, usually underground. Smouldering peat can burn at depths of up to two metres, which makes it difficult to extinguish. Only heavy rainfall can put out the smouldering fires. Burning peat also emits larger amounts of smoke than the burning of other forms of biomass.

Finally, seams of coal near the surface have also caught fire and may smoulder for a long time. Some coal seams that caught fire during the early 1980s are still smouldering.

Smoke haze from forest fires

The smoke from the forest fires travelled across the Southeast Asian region, reaching all the way to southern parts of Thailand and the Philippines but with the most severe effects being felt in Singapore, Malaysia and Brunei. Of course, the smoke in Indonesia itself was tremendous, although Java, with 115 million people, was mostly spared because of the prevailing winds. Nevertheless, about 70 million people were affected.

The ENSO phenomenon that led to drought conditions in Southeast Asia was also associated with high pressure over the region that prevented the smoke from dissipating and caused it to spread into relatively thin layers of great horizontal extent while maintaining its concentration. When the smoke reached urban areas, it often led to an atmospheric inversion, trapping emissions from cars and factories and thereby multiplying any negative health effects.

The smoke haze from the forest fires lasted from late July to December 1997. Little could be done to combat it once the fires were raging. The air pollution subsided only after the arrival of the monsoons. During the peak period of haze in September 1997, the ambient air pollution concentrations in Kuching, in Sarawak state, Malaysia, reached 930 micrograms per cubic metre, an astonishingly high level more than 10 times higher than normal. In many other cities in the region, air pollution indexes repeatedly reached unsafe levels.

During periods of severe air pollution, schools, factories and offices were closed, and people – especially children, the elderly, the sick and the infirm – were advised to stay indoors and restrict their activities. Facemasks were also distributed, although their use probably had little benefit. People who could leave the area, including many foreign nationals, did so. Nevertheless, in Indonesia at least, reports indicated that many people viewed the smoke haze as a nuisance, rather than as a major environmental disaster and potential health hazard.

Health effects of air pollution

There are potential short-term and long-term health effects of exposure to air pollution. In the short-term, high levels of air pollution lead to acute conditions, such as respiratory infections and mortality, including deaths from accidents and chronic conditions. The possible long-term health effects of exposure to air pollution are unknown and difficult to detect. The components of smoke haze, including polycyclic aromatic hydrocarbons, are known carcinogens whose effects may not be apparent for years. The consequences may be more severe for children, for whom the particulates inhaled are high relative to body size and who may be passing through critical periods of development.

Recent studies by the World Health Organization (1998) in the region have examined the possible health effects of the 1997 forest fires. Some negative health effects have been found in Malaysia. For example, outpatient visits in Kuching, Sarawak, increased two to three times during the peak period of smoke haze and outpatient visits for respiratory disease at Kuala Lumpur General Hospital increased from 250 to 800 per day.

Effects were found to be the greatest in children, the elderly and people with pre-existing respiratory problems. Suggestive data were assembled that indicated an increase in cases of asthma, acute respiratory infections and conjunctivitis from August to September 1997 at a number of major hospitals in Kuala Lumpur (Brauer and Hisham-Hashim, 1998).

Similar findings were reported by the World Health Organization (1998) for the state of Sarawak and for Singapore. In Singapore, there was an increase in levels of micro-particulate matter (PM_{10}) from 50 to 150 tg/m^3 during the last week of September 1997. This was associated with a 12 per cent increase in cases of upper respiratory-tract illness, a 19 per cent increase in cases of asthma and a 26 per cent increase in cases of rhinitis, based on health surveillance data from clinics. There were, however, no significant increases in hospital admissions or mortality.

Studies such as these, of healthcare-seeking behaviour or diagnoses based on visits to health facilities suffer from unknown selection effects. For example, the publicity associated with the smoke haze may have led to greater healthcare-seeking behaviour and to more diagnoses because of the heightened awareness of symptoms among both patients and healthcare providers. Unfortunately, no population-based morbidity measures were collected during this period in Singapore or Malaysia. Finally, it is important to note that no data or studies are available for Indonesia, the country that was most affected by the forest fires and smoke.

Possible solutions

The issue of stopping forest fires and the haze lies with weak regulation and poor institution of controls. This means that authorities are unable to differentiate companies that are compliant with forest clearing regulations from the ones that are not, making reward or punishment difficult.

A small number of solutions have been suggested. The first is to prevent these fires by the creation of a stronger and more coordinated regulatory agency to better enforce the prosecution of those lighting illegal fires. The second is to enhance the ability of authorities to better deal with the forest fires once they have been started by providing better training for law enforcers and increased utilization of technology to detect and locate forest fires. A third related solution is to get the community to be involved to assist reporting and fighting fires alongside authorities, hence increasing both the monitoring and controlling of the fires.

However, the problem would be likely to persist, as clearing forests by lighting fires remains one of the cheapest methods, hence the incentive for illegal fire starting remains.

Conclusion

The 1997 forest fires in Southeast Asia were an environmental disaster of huge proportions, in terms of their intensity, extent, duration and the number of people affected. The smoke haze from these fires had a deleterious effect on the health of the population in Malaysia. The presence of significant mortality effects in Malaysian cities that are several hundred miles away from the main fires strongly supports this.

In addition, there are the global consequences of the destruction of a massive area of rainforest, huge emissions of greenhouse gases and future global warming, suggesting the need for a wider international response as well. This last point is especially important because the 1997 forest fire and smoke-haze episode were not isolated events. Large forest fires occurred in other locations around the world (though with a smaller affected population) and in previous and subsequent years in Southeast Asia. In particular, forest fires raged again in the region in 1998 and 2000. In Indonesia, the poor record on the enforcement of existing policies and the absence of new policy initiatives has now been combined with major – and continuing – economic and political upheaval. These circumstances suggest that the recent disasters will probably be repeated. Successful efforts to prevent and contain forest fires, however, will have important economic and health benefits throughout the region.

Discussion questions

1   Despite the huge costs imposed on the countries of Southeast Asia, why has there not been an effective solution and how can a study on the costs be useful for determining the appropriate public policy?
2   Slash-and-burn is the cheapest way to clear a forest but the destruction can be massive, as it is not easily controlled. Discuss how governments can incentiv- ize people to adopt other methods of forest clearing.

Table 20.1 Summary of cost and benefit items of Southeast Asian smoke-haze of 1997

Private costs	*Social costs*	*Private benefits*	*Social benefits*
Costs that economic agents alone face when producing or consuming economic resources.	*Incidental costs created by production or consumption of goods and services. These are faced by third parties.*	*Benefits (monetary and non-monetary) accrued to economic agents alone when they produce or consume products.*	*Incidental benefits created by production or consumption of goods and services. These are faced by third parties.*
Farmers that set the fires are affected by the ill effects of the haze and are at physical risk, as these fires cannot be easily stopped once they are started.	Haze that travelled all over the Southeast Asian region caused health problems and affected daily life.	Burning of the forest was a cheap, fast and efficient method of clearing the forest for agricultural use, benefiting local farmers and plantations in Indonesia.	None

21 H5N1 avian influenza immunization programme

Introduction

In September 2005, the UN warned that an outbreak of avian influenza could kill between 5 and 150 million people; suddenly all of the world's attention was focused on this. This particular strain of influenza virus, commonly referred to as H5N1, infects not only various species of birds, including poultry and migrating waterfowl, but also mammals, which includes humans. While a typical influenza has a mortality rate of 0.1 per cent, WHO data indicated that 60 per cent of the cases classified as H5N1 resulted in death.

The good news was that currently the virus was only transmitted from infected animals to humans and that human-to-human transmission was not yet evident. However, there is now evidence that a more deadly form of the H5N1 virus has developed, increasing the risk that it will become a virus that can be transmitted from human to human. Added to this is the discovery of the virus in wild bird populations that migrate across continents.

There are also indications that new forms of H5N1 are carried in birds without producing any physical appearance of illness. This means that visual identification of sick birds (the most common means of surveillance used so far) may become impossible.

As international media attention shifts to the discovery of H5N1 in migratory birds and the risks posed by new strains of H5N1 that can be passed from human to human, there remains an urgent need to address the immediate problem faced by those engaged directly in the farming and processing of poultry. Small farmers, agricultural workers and poultry processing workers face a high risk of infection. Where virus outbreaks have occurred, small farmers and workers have also suffered the economic impact of the death or culling of poultry flocks and the drop in sales of eggs and processed poultry.

Methods of control

The two main methods of control and prevention in a possible influenza pandemic would be the culling of poultry (the main source of transmission to humans) as well as vaccinating both poultry and poultry workers against the virus. In terms of economic cost, as of January 2006, over US$10 billion has been spent and over 200 million birds have been killed in an effort to contain the H5N1 virus.

Alongside the culling of infected poultry, new farming practices such as vaccination and reducing contact between livestock and wild birds were enforced in order to prevent and contain any possible spread of the virus. This led to a rise in the cost of poultry farming while consumer confidence has been shattered by the health scare leading to a huge dip in demand resulted in devastating losses for many poultry farmers. For example in Vietnam, poultry output accounts for 0.6 per cent of the GDP. Poultry output fell by around 15 per cent and there were additional losses due to decreased egg production and reduced activity within distribution channels, in addition to the costs of government purchase of poultry vaccines and hiring workers for culling, clean-up and surveillance. This resulted in the direct cost incurred of approximately 0.12 per cent of GDP. While this might seem insignificant in a macroeconomic perspective, these losses were borne heavily by the poultry sector and related communities.

Elsewhere, poor farmers who did not have the means to comply with these new mandated practices risked losing their livelihoods altogether. Such dire situations led many farmers to commit suicide and others to stop cooperating with efforts to contain the virus, leading to more deaths as well as increased chances for the virus to mutate, possibly starting a pandemic.

If the main concern were the fear of a pandemic of a human-transmittable influenza, a more effective approach to the problem would be to simply produce vaccines and immunize the population against the H5N1 virus. According to a study by N. Khazeni *et al.* (2009), expanded adjuvant vaccination (a multi-part vaccine) is an effective and cost-effective mitigation strategy for an influenza A (H5N1) pandemic. However the highly mutational nature of the virus along with the high cost of producing a vaccine might limit the effectiveness of this method; by the time the vaccine is produced and distributed sufficiently among the population it is possible that a new strain of the virus would have started making its rounds.

Social costs

An interesting point to note is that the immediate cost of a pandemic does not come from actual death or sickness but rather the uncoordinated efforts of people trying to avoid being infected. This was the case during the Severe Acute Respiratory Syndrome (SARS) outbreak in 2003 where attempts to avoid infection by minimizing physical contact resulted in severe demand shocks to the service sector, such as tourism and retail sales. The supply side was also affected by workplace absenteeism and disruption of production processes. All of these impacts are further exacerbated by emergency public policy measures such as quarantines and restriction on international trade and travel. The immediate economic loss during SARS in East Asia was estimated at 2 per cent of GDP.

A study by the Centre for Disease Control and Prevention (CDC) (Meltzer *et al.*, 1999), suggested that a pandemic influenza in the US would cause between

100,000 and 200,000 deaths, more than 700,000 hospitalizations, 40 million outpatient visits and 50 million additional illnesses. It estimated the value of economic losses at between US$100 and US$200 billion. Extrapolating this number to the rest of the world, a global influenza pandemic would represent a loss of US$800 billion a year according to the World Bank's estimate (World Bank, 2005). An influenza epidemic could also be larger and longer lasting than SARS, as seen from the 1918 influenza epidemic (better known as 'Spanish 'flu'), which came in three waves over two years.

Other indirect impacts such as possible school closures, as seen with SARS, would not only result in a loss of productivity and 'learning hours' but also cause an estimated reduction of 16 per cent of the workforce who would have to take care of their children at home.

Conclusion

Although the H5N1 avian influenza provides great insecurity and uncertainty, the International Partnership on Avian and Pandemic Influenza was announced by the then US President George W. Bush to the High-Level Plenary Meeting of the United Nations General Assembly on 14 September 2005 in New York. The International Partnership on Avian and Pandemic Influenza is committed to protecting human and animal health as well as mitigating the global socioeconomic and security consequences of an influenza pandemic. The plan calls for international cooperation, responsibility and transparency in dealing with avian and pandemic influenza. While the cost of prevention might be high, we must remember that millions of lives depend on it.

Discussion questions

1   If there were no certainty about the effectiveness of the immunization measures, how much would be the optimal amount of resources that governments should spend to prevent a pandemic outbreak?
2   In most causes of pandemic outbreak there will be deaths. Suggest ways by cost–benefit analysis to value such deaths.

Table 21.1 Summary of cost and benefit items of H5N1 avian influenza immunization programme

Private costs	Social costs	Private benefits	Social benefits
Costs that economic agents alone face when producing or consuming economic resources.	*Incidental costs created by production or consumption of goods and services. These are faced by third parties.*	*Benefits (monetary and non-monetary) accrued to economic agents alone when they produce or consume products.*	*Incidental benefits created by production or consumption of goods and services. These are faced by third parties.*
Vaccination of poultry and poultry workers and culling of infected poultry amounted to over US$10 billion. Increased farming costs due to new farming practices enforced to reduce the spread of the virus.	Fall in demand for service sectors such as tourism and retail sales. Fall in productivity due to workplace absenteeism and disruption of production processes. Possible school closures incurring a loss of 'learning hours' as well as an estimated further reduction of 16% of the workforce, who would have to take care of their children.	The prevention of a possible global pandemic outbreak, that could potentially cost US$800 billion.	Enhanced hygiene practices and culling can prevent the spread of other diseases present.

22 Fangcheng Port project, Guangxi, China

Introduction

The Fangcheng Port project expanded Fangcheng Port by adding one container berth and one bulk cargo berth. Being a principal access point to the sea for the landlocked provinces in the region, it is one of the axes of development. This port specializes in handling international trade cargo and coastal distribution. The cost of the expansion project is estimated at US$100 million.

Air pollution of carbon monoxide and sulphur dioxide are not expected to rise above the National Atmosphere Environmental quality standard. Total suspended particulates, however, are the key source of atmospheric pollution and would be mitigated by a reduction in dust production and diffusion. Measures such as increasing the water content of coal and ores will help to bind fine grains together to reduce dust production and diffusion. Two watering vehicles will be utilized under the project to spray the cargo at regular intervals throughout the day. The cargo loading system will also be equipped with a water sprinkling facility. In addition, an area of 38 square metres will be planted with trees to reduce the impact of pollution at the terminals.

During construction, dredging and reclamation operations will cause water pollution. The main effects are the sedimentation of the water and seabed, toxic contamination of marine waters by resuspension of toxic substances and loss of marine fauna due to blasting during rock removal.

In addition, there will be surface run-off from ore, coal rain, wastewater and washing residue, and accidental overflow during oil refuelling to ships. Ore and coal wastewater and washing residue will be treated to meet standard water conditions before being released while a multifunction oil-spill vessel will be procured to deal with minor oil spills.

Noise pollution is minimal in the area during construction as there are few residents and the construction period coincides with the development of the urban area. Noise from port operations rarely affects residential areas and hence is not deemed to be an issue. Equipment that complies with industry noise control standards will be the main mitigation measure to avoid noise pollution and a greenbelt, planted between the port and urban areas, will further reduce the noise level.

The ecology of the area is not affected as the port region has low levels of organisms and species. The mariculture site in Fangcheng Bay is also not affected by the construction works as it is situated upstream and hence not affected by sedimentation impacts. However, to further minimize the impact on the marine ecology, works will be carried out in winter when aquatic organisms do not grow. Equipment will be utilized to ensure minimal floating silt.

The estimated economic internal rate of return (IRR) is about 21 per cent and the total cost of the environmental project is estimated to be 1 per cent of the construction costs. As this project does not involve any relocation issues and does not affect the livelihoods of the local fishermen, public opinion is in favour of the project. Both water and air quality of the port will be improved as new measures of mitigation are implemented. A dedicated wastewater treatment plant will be included in the project, reducing the level of water pollution from urban wastewater.

Highway component

Accompanying the expansion of the Fangcheng Port, a highway connecting Natan to Fangcheng Port was proposed, the Fangcheng Highway. This highway would reduce current traffic bottlenecks as well as serve to cope with the increased traffic expected from the expansion of the Fangcheng Port. The existing rural road has a capacity of less than 2,000 vehicles a day, is congested and would certainly be unable to meet the predicted traffic of 6,300 vehicles a day from the port expansion. The Asian Development Bank estimated the benefits to amount to an economic IRR of 21 per cent.

However, in order to build the highway, a land area of 345 hectares will be acquired and this will involve the resettlement of 2,096 families or 10,000 people. In addition, 35 per cent of this acquired land also runs through cultivation and farms within 300 m to 1 km of the highway will have to be resettled. The compensation of the resettlement will include both output loss and resettlement subsidies. The average compensation will be 120 yuan per square metre or a total of 414 million yuan.

There is relatively little environmental concern regarding the construction of the highway, as there is minimal disturbance to the natural environment. Excess soil from construction will be carefully disposed of and exposed areas will be replanted and reinforced with retaining walls and drains in order to prevent soil erosion.

Noise pollution and vibration concerns will be within acceptable limits during operation as the planned route avoids sensitive areas such as schools and hospitals, and there are currently no instruments and equipment sensitive to vibration close to the road.

Air pollution will be reduced, as the improvement of the road will allow greater speeds. Spot checks of exhaust emissions will also be carried out along the highway to ensure that vehicles are compliant with emission standards. Trees will be planted along the margins of the highway to reduce the effects of suspended dust and gas pollutants and watering will be done to further reduce dust pollution. Overall, the construction costs are estimated to be US$54 million while mitigation measures amount to US$4.8 million.

Discussion question

1 Using concepts of demand, supply and opportunity cost, analyse and discuss the suitability of the area chosen for the construction of the Fangcheng Port.

Table 22.1 Summary of cost and benefit items for Fangcheng Port project, Guangxi, China

Private costs	*Social costs*	*Private benefits*	*Social benefits*
Costs that economic agents alone face when producing or consuming economic resources.	*Incidental costs created by production or consumption of goods and services. These are faced by third parties.*	*Benefits (monetary and non-monetary) accrued to economic agents alone when they produce or consume products.*	*Incidental benefits created by production or consumption of goods and services. These are faced by third parties.*
Port component			
Building cost of US$10 million. Additional US$1 million for environmental mitigation.	Minor impacts from noise and on ecology from construction and operation of the port.	Increase in trade volume in the region and creation of new jobs.	Better air and water quality in the region from mitigation measures implemented for the project.
Highway component			
Construction costs of US$54 million. US$4.8 million for environmental mitigation and resettlement compensation.	Increase in noise pollution to nearby residential areas. Additional cost to relocated residents that cannot be accounted for.	Cost-savings from reduced travel time, especially for port cargo.	Better air and water quality in the region from mitigation measures implemented from the project.

23 Jamuna Bridge project in Bangladesh

Bisecting Bangladesh almost neatly into two equal halves, the Jamuna River is the largest of the three major rivers in Bangladesh and the fifth largest river in the world. In 1998, the Bangabandhu Bridge, more commonly known as Jamuna Bridge, was completed to provide the essential link between east and west Bangladesh.

Prior to the building of the bridge, all communication between the two sides depended on a ferry system, which was subject to the conditions of the mighty river. These ferries were often outdated, unreliable and costly to run, resulting in high transportation costs.

The physical divide had caused the more fertile, agrarian west to lag behind the east, which houses the capital Dhaka and the international port Chittagong, in terms of development. Building a bridge to connect the two halves of Bangladesh would stimulate economic growth as well as provide a link for the transmission of electricity, gas and telecommunications. The estimated savings by having power transmission pylons on the bridge compared to building a stand-alone power connector was US$108 million.

By having a four-lane carriageway as well as a railway track, the bridge would provide significant cost savings for passenger and freight movements. In the opening year, the annual average daily traffic for all vehicles was 2,294, which resulted in the economic internal rate of return (IRR) of 16.8 per cent, affirming the economic viability of the project.

The total project cost was estimated at US$696 million, which included construction, river diversion, supporting transport ways and contingency costs. The two main concerns with the project were the resettlement of the local population around the proposed building site of the bridge and the modification of river flow of the Dhaleswari River (the second largest spill channel of the Jamuna River).

The total area of land to be acquired was estimated to be 2,784 ha, in which 6,156 households would have to be relocated, in addition to another 5,906 households that would be indirectly affected. Indirect impacts included the disruption of agricultural activities due to earthworks and noise generated by transportation, electricity generation and construction.

The cost of resettlement would not only include compensation and mitigation efforts to resituate affected residents in their previous livelihoods, but would also include programmes to impart new skills to expand their employment opportunities.

The introduction of the large labour force employed for the project would benefit the local residents as they would be able to access a wide array of amenities 'such as marketplaces, mosques, movie theatres and banks, particularly at the larger camps'[1].

In order to ensure the viability of river training works and other affiliated works regarding the bridge, the northern intake of the Dhaleswari River had to be closed 'since a sudden onrush of floodwater entering through the northern intake of the Dhaleswari River could cause irreparable damage to the bridge'[2].

The closure would reduce the available area for fish farming by 11,000 hectares, thereby reducing annual fish production by 500 tons, worth an estimated Tk16 million. Flooding would also be reduced in the region south of the closure with the estimated reduction in flood damages amounting to Tk25 million. The reduction in flooding also has an important positive spillover effect of enabling the use of higher-yield cropping equipment, which increases agricultural production and increases income by an average of 50 per cent for the 36,500 farming households in the affected area. The benefit of the increase in agricultural yield is estimated to be Tk98 million. In total, the net benefit of the closure of the north intake of the Dhaleswari River is an estimated Tk107 million.

However, the estimates for the cost of the reduction in fish production only includes fish farms and does not account for losses by professional fishermen and rural households involved in opportunistic fishing. Hence, the full social impact cannot be accurately determined. Similar difficulties arise when attempting to compensate residents in the affected regions, as transient labourers and squatters with no fixed address may be hard to reach both to be informed of the relocation compensation programme as well as the actual administering of the compensation.

Even though we can see that there are obvious benefits from the project and that society on a whole is better off, the impacts are also distributive. For example, crop farmers gain while a large proportion of fish farmers lose their livelihoods. This adjustment in the relative sizes of the region's production might have unexpected and far-reaching impacts on the direction of future development and environment.

Discussion question

1   As mentioned in the last paragraph, the bridge will improve the livelihoods of crop farmers at the expense of fish farmers. Even if the overall net effect is deemed positive, how much sacrifice is acceptable for 'the greater good'?

Table 23.1 Summary of cost and benefit items for Jamuna Bridge project, Bangladesh

Private costs	Social costs	Private benefits	Social benefits
Costs that economic agents alone face when producing or consuming economic resources.	*Incidental costs created by production or consumption of goods and services. These are faced by third parties.*	*Benefits (monetary and non-monetary) accrued to economic agents alone when they produce or consume products.*	*Incidental benefits created by production or consumption of goods and services. These are faced by third parties.*
Building cost of the bridge estimated to be US$696 million. Compensation cost for the resettlement benefit package.	A third of the fish farming area would have to be repurposed and fish yield estimated to fall by Tk16 million. Increase in traffic disturbance and noise pollution in the vicinity of the bridge.	Increased connectivity between east and west of Bangladesh, enabling greater economic cooperation. Cost savings from using the bridge as a transmission link for gas, electricity and telecommunications, instead of building separate generation facilities on the other side.	Increased access to amenities available to local community due to introduction of labour force. Increased agricultural production due to reduced flooding, enabling the use of high yield cropping equipment.

24 Construction of Suvarnabhumi Airport, Bangkok, Thailand

Opened on 28 September 2006, the Suvarnabhumi Airport took over from the ageing Don Mueang Airport, even inheriting its airport code BKK, to become Thailand's main international airport. Suvarnabhumi means the Golden Land in Sanskrit, and was chosen by King Bhumibol Adulyadej. It refers to a golden kingdom hypothesized to have existed in the area where Lower Burma is today (Hazra,1982, p. 58)[1].

Located in Bang Phli district of the Samut Prakan Province, about 25 km east of downtown Bangkok, the Suvarnabhumi Airport has the world's tallest control tower as well as the world's third largest single-building airport terminal. With the capacity to handle up to 45 million passengers annually, it has become the fifth busiest airport in Asia.

The earliest conception of a second international airport for Bangkok began in the early 1960s. However during the 46 years from then and the eventual completion of the airport, progress was plagued by various delays: budget overruns, construction flaws, corruption allegations, and political and economic instabilities. Despite the long time that it took to become a reality, the Suvarnabhumi Airport is 'being touted as the transportation and logistics centre for South East Asia'[2] (Pantumsinchai, 2006, p. 47)

The total investment cost is estimated at 155 billion baht (roughly US$5 billion), which includes costs for land reclamation (as the airport is built over swamp land), construction, supporting infrastructure and getting the airport operational.

In addition to this, another 30 billion baht has been set aside for a 28 km overhead rail link to be built to connect the airport to downtown Bangkok, cutting the travelling time down to a mere 15 minutes. A number of roads are also being constructed to increase the accessibility of the new airport.

This increase in transportation links represents a positive externality, as residents who are able to utilize these new infrastructures will gain from routes that are more direct and have shorter travelling times.

One thing that arose for this project was the issue of noise pollution for the residents in the vicinity of the airport. An Environmental Impact Assessment performed by the Environmental Engineering Association of Thailand has concluded that the area encompassing 70 square kilometres around the airport is a high impact noise zone which includes 50 residential buildings.

According to the report:

> The area affected by noise encompasses 70 sq km around the airport. The high impact noise zone, where Noise Exposure Forecast (NEF) is over 40, includes 50 residential buildings. These buildings will be purchased from the owners since they will not be fit to live in once the airport is in operation. The moderate impact zone, where NEF is between 35 and 40, includes almost 600 residential buildings and education institutions. The owners of these buildings will to be compensated for the noise exposure risks, which will affect their quality of life and health. Noise reduction measures will also be introduced. Thirteen noise monitoring stations will measure noise levels around the airport for further noise exposure limits during airport operation.
>
> (Pantumsinchai, 2006, pp. 47–48)

In a separate audit commissioned by the Office of the Auditor General of Thailand (2008), the cost of compensating residents to relocate and soundproof the remaining residential infrastructure may amount to 12 billion baht. This large amount shows that the negative externality arising from the project is significant and should have been considered, and indeed has been duly considered, by the Thai government. The impacts identified from the study include the disruption of daily lives of the people living near the take-off and landing routes, the medical cost arising from damage to hearing from exposure to the loud noise for extended periods of time, and cracks in the walls and falling tiles from shaking caused by the noise.

There are, however, plans to build an Aeropolis around the new airport. Building an Aeropolis will allow control over the future development of the area instead of letting development 'happen naturally and haphazardly as seen in the past' (Pantumsinchai, 2006, p. 50)[3]. For example, the current practice of burning fields to clear land for crop growing raised airport safety concerns.

In addition, if an Aeropolis is being planned, the cost of relocating the residents in the area can be considered and weighted against its own set of benefits from building the Aeropolis, and not simply as a cost of the airport.

Discussion questions

1   Since the announcement of the construction of the new airport, large numbers of people moved to areas in the vicinity of the new airport, expecting to benefit from the progress in the communities and to be compensated. This significantly raised the compensation budget required by the government. Is the compensation necessary? Does the migration indicate that the compensation is too high?

2   Suggest ways to measure the economic cost of noise pollution.

Table 24.1 Summary of cost and benefit items in the construction of Suvarnabhumi Airport, Bangkok, Thailand

Private costs	Social costs	Private benefits	Social benefits
Costs that economic agents alone face when producing or consuming economic resources.	*Incidental costs created by production or consumption of goods and services. These are faced by third parties.*	*Benefits (monetary and non-monetary) accrued to economic agents alone when they produce or consume products.*	*Incidental benefits created by production or consumption of goods and services. These are faced by third parties.*
Building cost of the airport, which would make up almost all, or a large proportion of, the above-mentioned 155 billion baht. Additional 30 billion baht on supporting infrastructure such as the 28km overhead rail link with downtown Bangkok.	Staff would have to incur greater travelling costs and inconvenience due to the relocation. Local communities will be faced with an increase in daily expenses resulting from a higher cost of living.	Considerable positive economic impacts such as increased employment, export and foreign investment in the aviation industry. Enhanced competitiveness in the tourism industry. Greater job opportunities and incremental income for local population due to higher investment.	Better quality of life and mental health expected near the old airport due to reduced traffic, noise disturbance and congestion.

25 Speed limit regulation for highways in Japan

Introduction

Speed limits are something all of us are familiar with; wherever we live, the chances are our roads and highways are littered with signs indicating the maximum allowed speed on that stretch of road as well as speed cameras vigilantly awaiting drivers who violate the limit.

While speed limits do inconvenience us by preventing us from getting to where we want to go more quickly, it does actually reduce the chance of accidents occurring. Hence, the trade-off is between saving time and the increased risks as well as the accompanying cost of injury and even death. The following case utilizes a study done on expressway speed limits in Japan, in order to understand if relaxing speed limits would be sound.

Purpose

In Japan, prefectural police agencies set speed limits without any economic analysis but rather based on intuitive reasoning. This often results in speed limits being set lower than the design standards of the highway. As prefectural police agencies have autonomous control over the speed limit in their jurisdiction, there are cases of single highway routes being subjected to different speed limits in different sections of the highway. These causes inefficiency in the use of the highway and this project aims to apply cost–benefit analysis to determine if speed limits in Japan's highways should be relaxed.

There exist three different categories of design speeds for expressways in Japan, namely 80 km/h, 100 km/h and 120 km/h. The design speed for a particular stretch of the expressway is determined by taking several factors into account, such as expected traffic volume, land-use (urban or rural) and topography as well as other physical constrains to road geometry. Physical constraints can be overcome by constructing the appropriate structure but cost concerns would demand that a compromise be made between design speed and the cost of construction. For example, high traffic volume would justify a higher design speed as this yields a relatively higher time saving benefit. Despite the design speed of several sections of the expressway being 120 km/h, the maximum speed limit in the whole of

Table 25.1 Monetary cost (yen) of time for different vehicle types

	Car	Bus	Small truck	Truck
Yen/minute – by vehicle type	62.86	519.74	56.81	87.44

Japan is capped at 100 km/h. We shall also examine if the speed limit should be allowed to go beyond this cap to match the design speed.

In the following cost–benefit analysis, the Joban Expressway will be used due to data availability and the varying speed limits present in different sections of the route. The formula used for this analysis will be provided at the end of this case study.

Private benefits

The main benefit of raising the speed limit on highways would be the reduction in the cost of travel time. As actual speed corresponds with regulated speeds, a higher speed limit cap would mean that vehicles would travel at a faster speed, and hence this would reduce the amount of time spent in transit. This would translate into companies and commuters not having to suffer needless and costly delays.

As mentioned earlier, time is money or rather there are opportunity costs of time. The time spent travelling could be utilized in another form of productive work or for leisure, both of which have a certain value attached to them.

Table 25.1 shows the monetay cost of time for each vehicle type. From the table, we can see that the monetay cost of time for buses is significantly higher than other vehicle types, perhaps due to the higher density of people per bus and by extension, a higher value gained with time savings. Trucks come in second, possibly because trucks are the common mode for transporting goods.

Private costs

By travelling at a higher speed, vehicles would incur a higher vehicle operation cost. This is due to vehicles being subjected to harsher wear and tear, requiring a higher maintenance cost. In addition, fuel economy is poorer at higher speeds mainly due to wind resistance and, as a result, there will be increased fuel costs.

Table 25.2 shows the unit operation cost of different types of vehicles. Speeds above 90 km/h are linearly extrapolated.

Easing the speed limit restriction would also incur a higher accident cost. As actual driving speed increases, drivers have less time to react to any adverse change in conditions, which then raises the chance of an accident occurring. In the *Japanese Cost–Benefit Analysis Manual,* the cost of accidents on expressways is given as a simple expression (Ministry of Land, Infrastructure and Transport, 2003):

$$\text{Accident Cost (thousand yen/year)} = 270 \times \text{Traffic Volume (thousand vehicles/day)} \times \text{Length of Road (km)}.$$

Table 25.2 Unit operating cost (yen) of different vehicle types and speeds

Speed (km/h)	Car	Bus	Small truck	Truck
80	6.50	28.58	13.81	21.59
85	6.65	29.09	13.97	22.36
90	6.85	29.74	14.18	23.36
100	7.25	31.04	14.60	25.36
120	8.01	33.64	15.44	29.36

Another minor cost would be the cost of implementing the new speed limits. The commuters of the affected region would have to be informed and signage would have to be replaced. Databases, street directories and GPS systems would all need to be updated. While this cost may not be as significant as other costs, the logistical hassle might provide a barrier to change in the implementation of new speed limits.

External factors

A main concern of raising the speed limit of Japanese highways would be the increase in environmental pollution, such as air and noise pollution. Vehicles emit carbon dioxide (a greenhouse gas), unburned hydrocarbons, soot (which contributes to smog) and nitrogen oxides (which cause acid rain). Recommending the relaxation of speed limits would be moving in opposition to the recent trend of fighting against global warming, in addition to the increased health risks and building maintenance costs due to acid rain.

At higher speeds, tyre roar from passing vehicles would become more noticeable and higher speeds would kick up more dust into the surrounding area, possibly disrupting both productive and leisure activities taking place in the region of the expressway.

The *Japanese Cost–Benefit Analysis Manual* for the road sector in Japan recommends some formulae to estimate the different components of environmental impacts, namely air pollution, greenhouse gases and noise. They are used to calculate the impact of different types of pollution at various speeds. Then the environmental costs are calculated accordingly to the type of environment, as seen in Table 25.3 below.

External benefits, on the other hand, could be the easing of congestion on other forms of transport on parallel routes. As speed limits are raised, commuters who originally chose other modes of transport now have a new competitive option to maximize their time savings or minimize their time costs. Other commuters who chose to stick with their original mode of transport would then be able to enjoy less congestion, thereby increasing social welfare.

Table 25.3 Unit costs of different environmental effects

Type of impact	Coefficients for converting environmental impact into monetary terms			
	Densely urbanized areas	Other urbanized areas	Rural areas (flat land)	Rural areas (mountainous)
Air pollutants (1,000 yen/tonne)	2,920	580	200	10
Noise (1,000 yen / dB(A) / year)	2,400	475.2	165.6	7.2
Greenhouse gases (1,000 yen/tonne)	2.3			

Source: Adapted from Guidelines for Evaluation of Road Investment Projects (Committee on Evaluation of Road Investment Projects, 1998).

Conclusion

For the Joban Expressway, the costs and benefits of increasing the regulated speed up to the design speed, meaning that some parts of the expressway will have a speed limit of 120 km/h, is shown in Table 25.4.

As seen from Table 25.4, increasing the speed limit to match the design speed of the Joban Expressway gives a net benefit of 5.9 billion yen a year or 4.6 per cent of the total transport cost.

However, in the computation of accident costs, there might have been factors that were left out. Perhaps in non-fatal accidents, the cost can simply be the damage to vehicles, medical bills and the opportunity costs of time while the vehicle owners are deprived of their modes of transport. In cases of fatal accidents, how are we supposed to calculate the costs of a life lost? Should we use life insurance as a gauge? Or perhaps we should take the person's wage and multiply it by the working life-span remaining should the person have not had an accident and we would get a figure that would indicate the loss to society in terms of productivity. There is a wide array of external factors that would be immeasurable such as the trauma inflicted on loved ones and broken families resulting in a less nurtured upbringing potentially leading to children not reaching their potential. These costs

Table 25.4 Valuing costs and benefits of speed regulation

Costs and benefits	Change in benefits (million yen/year)				Net benefits (million yen/ year)
	Travel time	Vehicle operation	Accident cost	Environmental impacts	
Total	7,847	−1,509	−323	−120	5,895

are difficult to internalize as no one can predict nor accurately quantify the spiralling effects of death.

Another point regarding accidents is that accident rates are consistently higher in places where drivers exceed the design speed. This differs from the commonly held view that more speed causes more accidents; rather, it is exceeding the design speed of the road that causes the chaos.

Hence, in this analysis, we find that there is a benefit in raising the speed limit to match the maximum design speed of the road. In addition, upgrading existing roads to enable a higher design speed would also seem like an ideal solution, not only to increase time cost savings but to mitigate accident costs.

Lessons learned

In transport related cases, time costs are often the main benefit touted by proponents of increasing road infrastructure or in this case, the easing of speed limits. Time cost consideration for businesses is tied to the wage costs of hiring a worker; the worker has to be paid even if the vehicle is not moving, for example, being stuck in a traffic jam, as long as time elapses.

As for regular commuters, deriving their time cost would not be as direct as they do not have an apparent indicator (wage rate). It is much harder to determine the value that people attach to their time; in fact, this value might not be immediately obvious to the people themselves. Instead, we use the revealed preference method, which uses observed behaviour in order to relate to their valuation of a non-marketed good, which in this case is time.

Discussion questions

1   Would you be supportive of a relaxation of speed limits and shorter travelling times in exchange for increased risk? How high should speed limits be set?
2   Since the value of one's own life should be infinite or at least very great, why then do some people consistently speed and exceed the speed limit? Is this behaviour irrational?

Table 25.5 Summary of cost and benefit items in speed limit regulation for highways in Japan

Private costs	Social costs	Private benefits	Social benefits
Costs that economic agents alone face when producing or consuming economic resources.	*Incidental costs created by production or consumption of goods and services. These are faced by third parties.*	*Benefits (monetary and non-monetary) accrued to economic agents alone when they produce or consume products.*	*Incidental benefits created by production or consumption of goods and services. These are faced by third parties.*
Increase in vehicle operation cost. Increase in accident cost. Frictional costs in changing regulated speed limit.	Environmental pollution.	Reduction in travel time costs.	Easing of congestion by other forms of transport, such as trains.

Further Reading

Abelson, P. (1979). *Cost Benefit Analysis – Environment and Problems*, London, Saxon House.

Adler, M. D. and Posner, E. A. (2001). *Cost–Benefit Analysis – Legal, Economic and Philosophical Perspectives*, Chicago and London, The University of Chicago Press.

Anthony, E. B., Greenberg, D. H., Vining, A. R. and Weiner, D. L. (2011). *Cost–Benefit Analysis – Concepts and Practice*, Upper Saddle River, NJ, Pearson Prentice Hall.

Arnold, F. S. (1995). *Economic Analysis of Environmental Policy and Regulation*, New York, John Wiley & Sons.

Bateman, I. J. and Willis, K. G. (1999). *Valuing Environmental Preferences – Theory and Practice of the Contingent Valuation Method in the US, EU & Developing Countries*, Oxford, Oxford University Press.

Bellinger, W. K. (2007). *The Economic Analysis of Public Policy*, London, Routledge Taylor and Francis Group.

Brent, R. J. (1990). *Project Appraisal for Developing Countries*, New York, Harvester Wheatsheaf.

Brent, R. J. (2006). *Applied Cost–Benefit Analysis*, Cheltenham, Edward Elgar Publishing Limited.

Cairncross, F. (1992). *Costing the Earth*, Cambridge, MA, Harvard Business School Press.

Campbell, H. and Brown, R. (2003). *Benefit–Cost Analysis – Financial and Economic Appraisal Using Spreadsheets*, Cambridge, Cambridge University Press.

Campen, J. T. (1986). *Benefit, Cost and Beyond – The Political Economy of Benefit Cost Analysis*, New York, Ballinger Publishing Company.

Champ, P. A., Boyle K. J. and Brown T. C. (2003). *A Primer on Nonmarket Valuation*, Boston, Kluwer Academic Publishers.

Clark, J. L. (1998). *The Economic Approach to Environmental and Natural Resources*, New York, The Dryden Press.

Cohen, M. A. (2005). *The Costs of Crime and Justice*, New York, Routledge Taylor & Francis Group.

Curry, S. and Weiss, J. (1993). *Project Analysis in Developing Countries*, London, Macmillan Press Limited.

Daly, H. E. and Townsend, K. N. (1993). *Valuing the Earth – Economics, Ecology and Ethics*, Cambridge, MA, The MIT Press.

Dasgupta, P., Sen, A. and Maglin, S. (1972). *Guidelines for Policy Evaluation*, Vienna, United Nations Industrial Development Organization (UNIDO).

Dinwiddy, C. and Teal, F. (1996). *Principles of Cost–Benefit Analysis for Developing Countries*, Cambridge, Cambridge University Press.

Dixon, J. A., Scura, L. F., Carpenter, R. A. and Sherman, P. B. (1994). *Economic Analysis of Environmental Impacts*, London, Earthscan Publications Limited.

Drummond, M. F., O'Brien, B. J., Stoddart, G. L. and Torrance, G. W. (2000). *Methods for the Economic Evaluation of Health Care Programmes*, New York, Oxford University Press.

English, J. M. (1984). *Project Evaluation – A Unified Approach for the Analysis of Capital Investments*, New York, Macmillan Publishing Co.

Fabrycky, W. J., Thusen, G. J. and Verma, D. (1998). *Economic Decision Analysis*, Upper Saddle River, NJ, Prentice Hall International Inc.

Ferrara, D. A. (2010). *Cost–Benefit Analysis of Multi-level Government – The case of EU Cohesion Policy and of US Federal Investment Policies*, London and New York, Routledge, Taylor & Francis Group.

Fiorino, D. J. (1995). *Making Environmental Policy*, Berkeley, CA, University of California Press.

Fuguitt, D. and Wilcox, S. J. (1999). *Cost–Benefit Analysis for Public Sector Decision Makers*, London, Quorum Books.

Gramlich, E. M. (1990). *A Guide to Benefit–Cost Analysis*, Englewood Cliffs, NJ, Prentice Hall.

Haab, T. C. and McConnell, K. E. (2002). *Valuing Environmental & Natural Resources – The Econometric Non-market Valuation*, Cheltenham, Edward Elgar Publishing Limited.

Hanley, N. and Splash, C. L. (1993). *Cost–Benefit Analysis and the Environment*, Cheltenham, Edward Elgar Publishing Limited.

Hanley, N. and Roberts, C. J. (2002). *Issues in Environmental Economics*, London, Blackwell Publishing.

Heal, G. (1998). *Valuing the Future – Economic Theory and Sustainability*, New York, Columbia University Press.

Hecht, J. E. (2004). *National Environmental Accounting – Bridging the Gap Between Ecology and Economy*, Washington, DC, RFF Press.

Irvin, G. (1978). *Modern Cost–Benefit Methods – An Introduction to Financial, Economic and Social Appraisal of Development Projects*, London, Macmillan Education.

Johansson, P. O. (1987). *The Economic Theory and Measurement of Environmental Benefits*, Cambridge, Cambridge University Press.

Johansson, P. O. (1993). *Cost–Benefit Analysis of Environmental Change*, Cambridge, Cambridge University Press.

Johansson, P. O. (1995). *Evaluating Health Risks – An Economic Approach*, Cambridge, Cambridge University Press.

Johnson, R. L. and Johnson, G. V. (1990). *Economic Valuation of Natural Resources – Issues, Theory and Applications*, Boulder, CO, Westview Press.

Klein, T. A. (1977). *Social Costs and Benefits of Business*, Englewood Cliffs, NJ, Prentice Hall.

Kneese, A. V. (1984). *Measuring the Benefits of Clean Air and Water*, Washington, DC, RFF Press.

Kula, E. (1992). *Economics of Natural Resources and the Environment*, London, Chapman and Hall.

Layard, R. (1992). *Cost–Benefit Analysis*, London, Penguin Books.

Layard, R. and Glaister, S. (1994). *Cost–Benefit Analysis*, New York, Cambridge University Press.

Lohani, B., Evans. J. W., Ludwig, H., Everitt, R. R., Carpenter, R. A. and Tu, S. L. (1997). *Environmental Impact Assessment for Developing Countries in Asia*, Manila, Asia Development Bank.

Louviere, J. J., Hensher, D. A., Swait, J. D. and Adamowicz, W. (2000). *Stated Choice Methods – Analysis and Application*, Cambridge, Cambridge University Press.

Markandya, A., Cistulli, V., Harou, P. and Bellu, L. G. (2002). *Environmental Economics for Sustainable Growth – A Handbook for Sustainable Growth*, Cheltenham, Edward Elgar Publishing.

Marshall, A. (1890). *Principles of Economics*, 8th edition (1920), London, Macmillan and Co, Ltd.

McAllister, D. M. (1990). *Evaluation in Environmental Planning – Assessing Environmental, Social, Economic and Political Trade-offs*, Cambridge, MA, The MIT Press.

Mishan, E. J. (1972). *Elements of Cost–Benefit Analysis*, London, George Allen & Unwin Limited.

Mishan, E. J. (1988). *Cost–Benefit Analysis*, London, Unwin Hyman.

Mishan, E. J. (1993). *The Costs of Economic Growth*, London, Weidenfeld & Nicolson Limited.

Mishan, E. J. and Quah, E. (2007) *Cost–Benefit Analysis*, 5th edition, London, Routledge, Taylor & Francis Group.

Modak, P. and Biswas, A. K. (1999). *Conducting Environmental Impact Assessment for Developing Countries*, New York, United Nations University Press.

Ortolano, L. (1997). *Environmental Regulation and Impact Assessment*, New York, John Wiley & Sons.

Pearce, D. (1995). *Blueprint 4 – Capturing Global Environmental Value*, London, Earthscan Publications Limited.

Pearce, D., Atkinson, G. and Mourato, S. (2006). *Cost–Benefit Analysis and the Environment: Recent Developments*, Paris, OECD.

Pearce, D. W. and Nash, C. A. (1981). *The Social Appraisal of Projects – A Text in Cost–Benefit Analysis*, London, The Macmillan Press.

Puttaswamaiah, K. (2002). *Cost–Benefit Analysis – Environment and Ecological Perspectives*, New Brunswick, NJ, Transaction Publishers.

Ray, A. (1984). *Cost–Benefit Analysis – Issues of Methodologies*, Baltimore, MD, John Hopkins University Press.

Rogers, P. P. and Jalal, K. F. (1997). *Measuring Environmental Quality in Asia*, Cambridge, MA, Harvard University Press.

Schofield, J. A. (1987). *Cost–Benefit Analysis in Urban and Regional Planning*, London, Allen & Unwin.

Sewell, W. R. D. and Roston, J. (1970). *Recreational Fishing Evaluation*, Quebec, Queen's Printer for Canada.

Stavins, R. N. (2000). *Economics of the Environment – Selected Readings*, New York, W. W. Norton and Company.

Sterner, T. (2003). *Policy Instruments for Environmental and Natural Resource Management*, Washington, DC, RFF Press.

Sugden, R. and Williams, A. (1978). *The Principles of Practical Cost–Benefit Analysis*, Oxford, Oxford University Press.

Takayama, A. (1994). *Analytical Methods in Economics*, London, Harvester Wheatsheaf.

Walshe, G. and Daffern, P. (1990). *Managing Cost Benefit Analysis*, London, The Macmillan Press.

Weimer, D. L. and Vining, A. R. (1989). *Policy Analysis – Concepts & Practice*, Englewood Cliffs, NJ, Prentice Hall.

Zerbe, R. O. and Bellas, A. S. (2006). *A Primer for Benefit–Cost Analysis*, Northampton, MA, Edward Elgar Publishing Limited.

Notes

Foreword

1 Mainstream economists habitually ignore – or regard as a blip – the occasional seeming behavioural anomaly which, however, may exercise the minds of some practitioners of the art.

1 Introduction

1 Strictly speaking, the opportunity cost would not be zero as the forgone leisure and household production should carry some value.

2 History and scope of cost–benefit analysis

1 The term 'formal' is used here as the US Army Corps of Engineers were conducting studies not unlike CBA from as far back as 1902 (Hammond, 1966).
2 Alfred Marshall (1842–1924) was an influential economist in the late nineteenth and early twentieth centuries. His book *Principles of Economics* (1890) became the dominant economics textbook in England during that period.
3 The term was coined in the late 1930s from the writings of two eminent welfare economists, Sir John Hicks (1939) and Nicholas Kaldor (1939).

4 Benefit transfers

1 Christabelle Soh is a teacher with the Ministry of Education, Singapore.
2 The United States Department of Agriculture's Natural Resources Conservation Service (NRCS) maintains a database of economic values of recreational activities that NRCS economists are encouraged to utilize.
3 Here, it must be clarified that the issue is not about adjusting for inflation over time (we do not consider adjustments for inflation real adjustments); it is adjusting for differences in relative shadow price over time.
4 Environmental Valuation Reference Inventory.
5 ValueBase[SWE] is a database that tracks economic valuation studies on environmental change in Sweden.

6 Value of a statistical life in Singapore

1 Chia Wai Mun is an Assistant Professor with the Economics Department of Nanyang Technological University, Singapore.
2 These are variables that take on the value '1' if an attribute is present and '0' if it is not (e.g. for a 50–60-year-old age group dummy variable, if a participant falls within the age group, it would be coded as '1' and '0' if not.

7 Estimating the economic cost of air pollution on health

1 Chia Wai Mun is an Assistant Professor with the Economics Department of Nanyang Technological University, Singapore

9 Pair-wise comparison: a novel approach

1 The number of combinations is $n(n+1)/2$ where n is the number of items.
2 In general, the number of times an item can be chosen over others by a single individual is $n-1$ where n is the number of items.
3 If there are x number of respondents and n number of items, the maximum number of times an item can be chosen by the whole sample would be $x(n-1)$.
4 For a more detailed discussion on intransitivity and pair-wise comparison, refer to Peterson and Brown (1998).

10 Behavioural effects and cost–benefit analysis: lessons from behavioural economics

1 Jack L. Knetsch is an Emeritus Professor with the Economics Department of Simon Fraser University, Vancouver, Canada.

11 The Three Gorges Dam project, China

1 The Three Gorges is a natural rock feature that is about 200 km (125 miles) long and has steep slopes composed of thick limestone rocks.
2 http://news.xinhuanet.com/english/2009-05/18/content_11395483.htm.
3 http://china.org.cn/english/culture/70271.htm.
4 http://news.nationalgeographic.com/news/2006/12/061214-dolphin-extinct.html.

12 Flue gas desulphurization in Mae Moh, Thailand

1 http://www.isf.uts.edu.au/publications/tarlo2002whybrowncoal.pdf.
2 http://www.greenpeace.org/raw/content/seasia/en/press/reports/all-emission-no-solution-en.pdf.
3 http://www.jica.go.jp/english/operations/evaluation/oda_loan/post/2004/pdf/2-04_smry.pdf.

13 Hosting international events: cases from the Beijing Olympics 2008 and the inaugural Youth Olympics in Singapore 2010

1 http://en.beijing2008.cn/news/olympiccities/beijing/n214570334.shtml.
2 http://www.reuters.com/article/idUSPEK12263220070605.

15 Qinghai–Tibet railway: investment to improve travel time, promote tourism and economic growth

1 http://www.chinatibettrain.com/beijinglhasa.htm.
2 http://atwonline.com/news/story.html?storyID=6452&cid=0&sig2=9EAUZ0KVMuO VF-hr5hw0cw.
3 http://news.xinhuanet.com/english/2009-06/30/content_11626203.htm.

17 Preservation of the Amazon rainforest

1 Animal output accounts for only 30 per cent of agricultural output while taking up 63 per cent of agricultural land. The value of cattle-raising was estimated to be US$20/hectare. Annual crops which generated an annual output of US$210 per hectare accounted for 37 per cent of total agricultural output. However, it takes up 35 per cent of agriculture land when including the fallow land, thus leading to a value of US$43 per hectare. Perennial crops (black pepper, oranges, coffee, cocoa, banana, passion fruit and cotton) do not require fallow land and the output was US$377/hectare, accounting for more than 12 per cent of total agricultural output while taking up less than 2 per cent of the area.
2 http://wwf.panda.org/?196057/Amazing-Discoveries-in-the-Amazon-New-Species-Found-Every-Three-Days-Over-Last-Decade.

20 Southeast Asian haze of 1997

1 Hon, Pricilla M.L. (2006).

23 Jamuna Bridge project in Bangladesh

1 Asian Development Bank. Summary Environmental Impact Assessment of the Jamuna Bridge Railway Link Project in the People's Republic of Bangladesh – Appendix 5, p. 339.
2 Asian Development Bank. Summary Environmental Impact Assessment of the Jamuna Bridge Railway Link Project in the People's Republic of Bangladesh – Appendix 5, p. 331.

24 Construction of Suvarnabhumi Airport, Bangkok, Thailand

1 http://en.wikipedia.org/wiki/Suvarnabhumi.
2 Environmental Concerns for Suvarnabhumi Airport and Aeropolis, http://www.eeat. or.th/images/EnvironmentalConcernsforSuvarnabhumiAirportandAeropolis.pdf.
3 Environmental Concerns for Suvarnabhumi Airport and Aeropolis, http://www.eeat. or.th/images/EnvironmentalConcernsforSuvarnabhumiAirportandAeropolis.pdf.

Bibliography

Aabø, S. (2005). Are Public Libraries Worth their Price? A Contingent Valuation Study of Norwegian Public Libraries, *New Library World*, Vol. 106 (11/12), pp. 487–495.

Abelson, P. (2003). The Value of Life and Health for Public Policy, *Economic Record*, Vol. 79, pp. S2–S13.

Africa Development Fund (2007). *Nairobi–Thika Highway Improvement Project – Appraisal Report*, Tunisia, Africa Development Fund.

Alberini, A., Cropper, M. L., Fu, T. T., Krupnick, A., Liu, J. T., Shaw, D. and Harrington, W. (1997). Valuing Health Effects of Air Pollution in Developing Countries – the Case of Taiwan, *Journal of Environmental Economics and Management*, Vol. 34, pp. 107–126.

Alberini, A., Cropper, M., Krupnick, A. and Simon, N. (2004). Does the Value of a Statistical Life Vary with Age and Health Status? Evidence from the United States and Canada, *Journal of Environmental Economics and Management*, Vol. 48 (1), pp. 769–792.

Amirnejah, H., Khalilian, S., Assareh, M. H. and Ahmadian, M. (2006). Estimating the Existence Value of North Forests of Iran by Using a Contingent Calculation Method, *Ecological Economics*, Vol. 58 (4), pp. 665–675.

Andersen, L. E. (1997). *A Cost–Benefit Analysis of Deforestation in the Brazilian Amazon*, Institute for Applied Economics Research (IPEA) in Rio de Janeiro, Discussion Paper No. 455, retrieved 15 June 2011 from www.sae.gov.br/site/wp-content/uploads/td_0455. pdf.

Arkes, H. R. and Blumer, C. (1985). The Psychology of Sunk Costs, *Organizational Behavior and Human Decision Processes*, Vol. 35, pp. 124–140.

Asian Development Bank (1997). *Environmental Impact Assessment for Developing Countries in Asia, Vol. 2: Selected Case Studies*, Chapter 1, pp. 1-1–1-22, Manila, Asian Development Bank.

Asian Development Bank (2007). *Greater Colombo Wastewater Management Project, Sri Lanka*, PPTA 4531 – SRI.

Asian Development Bank. Summary Environmental Impact Assessment of the Jamuna Bridge Railway Link Project in the People's Republic of Bangladesh – Appendix 5, retrieved 15 June 2011 from http://www.adb.org/Documents/Books/Env_and_Eco/ appendix-5.pdf.

Bateman, I. J., Jones, A. P., Nishikawa, N. and Brouwer, R. (2000). Benefit Transfer in Theory and Practice – A Review, *CSERGE Working Paper GEC 2000–25*, retrieved 15 June 2011 from http://www.uea.ac.uk/env/cserge/pub/wp/gec/gec_2000_25.pdf.

Bateman, I. J., Day, B. H. and Lake, I. (2004). The Valuation of Transport-Related Noise in Birmingham, *Technical Report to the Department for Transport*, retrieved 15 June 2011 from http://www.dft.gov.uk/pgr/economics/.

Berfield, S. (1996). The Price of Pollution, *Asiaweek*, 26 April, pp. 34–39.

Blomquist, G. C. and Whitehead, J. C. (1998). Resource Quality Information and Validity of Willingness to Pay in Contingent Valuation, *Resource and Energy Economics*, Vol. 20, pp. 179–196.

Boardman, A., Greenberg, D., Vining, A. and Weimer, D. (2006). *Cost Benefit Analysis – Concepts and Practice*, 3rd edition, Englewood Cliffs, NJ, Prentice Hall.

Boyle, K. J. and Bergstrom, J. C. (1992). Benefit Transfer Studies – Myths, Pragmatism, and Idealism, *Water Resources Research*, Vol. 28 (3), pp. 657–663.

Brauer, M. and Hisham-Hashim, J. (1998). Fires in Indonesia – Crisis and Reaction, *Environmental Science and Technology*, Vol. 32 (7), pp. 404A–407A.

Brown, K. and Pearce, D. W. (1994). The Economic Value of Carbon Storage in Tropical Forests, in Weiss, J. (ed.), *The Economics of Project Appraisal and the Environment*, Aldershot, Edward Elgar.

Chin, A. and Knetsch, J. L. (in progress). The Choice of Measure Matters – Are Many Transport Project Valuations Seriously Biased?, *Working Paper*.

China Three Gorges Project (2002). *Biggest Flood Control Benefit in the World*, retrieved 12 June 2011 from http://www.ctgpc.com/benefifs/benefifs_a.php.

China Tibet Train, Train to Tibet Official Website, retrieved 12 June 2011 from http://www.chinatibettrain.com/beijinglhasa.htm.

Chuenpagdee, R., Knetsch, J. and Brown, T. (2001). Coastal Management Using Public Judgments, Importance Scales, and Predetermined Schedules, *Coastal Management*, Vol. 29, pp. 253–270.

Clawson, M. and Knetsch, J. L. (1966). *Economics of Outdoor Recreation*, Baltimore, MD, Johns Hopkins University Press.

Cohen, D. and Knetsch, J. L. (1992). Judicial Choice and Disparities Between Measures of Economic Values, *Osgoode Hall Law Journal*, Vol. 30, pp. 737–770.

Committee on Evaluation of Road Investment Projects (1998). *Guidelines for Evaluation of Road Investment Projects*, Tokyo, Japan (in Japanese).

Davis, R. K. (1963). Recreation Planning as an Economic Problem, *Natural Resources Journal*, Vol. 3, pp. 239–249.

Day, B., Bateman, I. and Lake, I. (2007). Beyond Implicit Prices – Recovering Theoretically Consistent and Transferable Values for Noise Avoidance from a Hedonic Property Price Model, *Environmental and Resource Economics*, Vol. 37 (1), pp. 211–232.

Department of Statistics, Singapore (n.d.) Singstat Time Series Online [database], retrieved 15 June 2011 from https://app.sts.singstat.gov.sg/dots_index.asp.

Department of Statistics, Singapore. *Monthly Digest of Statistics*, retrieved 15 June 2011 from http://www.singstat.gov.sg/pubn/reference.html.

Dewenter, R., Haucap, J., Luther, R. and Rötzel, P. (2007). Hedonic Prices in the German Market for Mobile Phones, *Telecommunications Policy*, Vol. 31 (1), pp. 4–13.

Dixon, J. A., Scura, L. F., Carpenter, R. A. and Sherman, P. B. (1994). *Economic Analysis of Environmental Impacts*, London, Earthscan Publications Ltd.

Dupuit, J. (1844). De la mesure de l'utilité des travaux publics, *Annales des Ponts et Chaussées*, translated by R. Barback (1952) in *International Economic Papers*, Vol. 2, pp. 83–110.

Eckstein, O. (1958). *Water Resources Development*, Cambridge, MA, Harvard University Press.

Ehrenkranz, N. J., Ventura, A. K., Guadrado, R. R., Bond, W. L. and Porter, J. E. (1971). Pandemic Dengue in Caribbean Countries and the Southern United States – Past, Present and Potential Problems, *New England Journal of Medicine*, Vol. 285, pp. 1460–1469.

Einio, M., Kaustia, M. and Puttonen, V. (2008). Price Setting and the Reluctance to Realize Losses in Apartment Markets, *Journal of Economic Psychology*, Vol. 29, pp. 19–34.

Envalue [database] retrieved 15 June 2011 from http://www.environment.nsw.gov.au/envalueapp/.

European Commission (2000). *Analysis of the Fundamental Concepts of Resource Management*, retrieved from http://ec.europa.eu/environment/enveco/waste/pdf/guareport.pdf.

EVRI [database], retrieved 15 June 2011 from https://www.evri.ca/Global/Home Anonymous.aspx.

Fisher, A. L., Chestnut, G. and Violette, D. M. (1989). The Value of Reducing Risks of Death – A Note on New Evidence, *Journal of Policy Analysis and Management*, Vol. 8 (1), pp. 88–100.

Fleming, C. M. and Cook, A. (2008). The Recreational Value of Lake McKenzie, Fraser Island – An Application of the Travel Cost Method, *Tourism Management*, Vol. 29 (6), pp. 1197–1205.

Food and Agriculture Organisation (2010). *Global Forest Resources Assessment 2010 – Key Findings*, retrieved 11 June 2011 from http://foris.fao.org/static/data/fra2010/KeyFindings-en.pdf.

Freeman, A. M. (1993). *The Measurement of Environmental and Resource Values: Theory and Method*, Washington, DC, Resources for the Future.

Groothuis, P. A. (2005). Benefit Transfer – A Comparison of Approaches, *Growth and Change*, Vol. 36 (4), pp. 551–564.

Gubler, D. J. (1991). Dengue Haemorrhagic Fever – A Global Update (editorial), *Virus Information Exchange News*, Vol. 8, pp. 2–3.

Gubler, D. J. and Trent, D. W. (1994). Emergence of Epidemic Dengue/Dengue Haemorrhagic Fever as a Public Health Problem in the Americas, *Infectious Agents and Disease*, Vol. 2, pp. 383–393.

Gubler, D. J. and Clark, G. G. (1995). Dengue/Dengue Haemorrhagic Fever – the Emergence of a Global Health Problem, *Emerging Infectious Diseases*, Vol. 1, pp. 55–57.

Gürlük, S. and Rehber, E. (2008). A Travel Cost Study to Estimate Recreational Value for a Bird Refuge at Lake Manyas, Turkey, *Journal of Environmental Management*, Vol. 88 (4), pp. 1350–1360.

Haab, T., Whitehead, J. C. and McConnell, T. (2000). The Economic Value of Marine Recreational Fishing in the Southeast United States – 1997 Southeast Economic Data Analysis. *NOAA Technical Memorandum NMFS-SEFSC-446*, Department of Economics, East Carolina University and Department of Agricultural and Resource Economics, University of Maryland, retrieved 15 June 2011 from http://www.st.nmfs.noaa.gov/st5/RecEcon/Publications/SE_vol2.pdf.

Halstead, S. B. (1980). Dengue Haemorrhagic Fever – A Public Health Problem and a Field for Research, *Bulletin of the World Health Organization*, Vol. 58, pp. 1–21.

Halstead, S. B. (1992). The 20th Century Dengue Pandemic – Need for Surveillance and Research, *World Health Organization Statistics Quarterly*, Vol. 45, pp. 292–298.

Hammack, J. and Brown, G. M. (1974). *Waterfowl and Wetlands – Toward Bio-Economic Analysis*, Baltimore, MD, Johns Hopkins Press.

Hammitt, J. K. and Zhou, Y. (2006). The Economic Value of Air-Pollution-Related Health Risks in China – A Contingent Valuation Study, *Environmental and Resource Economics*, Vol. 33 (2), pp. 399–423.

Hammond, R. J. (1966). Convention and Limitation in Benefit–Cost Analysis, *Natural Resources Journal*, Vol. 6, pp. 195–222.

Hanemann, M., Loomis, J. and Kanninen, B. (1991). Statistical Efficiency of Double-bounded Dichotomous Choice Contingent Valuation, *American Journal of Agricultural Economics*, Vol. 73 (4), pp. 1255–1263.

Hazra, K. L. (1982). *History of Theravada Buddhism in South–East Asia*, New Delhi, Munshiram Manoharlal.

Henderson, A. M. (1941). Consumer's Surplus and the Compensation Variation, *Review of Economic Studies*, Vol. 8, p. 117.

Hicks, J. (1939). The Foundation of Welfare Economics, *The Economic Journal*, Vol. 49 (196), pp. 696–712.

Hicks, R., Steinbeck, S., Gautam, A. and Thunberg, E. (1999). Volume II – The Economic Value of New England and Mid-Atlantic Sportfishing in 1994, *NOAA Technical Memorandum NMFS-F/SPO-38*, retrieved 15 June 2011 from http://www.st.nmfs.noaa.gov/st5/RecEcon/Publications/tm_f-spo-38-1999.pdf.

Hirsch, W. Z. (1965). Integrating View of Federal Program Budgeting, *Memorandum RM-4799-RC*, retrieved 15 June 2011 from http://www.rand.org/content/dam/rand/pubs/research_memoranda/2009/RM4799.pdf.

Hirsch, W. Z. (1966). Toward Federal Program Budgeting. *Public Administration Review*, Vol. 26 (4), pp. 259–269.

Hon, P. M. L. (2006). *Chapter 4 – Singapore*, in Glover, D. and Jessup, T. (eds.), *Indonesia's Fires and Haze – The Cost of Catastrophe*, Singapore, Institute of Southeast Asian Studies, retrieved 12 June 2011 from http://www.idrc.ca/en/ev-102684-201-1-DO_TOPIC.html.

Horowitz, J. and McConnell, K. (2002). A Review of WTA/WTP Studies, *Journal of Environmental Economics and Management*, Vol. 44, pp. 426–447.

Jeong, H. and Haab, T. (2004). The Economic Value of Marine Recreational Fishing – Applying Benefit Transfer to Marine Recreational Fisheries Statistics Survey (MRFSS), *AEDE Working Paper AEDE-WP-0039-04*, Department of Agricultural, Environmental, and Development Economics, The Ohio State University, retrieved 15 June 2011 from http://ageconsearch.umn.edu/bitstream/28322/1/wp040039.pdf.

Jeuland, M., Lucas, M., Clemens, J. and Whittington, D. (2010). Estimating the Private Benefits of Vaccination Against Cholera in Beira, Mozambique – a Travel Cost Approach, *Journal of Development Economics*, Vol. 91 (2), pp. 310–322.

Johannesson, M., Johansson, P. O. and Löfgren, K. G. (1997). On the Value of Changes in Life Expectancy – Blips Versus Parametric Changes, *Journal of Risk and Uncertainty*, Vol. 15, pp. 221–239.

Johansson, P. O. (2002). On the Definition and Age-Dependency of the Value of a Statistical Life, *Journal of Risk and Uncertainty*, Vol. 25 (3), pp. 251–263.

Johnson, E. J., Hershey, J., Meszaros J. and Kunreuther, H. (1993). Framing Probability Distortions, and Insurance Decisions, *Journal of Risk and Uncertainty*, Vol. 7, pp. 35–51.

Kachelmeier, S. J. and Shehata, M. (1992). Estimating Risk Preferences Under High Monetary Incentives – Experimental Evidence from the People's Republic of China, *American Economic Review*, Vol. 82, pp. 1120–1140.

Kahneman, D. and Knestch, J. (1992). Valuing Public Goods – The Purchase of Moral Satisfaction, *Journal of Environmental Economics and Management*, Vol. 22, pp. 57–70.

Kahneman, D., Knetsch, J. L. and Thaler, R. H. (1986) Fairness as a Constraint on Profit Seeking – Entitlements in the Market, *American Economic Review*, Vol. 76, pp. 728–741.

Kahneman, D., Knetsch, J. L. and Thaler, R. H. (1990). Experimental Tests of the Endowment Effect and the Coase Theorem, *Journal of Political Economy*, Vol. 98, pp. 728–741.

Kahneman, D., Ritov, I. and Schkade, D. (1999). Economic Preferences or Attitude Expressions? An Analysis of Dollar Responses to Public Issues, *Journal of Risk and Uncertainty*, Vol. 19 (1–3), pp. 203–235.

Kaldor, N. (1939). Welfare Propositions in Economics and Interpersonal Comparisons of Utility, *The Economic Journal*, Vol. 49 (195), pp. 549–552.

184   *Bibliography*

Khatun, F. A. (1997). The Cost of Particulate Air Pollution in Dhaka City, *The Bangladesh Development Studies*, Vol. XXV (1 and 2), Bangladesh Institute of Development Studies.

Khazeni, N., Hutton, D. W., Garber, A. M. and Owens, D. K. (2009). Effectiveness and Cost-effectiveness of Adjuvant Vaccination and Antiviral Prophylaxis for an Influenza A (H5N1) Pandemic, *Annals of Internal Medicine*, Vol. 151 (12), pp. 840–53.

Klocek, C. A. (2004). Estimating the Economic Value of Canaan Valley National Wildlife Refuge: a Contingent Valuation Approach, *Dissertation*, Davis College of Agricultural Forestry and Consumer Sciences, West Virginia University.

Knetsch, J. and Sinden, J. (1984). Willingness To Pay and Compensation Demanded – Experimental Evidence of an Unexpected Disparity in Measures of Value, *The Quarterly Journal of Economics*, Vol. 99, pp. 507–521.

Knetsch, J. L. (1989). The Endowment Effect and Evidence of Non-reversible Indifference Curves, *The American Economic Review*, Vol. 79, pp. 1277–1284.

Knetsch, J. L. (1990). Environmental Policy Implication of Disparities Between Willingness To Pay and Compensation Demanded Measures of Values, *Journal of Environmental Economics and Management*, Vol. 18, pp. 227–237.

Knetsch, J. L. (2000). Environmental Valuations and Standard Theory – Behavioural Findings, Context Dependence, and Implications, in Tietenberg, T. and Folmer, H. (eds.), *The International Yearbook of Environmental and Resource Economics 2000/2001*, pp. 267–299, Cheltenham, Edward Elgar Limited.

Kneisner, T. J., Viscusi, W. K., Woock, C. and Ziliak, J. P. (2006). *Pinning Down the Value of Statistical Life*, Center for Policy Research, Maxwell School, Syracuse University, Paper 80.

Kniesner, T. J. and Viscusi, W. K. (2006). Value of a Statistical Life – Relative Position vs. Relative Age, *American Economic Review, Papers and Proceedings*, Vol. 95, pp. 142–146.

Kong, F., Yin, H. and Nakagoshi, N. (2007). Using the GIS and Landscape Metrics in the Hedonic Price Modelling of the Amenity Value of Urban Green Space – a Case Study in Jinan City, China, *Landscape and Urban Planning*, Vol. 79, pp. 240–252.

Krupnick, A. J., Harrison, K., Nickell, E. and Toman, M. (1993). The Benefits of Ambient Air Quality Improvements in Central and Eastern Europe – A Preliminary Assessment, *Discussion Paper ENR93-19*, Washington, DC, Resources for the Future.

Krupnick, A., Alberini, A., Cropper, M., Simon, N., O'Brien, B., Goeree, R. and Heintzelman, M. (2002). Age, Health and Willingness to Pay for Mortality Risk Reductions – A Contingent Valuation Study of Ontario Residents, *Journal of Risk and Uncertainty*, Vol. 24, pp. 161–186.

Krutilla, J. and Eckstein, O. (1958). *Multiple Purpose River Development, Studies in Applied Economic Analysis*, Baltimore, MD, Johns Hopkins Press.

LeDuc, J. W. (1996). World Health Organization Strategy for Emerging Infectious Diseases, *Journal of the American Medical Association*, Vol. 275, pp. 318–320.

Loehman, E. T., Berg, S. V., Arroyo, A. A., Hedinger, R. A., Schwartz, J. M., Shaw, M. E., Fahien, R. W., De, V. H., Fishe, R. P. and Rio, D. E. (1979). Distributional Analysis of Regional Benefits and Costs of Air Quality Control, *Journal of Environmental Economics and Management*, Vol. VI, pp. 222–243.

Loomis, J. (2005). Updated Outdoor Recreation Use Values on National Forests and Other Public Lands, *General Technical Report PNW-GTR-658*, retrieved 15 June 2011 from http://www.fs.fed.us/pnw/pubs/pnw_gtr658.pdf.

Loomis, J., Hanemann, M., Kanninen, B. and Wegge, T. (1991). WTP to Protect Wetlands and Reduce Wildlife Contamination from Agricultural Drainage, in Dinar, A. and

Zilberman, D. (eds.), *The Economics and Management of Water and Drainage in Agriculture*, pp. 411–429, Norwell, MA, Kluwer Academic Publishers.

Lyon, R. M. (1990). Federal Discount Rate Policy, the Shadow Price of Capital, and Challenges for Reforms, *Journal of Environmental Economics and Management*, Vol. 18 (2), pp. S29–S50.

McKean, R. (1958). *Efficiency in Government through Systems Analysis with Emphasis on Water Resource Development*, New York, John Wiley.

Meltzer, M. I., Cox, N. J. and Fukuda, K. (1999). The Economic Impact of Pandemic Influenza in the United States – Implications for Setting Priorities for Intervention, *Emerging Infectious Diseases*, Vol. 5, September–October 1999.

Miller, T. R. (1990). The Plausible Range for the Value of Life – Red Herrings Among the Mackerel, *Journal of Forensic Economics*, Vol. 3, pp. 17–40.

Ministry of Environment, Singapore. *Annual Report*, retrieved 15 June 2011 from http://app2.nea.gov.sg/annualreport.aspx.

Ministry of Land, Infrastructure and Transport (2003). *Cost Benefit Analysis Manual* (in Japanese).

Mishan, E. J. (1971). *Cost Benefit Analysis*, UK, George Allen and Unwin.

Mishan, E. J. (1981a). *Economic Efficiency and Social Welfare*, UK, George Allen and Unwin.

Mishan, E. J. (1981b). *Introduction to Normative Economics*, UK, Oxford University Press.

Mishan, E. J. and Quah, E. (2007). *Cost–Benefit Analysis*, 5th edition, UK, Routledge.

MIT (2003). *The Future of Nuclear Power – An Interdisciplinary MIT Study*, retrieved 15 June 2011 from http://web.mit.edu/nuclearpower/.

Moeltner, K. and Woodward, R. (2009). Meta-Functional Benefit Transfer for Wetland Valuation: Making the Most of Small Samples, *Environmental and Resource Economics*, Vol. 42 (1), pp. 89–108.

Morichi, S. (2005). Cost Benefit Analysis of Speed Limit Regulation for Highways in Japan, *Journal of Eastern Asia Society for Transportation Studies*, Vol. 6, pp. 1008–1020.

Mullarkey, D. (1997). Contingent Valuation of Wetlands: Testing Sensitivity to Scope, *Dissertation*, Department of Agricultural and Applied Economics, Madison, University of Wisconsin.

Nellthorp, J., Bristow, A. L. and Day, B. (2007). Introducing Willingness-to-pay for Noise Changes into Transport Appraisal – An Application of Benefit Transfer, *Transport Reviews*, Vol. 27 (3), pp. 327–353.

Odean, T. (1998). Are Investors Reluctant to Realize their Losses?, *The Journal of Finance*, Vol. 53, pp. 1775–1798.

Office of the Auditor General of Thailand (2008). *The Environmental Impact on Government Policy – Lesson Learned from Thailand New International Airport*.

Ong, Q., Quah, E., Tan, K. C., Ho, K. W. and Knetsch, J. (2008). Happiness and Cross Category Paired Comparison of Public Amenities, *Working Paper*, Nanyang Technological University.

Organization for Economic Cooperation and Development (1994). *Project Appraisal – Integrating Economics and Environment*, Paris, OECD.

Organization for Economic Cooperation and Development (OECD) and International Energy Agency (IEA) (2007). *IEA Energy Technology Essentials – Nuclear Power*, retrieved 12 June 2011 from http://www.iea.org/techno/essentials4.pdf.

Ostro, B. (1992). Estimating the Health and Economic Effects of Particulate Matter in Jakarta – A Preliminary Assessment, *Fourth Annual Meeting of the International Society for Environmental Epidemiology*, 26–29 August, Cuernavaca, Mexico.

Ostro, B. (1994). Estimating the Health Effects of Air Pollutant – A Method with an Application to Jakarta, *Policy Research Working Paper*, No. 1301, Washington, DC, World Bank.

Otto, D., Monchuk, D., Jintanakul, K. and King, C. (2005). *The Economic Value of Iowa's Natural Resources*, Department of Economics, Iowa State University, retrieved 12 June 2011 from http://www.iowadnr.gov/sustainablefunding/files/econ_study.pdf.

Otto, D., Monchuk, D., Jintanakul, K. and King, C. (2007). *The Economic Value of Iowa's Natural Resources*, retrieved 15 June 2011 from http://www.card.iastate.edu/environment/items/DNR-Amenity.pdf.

Pantumsinchai, P. (2006). Environmental Concerns for Suvarnabhumi Airport and Aeropolis, *The Environmental Engineering Association of Thailand Yearbook and Directory 2006*, pp. 47–50, retrieved 12 June 2011 from http://www.eeat.or.th/articles/EnvironmentalConcernsforSuvarnabhumiAirportandAeropolis.pdf.

Pearce, D. W. (1993). *Economic Values and The Natural World*, Cambridge, MA, The MIT Press.

Pearce, D. W. (1996). Economic Valuation and Health Damage from Air Pollution in the Developing Countries, *Energy Policy*, Vol. 24 (7), pp. 627–630.

Pearce, D. W. and Crowards, T. (1995). *Assessing the Health Costs of Particulate Air Pollution in the UK*, CSERGE Working Paper GEC 95-27, Centre for Social and Economic Research on the Global Environment, University College London and University of East Anglia, retrieved 12 June 2011 from http://www.uea.ac.uk/env/cserge/pub/wp/gec/gec_1995_27.pdf.

Pearce, D. W., Whittington, D. and Georgiou, S. (1994). *Project and Policy Appraisal: Integrating Economics and Environment*, Paris, OECD.

Peterson, G. and Brown, T. (1998). Economic Valuation by the Method of Paired Comparison with Emphasis on Evaluation of the Transitivity Axiom, *Land Economics*, Vol. 74 (2), pp. 240–261.

Pigou, A. C. (1952). *Economics of Welfare*, 5th edition, London, Macmillan.

Pinheiro, F. P. (1989). Dengue in the Americas 1980–1987, *Epidemiological Bulletin of the Pan American Health Organization*, Vol. 10, pp. 1–8.

Poor, P. J. (1999). The Value of Additional Central Flyway Wetlands: the Case of Nebraska's Rainwater Basin Wetlands, *Journal of Agricultural and Resource Economics*, Vol. 24 (1), pp. 253–265.

Punyawadee, V., Phonthisuwan, R., Winichikule, N. and Satienperakul, K. (2006). Costs and Benefits of Flue Gas Desulphurization for Pollution Control at the Mae Moh Power Plant, Thailand, *EEPSEA Research Report*, No. 2006–RR4.

Putler, D. S. (1992). Incorporating Reference Price Effects Into a Theory of Consumer Choice, *Marketing Science*, Vol. 11, pp. 287–309.

Quah, E. and Tan, K. C. (1999). Pricing a Scenic View – the Case of Singapore's East Coast Park, *Impact Assessment and Project Appraisal*, Vol. 17(4), pp. 295–303.

Quah, E. and Boon, T. L. (2003). The Economic Cost of Particulate Air Pollution on Health in Singapore, *Journal of Asian Economics*, Vol. 14 (1), pp. 73–90.

Quah, E., Choa, E. and Tan, K. C. (2006). Use of Damage Schedules in Environmental Evaluation – The Case of Urban Singapore, *Applied Economics*, Vol. 38, pp. 1501–1512.

Quah, E., Chia, W. M. and Sng, H. Y. (2009). What is Human Life Worth? In Sng, H. Y. and Chia, W. M. (2010) (eds.), *Singapore and Asia – Impact of the Global Financial Tsunami and other Economic Issues*, Singapore, World Scientific.

Rabin, M. (1998). Psychology and Economics, *Journal of Economic Literature*, Vol. 36, pp. 11–46.

Reuters, 5 June 2007. Beijing to evict 1.5 million for Olympics games, retrieved 12 June 2011 from http://www.reuters.com/article/2007/06/05/us-olympics-beijing-housing-idUSPEK12263220070605.

Ridker, R. G. and Henning, J. A. (1967). The Determinants of Residential Property Values with Special Reference to Air Pollution, *The Review of Economics and Statistics*, Vol. 29 (2), pp. 246–257.

Roberts, L. A. and Leitch, J. A. (1997). *Economic Valuation of Some Wetland Outputs of Mud Lake, Minnesota-South Dakota, Agricultural Economics Reports*, Department of Agricultural Economics, North Dakota State University.

Rosenberger, R. S. and Loomis, J. B. (2003). *Benefit Transfer*, in Champ, P. A., Boyle, K. J. and Brown, T. C. (eds.), *A Primer on Nonmarket Valuation*, pp. 445–482, London, Kluwer Academic Publisher.

Roskill (Commission on the Third London Airport) (1970). *Papers and Proceedings Vol. VII, Part 1 – Proposed research methodology*, UK, Her Majesty's Stationery Office (HMSO).

Roskill (Commission on the Third London Airport) (1971). *Report*, UK, Her Majesty's Stationery Office (HMSO).

Rowe, R., Lang, C., Chestnut, L., Latimer, D., Rae, D., Bernow, S. and White, D. (1995). The New York Environmental Externalities Cost Study – Summary of Approach and Results, *European Commission, International Energy Agency and Organization for Economic Cooperation and Development Workshop on External Cost of Energy*, 30–31 January, Brussels.

Rutherford, M., Knetsch, J. and Brown, T. (1998). Assessing Environmental Losses – Judgments of Importance and Damage Schedules, *Harvard Environmental Law Review*, Vol. 20, pp. 51–101.

Sewell, W. R. D., Davis, J., Scott, A. D. and Ross, D. W. (1965). *Guide to Benefit–Cost Analysis*, Ottawa, Queen's Printer.

Shepard, D. S. and Zeckhauser, R. J. (1982). *Life-Cycle Consumption and Willingness-to-Pay for Increased Survival*, in Jones-Lee, M. W. (1982) (ed.), *Valuation of Life and Safety*, Amsterdam, North-Holland.

Shepard, D. S. and Zeckhauser, R. J. (1984). Survival Versus Consumption, *Management Science*, Vol. 30, pp. 423–439.

Shrestha, R. K., Stein, T. V. and Clark, J. (2007). Valuing Nature-Based Recreation in Public Natural Areas of the Apalachicola River Region, Florida, *Journal of Environmental Management*, Vol. 85 (4), pp. 977–985.

Sornmani, S., Okanurak, K. and Indaratna, K. (1995). *Social and Economic Impact of Dengue Haemorrhagic Fever in Thailand*, Bangkok, Mahidol University, Social and Economic Research Unit.

Squire, L. and van der Tak, H. (1975). *Economic Analysis of Projects*, Baltimore, MD, Johns Hopkins Press.

Stern, N. (2006). *Stern Review on the Economics of Climate Change*, UK, Her Majesty's Treasury.

SUDAM (Development of Amazonia) (1992). *Sustainable Development of the Amazon – Development Strategy and Investment Alternatives*, Rio de Janeiro.

Thaler, R. H. (1999). Mental Accounting Matters, *Journal of Behavioural Decision Making*, Vol. 12, pp. 183–206.

Thaler, R. H. and Benartzi, S. (2004). Save More Tomorrow – Using Behavioural Economics to Increase Employee Saving, *Journal of Political Economy*, Vol. 112, pp. S164–S182.

The Economist, 14 August 2008. Going for gold, retrieved 12 June 2011 from http://www.economist.com/node/11920899.

The Straits Times, 13 November 2010. S'pore workforce scores high in skills, retrieved 12 June 2011 from http://www.straitstimes.com/BreakingNews/Singapore/Story/STIStory_602805.html.

The US National Archives and Records Administration (1993). *Executive Order 12291*, Federal Register, Vol. 58 (190), retrieved 15 June 2011 from http://www.archives.gov/federal-register/executive-orders/pdf/12866.pdf.

The US National Archives and Records Administration (n.d.). *Executive Order 12291*, retrieved 15 June 2011 from http://www.archives.gov/federal-register/codification/executive-order/12291.html.

Thurstone, L. L. (1927). The Method of Paired Comparisons for Social Values, *Journal of Abnormal and Social Psychology*, Vol. 21, pp. 384–400.

Tkac, J. M. (2002). Estimating Willingness to Pay for the Preservation of the Alfred Bog Wetland in Ontario: a Multiple Bounded Discrete Choice Approach, *Master's Thesis*, Department of Agricultural Economics, Gill University.

Torres, M. (1997). Impact of an Outbreak of Dengue Fever – A Case Study from Rural Puerto Rico, *Human Organization*, Vol. 56, pp. 19–27.

US Bureau of the Budget (1952). *Circular on Water Resources Projects*, Budget Circular No. A-47, Washington, DC.

US Environmental Protection Agency (2000). *Guidelines for Preparing Economic Analyses*, Washington, DC, Environmental Protection Agency.

US Federal Inter-Agency Subcommittee on Evaluation Standards (1958). *Proposed Practices for Economic Analysis of River Basin Projects*, retrieved 12 June 2011 from ftp://ftp-fc.sc.egov.usda.gov/Economics/Technotes/1958ProposedPracticesForEconomicAnalysisOfRiverBasinProjects.pdf.

ValueBase [database] retrieved 15 June 2011 from http://www.beijer.kva.se/valuebase.htm.

Von Allmen, S. D., Lopez-Correa, R.H., Woodall, J.P., Morens, D.M., Chiriboga, J. and Casta-Velez, A. (1979). Epidemic Dengue Fever in Puerto Rico, 1977 – A Cost Analysis, *American Journal of Tropical Medicine and Hygiene*, Vol. 28, pp. 1040–1044.

Weisbrod, B. A. (1964). Collective-Consumption Services of Individual-Consumption Goods, *The Quarterly Journal of Economics*, Vol. 78 (3), pp. 471–477.

Whitehead, J. C. and Blomquist, G. C. (1991). Measuring Contingent Values for Wetlands: Effects of Information about Related Environmental Goods, *Water Resources Research*, Vol. 27 (10), pp. 2523–2531.

World Bank (2005). *Avian Flu – Economic Losses Could Top US$800 Billion*, retrieved 12 June 2011 from http://web.worldbank.org/WBSITE/EXTERNAL/NEWS/0, contentMD-K:20715408~pagePK:64257043~piPK:437376~theSitePK:4607,00.html.

World Health Organization (1998). Report of the Bi-regional Workshop on Health Impacts of Haze-Related Air Pollution, *Report RS/98/GE/17(MAA)*, Manila, World Health Organization, Regional Office for the Western Pacific.

World Health Organization (2006). *Report on Dengue*, 1–5 October 2006, Geneva, Switzerland.

Xinhua News Agency, 22 June 2007. Qinghai–Tibet Train Provides Translation Service, retrieved 12 June 2011 from http://www.china.org.cn/english/travel/214867.htm.

Xinhua News Agency, 20 December 2007. Qinghai–Tibet railway to handle 1.6 million passengers this year, retrieved 12 June 2011 from http://news.xinhuanet.com/english/2007-12/20/content_7286398.htm.

Xinhua News Agency, 6 March 2009. Chief auditor – Beijing Olympics' profit exceeds 1bn yuan, retrieved 12 June 2011 from http://news.xinhuanet.com/english/2009-06/19/content_11566718.htm.

Xinhua News Agency, 30 June 2009. Qinghai–Tibet Railway effective in boosting economic development, retrieved 12 June 2011 from http://news.xinhuanet.com/english/2009-06/30/content_11626203.htm.

Index